HELP YOURSELF TO ESSENTIAL
GERMAN GRAMMAR

A grammar reference and workbook
GCSE/Standard Grade

Linette Price
Marjorie Semple

 LONGMAN

Addison Wesley Longman Ltd
Edinburgh Gate, Harlow,
Essex CM20 2JE, England
and associated companies throughout the world

ISBN 0582 287464

First published 1998
Printed in Singapore

The publisher's policy is to use paper manufactured from sustainable forests.

Contents

Appendices   127

Introduction

Help Yourself to Essential German Grammar is a combined grammar reference book and workbook. It is designed for both self-study and class-based learning at the elementary and intermediate stages of learning German.

It is suitable for use as a one-year revision programme for Year 11 pupils at school and as preparation for GCSE or Standard Grade. It is also aimed at adult students taking intermediate German or GCSE, and for individuals studying on their own.

Preparation for GCSE and Standard Grade (Scotland)

Using this book will enable students to reach the level required to obtain basic and higher GCSE grades and foundation, general and credit levels at Standard Grade (Scotland).

Units 1–8 cover the structures and grammar required. Unit 9 goes beyond the requirements of most syllabuses, acting as a bridge to further study in German.

Presentation of grammar and vocabulary

The structures and exercises are carefully graded. Grammatical terms like 'noun' and 'verb' are only used where absolutely necessary and are explained when first used.

The vocabulary used in the exercises covers topics which are appropriate to communicative language teaching and learning at this level: everyday activities, personal and social life, the world around us, the world of work, the international world.

All vocabulary is carefully selected as being appropriate to the requirements of GCSE syllabuses.

Contents of the units

Each unit contains three chapters. Every chapter starts with *What do you know?* exercises which are designed to identify problem areas and assess the particular needs of students.

After the *What do you know?* exercises come the explanations of the grammar points. These present in plain language the structures and grammar needed in order to speak and write simple but correct German.

The grammar explanations are followed by *What have you learnt?* exercises, enabling students to apply and practise the grammar covered in the chapter.

At the end of each unit, a 'Revision test' helps the student to check that she or he has understood and remembered the grammar explained in the last three chapters.

Appendices

Appendices include verb tables and further information about language rules and usage which will be useful to students when doing the exercises and when communicating in German.

Glossaries and grammar index

The German–English and English–German glossaries provide all the vocabulary needed to complete the exercises. The 'Grammar index' enables both teacher and learner to find grammatical explanations for all grammar points covered in the book.

Key to exercises

Solutions to all exercises are given at the end of the book. These pages are perforated and can be removed for class use.

German spelling reforms

The authors would like to draw your attention to the proposed revisions in German spelling, which are currently being introduced and taught in German speaking schools. However, at the time of printing these revisions have not been fully ratified by all groups. The spellings in this edition are the unrevised spellings. It is anticipated that the spelling revisions will be fully in place by the academic year 2004/5. The older forms of spelling will still be deemed to be correct.

Further advice to students learning on their own

You can use this book in three ways: as a workbook, as a grammar reference, or as both.

Using the book as a workbook

The exercises and language points covered in Units 1 to 9 are carefully graded to enable you to work systematically through the book. Use the *What do you know?* exercises to find out your strengths and weaknesses, read through the grammar explanations and then do the *What have you learnt?* exercises to put the knowledge you have acquired to use. Finally, at the end of each unit, revise what you have learnt by doing the 'Revision test'.

Using the book as a grammar reference

To find out about a particular point of grammar, look up the chapter reference in the 'Grammar index' at the back of the book. Read the explanations carefully and do the relevant exercises (*What do you know? What have you learnt?* and 'Revision test').

Before you begin...

Here is some advice on how to tackle the various exercises.

1 Remember that the vocabulary needed to understand and complete the exercises is provided in the glossaries at the back of the book.

2 Before starting each exercise, read through it carefully to make sure you understand the point of the exercise and the meaning of the sentences. We suggest that you write out the answers in full and check your work carefully for spelling mistakes, agreement of adjectives, verb endings, etc.

3 Then, and only then, check your answers against the key to the exercises at the back of the book. Learn from any mistakes you make, and note down any vocabulary that you did not know.

Viel Glück!

Linette Price
Marjorie Semple

Die Familie Maier

CHAPTER 1   WHAT DO YOU KNOW?

Before looking at the explanations in this chapter, check what you know by doing the following exercises.

A Your penfriend Maria Maier has written to you describing the flat where her family lives. Insert **der**, **die**, **das** or **die** (plural) in the gaps provided.
e.g. ... Küche ist rechts von der Eingangstür.
→ <u>Die</u> Küche ist rechts von der Eingangstür.

Meine Wohnung

den 18. September

Lieber/Liebe X,
du fragst, wie unsere Wohnung aussieht. ... Küche ist rechts von der Eingangstür.
Neben der Küche ist ... Badezimmer. Links ist ... Wohnzimmer.
... Wohnung hat drei Schlafzimmer.
... Balkon hat eine sehr schöne Aussicht auf den Garten.
... Garten liegt vor und hinter dem Haus.
Hier ist ein Foto von dem Wohnhaus.
Kannst Du mir ein Foto von Deinem Haus schicken?
Schreib bald!
Maria

B Maria tells you more about her family. Put the verb in brackets in its correct form (present tense) to complete the sentence.
e.g. Ich (<u>tanzen</u>) gern.   →   Ich <u>tanze</u> gern.

Meine Brüder
1 Mein Bruder Peter ist sehr sportlich. Er (<u>spielen</u>) gern Tennis und Federball.
2 Mein jüngerer Bruder Moritz ist 13 Jahre alt. Er (<u>basteln</u>) sehr gerne.

Meine Eltern
3 Meine Mutter (<u>lernen</u>) abends Englisch in der Volkshochschule.
4 Mein Vater (<u>sammeln</u>) Briefmarken von der ehemaligen DDR.

Meine Großeltern
5 Mein Großvater (<u>hören</u>) gern Musik, obwohl er jetzt ziemlich taub ist.
6 Meine Oma (<u>wandern</u>) gern auf dem Lande.

Nouns and articles

1 In English *house, health,* and *Germany* are NOUNS. In German, nouns always have a capital letter even if they are not names or at the beginning of the sentence: **Haus, Gesundheit, Deutschland**.

2 In German, nouns are either MASCULINE, FEMININE, or NEUTER. This is their GENDER. Nouns can be SINGULAR (just one) or PLURAL (more than one).

3 In English, *the* is the DEFINITE ARTICLE. In German, **der** (masculine), **die** (feminine) and **das** (neuter) are the words for *the*. To show plural **der, die, das** become **die**:

	SINGULAR	PLURAL
MASCULINE	**der** Rock *the skirt*	**die** Röcke *the skirts*
FEMININE	**die** Bluse *the blouse*	**die** Blusen *the blouses*
NEUTER	**das** Hemd *the shirt*	**die** Hemden *the shirts*

See Appendix page 145 for a list of all the changes in the definite article

4 **Der, die, das** are often used where we would not use *the* in English:

a   with a few countries which are mostly feminine:

Die Schweiz   *Switzerland*   **Die** Türkei   *Turkey*

b   in an abstract/generalised sense:

Die Schule beginnt in zwei Wochen   *School begins in two weeks*
Der Tod kommt auf uns alle zu   *Death comes to us all*

c   with months, seasons and meals:

Der Juli war verregnet   *July was wet*
Der Frühling ist spät gekommen   *Spring came late*
Das Mittagessen ist um 12 Uhr   *Lunch is at 12 p.m.*

d   to express the price of something per quantity:

Zwei Mark **das** Kilo   *Two marks per kilo*

The present tense

5 A VERB expresses an action or a state. Examples of verbs are in bold type:

*She **is** the marketing director*   *We **are going** on holiday at Christmas*
*They **live** in a big house*   *He **has** a bad cold*

These verbs are all in the PRESENT TENSE, which describes what is happening now (or in the near future).

6 The INFINITIVE of the verb is the basic form, in English *to go, to make, to ring*, etc. In German it ends in **-en** or **-n**. This is the form you will find when you look up a verb in a dictionary:

gehen   *to go*   **klingeln**   *to ring*   **machen**   *to make*

7 In German, more than in English, the ending of the verb changes depending on who is doing the action. German has what are called WEAK VERBS, which follow a regular pattern, and STRONG VERBS, whose forms vary quite a lot. Here is the present tense of the weak verb **spielen** (*to play*):

SINGULAR		PLURAL	
ich spiele	*I play*	wir spielen	*we play*
du spielst	*you play (informal)*	ihr spielt	*you play (informal)*
Sie spielen	*you play (formal)*	Sie spielen	*you play (formal)*
er/sie/es spielt	*he/she/it plays*	sie spielen	*they play*

See Chapter 2 for more about the present tense and strong verbs

8 You can see from the example above that there are three different words for *you* in German.

INFORMAL	the familiar forms for people you know well, children, and animals **du** (singular form) and **ihr** (plural form)
FORMAL	the polite form **Sie** (with a capital S) for both singular and plural

9 The word for *one* (as in e.g. *One should not drink and drive*) in German is **man**. It is used much more commonly than *one* in English, and can also be translated by *you*, or *people*, for instance. With **man** the ending of the verb is the same as with **er/sie/es** (i.e. *he/she/it*):

man sagt, daß...   *people say that..., it is said that...*

CHAPTER 1   WHAT HAVE YOU LEARNT?

Now that you have studied the explanations on the previous pages, check that you have understood them by doing the following exercises.

A Maria describes the area she lives in. From the verbs given, decide which one best fits each gap, and put it into the correct form of the present tense.
e.g. Das Kino ... die neuesten Filme.

   → *zeigen* → Das Kino <u>zeigt</u> die neuesten Filme.

Was gibt es in der Gegend zu tun?

1 Berlin ist eine sehr interessante Stadt. In unserem Stadtteil gibt es eine Disko, ein Kino, ein Museum und ein Sportzentrum. In der Disko ... man und man ... Musik. Das Kino ... die neuesten Filme.

hören   zeigen   tanzen

2 Ich ... jede Woche das Sportzentrum. Da ... ich Squash und danach ... ich mir eine Cola.

spielen   kaufen   besuchen

3 Meine Freunde und ich ... ungefähr zweimal pro Jahr das Museum. In dem Museum sind Ausstellungen über die regionale Geschichte. Ich ... gerne hier in Berlin. Es gibt immer viel zu tun.

besichtigen   wohnen

4 An der Ecke ist eine Bibliothek. Dort ... ich meine Hausaufgaben. Meine Freunde und ich ... auf den Computers. Die Bibliothek ist prima!.

arbeiten   machen

5 Berlin hat mehrere Seen und Wälder. Im Sommer ... wir auf dem Wannsee. Im Herbst ... meine Schulklasse eine Wanderung im Grünewald.

machen   segeln

B Your reply to Maria describing the house where you live is not enthusiastic. Replace the English words in brackets with the German equivalent.
e.g. [The house] ist jetzt zu klein.   →   <u>Das Haus</u> ist jetzt zu klein.

Mein Haus

Hier ist ein Foto von meinem Haus.

[The kitchen] ist zu eng und [the bathroom] zu groß.

[The curtains] im Wohnzimmer sind scheußlich. [The bookcase] nimmt zu viel Platz ein. [The patio] ist für kleine Kinder sehr gefährlich. [The house] liegt direkt an einer Hauptstraße. [The windows] sind undicht. Ja, mir gefällt das Haus gar nicht!

UNIT

1

A Maria is talking to a new friend about her room. Check the gender of each underlined word and then insert **ein/eine** (if it's required).

e.g. Neben der Tür ist … <u>Kleiderschrank</u>. → Neben der Tür ist <u>ein</u> Kleiderschrank.

Mein Zimmer

FREUND Hast du dein eigenes Zimmer?

MARIA Ja. Mein Zimmer ist ziemlich groß. Neben der Tür ist … <u>Kleiderschrank</u> und … <u>Kommode</u>.

FREUND Hat das Zimmer … <u>Fenster</u>?

MARIA Das Fenster ist auf der rechten Seite des Kleiderschranks. Unter dem Fenster ist … <u>Gästebett</u>. In der Mitte ist … kleiner <u>Teppich</u>.

FREUND Hast du Bilder oder Posters an der Wand?

MARIA An der Wand über meinem Bett sind … <u>Posters</u> von meinen Lieblingssportlern. Wie sieht dein Zimmer aus?

B Mutti comes home from work and finds it unnaturally quiet. She asks each person in turn **Was machst du?** Put the verb in brackets into the correct form of the present tense.

e.g. Ich (<u>sehen</u>) fern. → Ich <u>sehe</u> fern.

Was macht die Familie?

MUTTI Peter! Wo bist du?

PETER Ich bin im Wohnzimmer. Ich [<u>sehen</u>] fern.

MUTTI Wo ist dein Bruder?

PETER Moritz ist noch nicht zu Hause. Er [<u>treffen</u>] um drei Uhr seinen Freund am Kinderspielplatz.

MUTTI Ist Maria zu Hause?

MARIA Ich bin hier in meinem Schlafzimmer. Ich bin müde. Ich [<u>lesen</u>].

MUTTI Was macht dein Vater?

VATI Ich [<u>schreiben</u>] einen Brief an Tante Irmi. Opa Maier [<u>sitzen</u>] mit mir im Wohnzimmer und [<u>schlafen</u>].

OMA Und ich bin hier in der Küche und [<u>schneiden</u>] Brot für das Abendessen.

How to use **ein, eine, ein**

1 The word for *a* or *an* in German is **ein**, **eine** or **ein**. This is the INDEFINITE ARTICLE. The negative *not a* (**kein**) is formed in the same way. These words agree in gender and number with the noun, that is, their form varies depending on whether the noun is masculine, feminine or neuter and whether it is singular or plural. They also change according to the FUNCTION their noun plays in the sentence, for instance whether it is subject or object *(see Section 2 below)*:

	SINGULAR	PLURAL
MASCULINE	**ein** Brief *a letter*	**keine** Briefe *no letters*
FEMININE	**eine** Ausnahme *an exception*	**keine** Ausnahmen *no exceptions*
NEUTER	**ein** Paket *a parcel*	**keine** Pakete *no parcels*

2 The forms above are used when the noun is the subject of the sentence. This is the NOMINATIVE case:

Ein Student muß fleißig arbeiten   A *student has to work hard*
Eine Frau kommt ins Zimmer   A *woman comes into the room*
Das ist doch **kein** Problem   *That's no problem*

> See Appendix page 144 for an explanation of subject/nominative

3 There are times when there will be no word for *a* or *an* in German even though there is one in English:

 a when talking about someone's profession or nationality:

Er arbeitet als Lehrer   *He works as **a** teacher*
Sie ist Deutsche   *She is **a** German*

 b in some set phrases:

Sie haben Fieber   *You have **a** temperature*
ein Zimmer mit Bad   *a room with **a** bathroom*

4 There is often no word in German for *some* or *any*:

Haben Sie Geld?   *Have you got **any** money?*
Mein Vater kauft Eier   *My father is buying **some** eggs*

Help Yourself to Essential German Grammar

More about the present tense...

5 In English the present tense has three different forms: *I play, I am playing, I do play.* German has just one form to express all three of these:

Was **macht** sie? Sie **klingelt**.   *What is she doing? She is **ringing** the bell*
Ich **wohne** in einem Vorort   *I live in a suburb*
Anna **singt** gut   *Anna does sing well*

6 Like the English *is/are coming*, etc., the present tense in German can also express the idea of the future, usually the near future:

Sie **kommen** morgen   *They **are coming** tomorrow*

7 Some verbs in German do not follow the regular pattern of the weak verbs we saw in Chapter 1. The endings are the same as for a weak verb. But an **a** or **e** in the first part of the verb (the STEM) changes in the **du** and **er/sie/es** forms. These irregular verbs are called STRONG VERBS.

a With verbs like **tragen** *(to carry)* the **a** becomes **ä**:

ich trage	wir tragen
du trägst	ihr tragt
Sie tragen	Sie tragen
er/sie/es trägt	sie tragen

Du schläfst ein   *You are falling asleep*
Sie fällt hin   *She falls down*
Der Zug fährt nach Bonn   *The train is going to Bonn*

b With verbs like **geben** *(to give)* the **e** changes to an **i**:

ich gebe	wir geben
du gibst	ihr gebt
Sie geben	Sie geben
er/sie/es gibt	sie geben

Er gibt auf   *He gives up*
Sie trifft ihren Freund   *She is meeting her friend*

You will find a full list of strong verbs on Appendix pages 130–135

CHAPTER 2   WHAT HAVE YOU LEARNT?

A Maria is trying to persuade her mother to buy something from an advertisement in the paper for a sale in a local electrical shop. Fill in the gaps with **ein/eine** or *leave them blank* if you think no extra word is necessary.

e.g. ... Kassettenrekorder kostet nur DM 89,-.

→ Ein Kassettenrekorder kostet nur DM 89,-.

Im Sonderangebot

1

MARIA   ... Kassettenrekorder kostet nur DM 89,- und ... Stereoanlage kostet DM 249,-. Und schau mal Mutti, ... Kopfhörer kostet DM 18,-. ... Mini-CD-Spieler kostet DM 149,-, und hier gibt es noch was: ... Packung von fünf Kassetten DM 9,89. ... Hi-Fi System kostet nur DM 429,-!

2

MARIA   Na ja, aber Gabis CD-Spieler allein hat DM 400 gekostet.

MUTTER   Aber Maria, Gabi arbeitet jetzt. Sie ist ... Empfangsdame in einem Hotel, nicht wahr?

MARIA   Wir haben aber keinen CD-Spieler.

MUTTER   Maria, ich kriege langsam ... Kopfschmerzen. Wir brauchen keinen CD-Spieler. Vati und ich haben auf jeden Fall nur Schallplatten.

3

MARIA   Ich muß irgendwie ... Geld verdienen.

MUTTER   Dann kannst du ruhig die Stellenangebote auch durchlesen!

B Now it is your turn to practise your German, by telling Maria what you do in each of the following places at home. Replace the words in English in brackets with the German equivalent.

e.g. Ich [write] im Wohnzimmer.   →   Ich schreibe im Wohnzimmer.

Zu Hause

1 Ich [write] im Wohnzimmer Briefe und [watch TV].
2 Wir [eat] und [drink] in der Küche.
3 Ich [listen to] in meinem Zimmer Musik und [sleep].
4 Wir [sit] im Sommer im Garten.
5 Meine Eltern [work] gern im Garten.

UNIT

1

A Frau Maier works in a Kindergarten. Today the children are learning words for parts of the body. Complete each sentence with a number, and where there are two or more of something change the word into the plural.

e.g. Ich habe ... Auge ...   →   Ich habe <u>zwei</u> Augen.

Mein Körper

Ich habe ... Auge ... , ... Ohr ... , und ... Finger ... an einer Hand.

B Frau Maier describes her journey to work. Fill in the gaps with the correct form of the separable verb shown at the end of the sentence.

e.g. Ich ... um sechs Uhr ...   *aufstehen*   →   Ich <u>stehe</u> um sechs Uhr <u>auf</u>.

Meine Alltagsroutine

1 Der Bus ... pünktlich um viertel nach sieben ...   *ankommen*
2 Ich ... in den Bus ...   *einsteigen*
3 Ich ... an der Bushaltestelle direkt vor meinem Kindergarten ...   *aussteigen*

C Herr Maier describes the start to his day. Fill in the gaps in each sentence with the correct form of the reflexive verb shown at the end of the sentence.

e.g. Ich ... ... schnell.   *sich waschen*   →   Ich <u>wasche mich</u> schnell.

Meine tägliche Routine

1 Zuerst gehe ich ins Badezimmer. Ich ... ... schnell.   *sich waschen*
2 Ich ... ...   *sich rasieren*
3 Ich ... ... im Schlafzimmer vor dem Spiegel.   *sich kämmen*

D In the garden of Frau Maier's Kindergarten three children are playing. Complete the dialogue using the correct form of **sein** in the present tense.

e.g. Ich ... Batman.   →   Ich <u>bin</u> Batman.

Was spielen wir?

1 KIND Ich ... Batman, und du ... Robin.
2 KIND Nein, er ... Superman. Wir ... Batman und Robin.
3 KIND Superman ... besser als Batman.

Plural form of nouns

1 To express the idea that there are two or more of something (PLURAL) in English we usually add -s, e.g. *tables*, *books*. In German nouns change in a variety of ways to show that they are plural. The most common changes can be grouped into seven categories:

NO CHANGE	der Koffer	die Koffer	*the suitcase(s)*
	der Lehrer	die Lehrer	*the teacher(s)*
UMLAUT + -E	die Stadt	die Städte	*the town(s)*
	die Hand	die Hände	*the hand(s)*
-N	die Flasche	die Flaschen	*the bottle(s)*
	die Dusche	die Duschen	*the shower(s)*
-EN	die Frau	die Frauen	*the woman (women)*
	der Student	die Studenten	*the student(s)*
UMLAUT	der Garten	die Gärten	*the garden(s)*
	der Vogel	die Vögel	*the bird(s)*
-E	der Tag	die Tage	*the day(s)*
	der Film	die Filme	*the film(s)*
UMLAUT + -ER	der Mann	die Männer	*the man (men)*
	das Haus	die Häuser	*the house(s)*

Note: When you learn a noun in German, you should always learn its gender and its plural:

Die Flasche**n** sind schmutzig   *The bottles are dirty*
Die Häus**er** sind neu   *The houses are new*
Die Frau**en** arbeiten   *The women are working*

Separable verbs

2 SEPARABLE VERBS have a part called a PREFIX which separates from the basic verb when used in straightforward sentences. The prefix is attached to the front of the verb in the infinitive:

abfahren *(to depart)*   **an**fangen *(to begin)*   **auf**machen *(to open)*
aussehen *(to look like)*   **mit**kommen *(to come too)*   **zu**hören *(to listen)*

These separable verbs are similar to English verbs such as *go out, come in, start off* and so on, and their prefixes can often be translated literally. For instance **ab** *away, off*; **aus** *out*; and **zurück** *back* can be combined with **gehen** to give us:

abgehen *(to go away)*   **aus**gehen *(to go out)*   **zurück**gehen *(to go back)*

The separable prefix goes to the end of the sentence in a straightforward statement or question:

Wann **fährt** der Zug **ab**?	When does the train leave?
Die Schule **fängt** um neun Uhr **an**	School begins at 9 a.m.
Füllen Sie dieses Formular **aus**!	Fill out this form

Reflexive verbs

3   When we say *I wash* in English, what we really mean is *I wash myself*. In German, the word for *myself, yourself, himself*, etc. must always be there. These verbs which often describe what one does to oneself (or a thing does to itself) are called REFLEXIVE VERBS, and the word for *myself*, etc. is called a REFLEXIVE PRONOUN:

sich waschen	ich wasche **mich**	*I wash*
to wash (oneself)	du wäschst **dich**	*you wash*
	Sie waschen **sich**	*you wash (formal)*
	er/sie/es wäscht **sich**	*he/she/it washes*
	wir waschen **uns**	*we wash*
	ihr wascht **euch**	*you wash (informal)*
	Sie waschen **sich**	*you wash (formal)*
	sie waschen **sich**	*they wash*

| Wir amüsieren **uns** hier | We're enjoying ourselves here |
| Die Automaten befinden **sich** dort | The vending machines are (situated) there |

To be = **sein**

4   The verb **sein** *(to be)* is very irregular. The present tense is as follows:

SINGULAR		PLURAL	
ich **bin**	*I am*	wir **sind**	*we are*
du **bist**	*you are (informal)*	ihr **seid**	*you are (informal)*
Sie **sind**	*you are (formal)*	Sie **sind**	*you are (formal)*
er/sie/es **ist**	*he/she/it is*	sie **sind**	*they are*

| Ich **bin** 16 Jahre alt | *I am 16 years old* |
| Boppard **ist** eine kleine Stadt | *Boppard is a small town* |

CHAPTER 3   WHAT HAVE YOU LEARNT?

A   You're describing your room to Maria. Insert a number in the gaps to show how
many of the following objects there are in your room, and where necessary change
the noun to show it is plural.
e.g. In meinem Zimmer habe ich … Vorhang …
   →   In meinem Zimmer habe ich 2 Vorhänge.

In meinem Zimmer
1   In meinem Zimmer habe ich … Vorhang … und … Kleiderschrank …
2   Neben meinem Bett habe ich … Nachttisch …
3   An der Wand habe ich … Foto … und … Bild …
4   Das Zimmer hat … Fenster …
5   Ich habe … Bücherregal … , … Kassettenrekorder … und … Fernseher.

B   You write to Maria and describe your morning routine.
Complete the sentence with
either the missing prefix of the separable verb
or the reflexive pronoun
to give the sense of the English verb in brackets.
e.g. Ich wache um sieben Uhr …   [wake up].   →   Ich wache um sieben Uhr auf.

Ich stehe langsam auf
1   Ich wache um sieben Uhr …   [wake up]
    Zuerst höre ich etwas Musik.
2   Ich stehe nur langsam …   [get up]
    Dann gehe ich ins Badezimmer.
3   Ich wasche …   [wash myself]
    Danach gehe ich ins Schlafzimmer zurück.
4   Ich kämme …   [comb my hair]
    Ich frühstücke schnell.
    Ich verlasse das Haus um 8.25 Uhr.
5   Der Bus kommt um 8.30 Uhr …   [arrive]
    Ich steige in den Bus …   [get on]
    Die Fahrt zur Schule dauert 15 Minuten.
6   Ich steige vor der Schule …   [get off]
    Die Schule beginnt um neun Uhr.

Revision test 1–3

A Test yourself to see if you know the gender of all these items which are in the Maier's kitchen. Put (**die**) after feminine nouns; (**der**) after masculine nouns and (**das**) after neuter nouns.

e.g. Besteck (…) → Besteck (<u>das</u>)

Im Kaufhaus

1 Besteck (…)	2 Messer (…)	3 Gabel (…)	4 Löffel (…)
5 Geschirr (…)	6 Teller (…)	7 Untertasse (…)	8 Tasse (…)
9 Glas (…)	10 Bier (…)	11 Wein (…)	12 Sekt (…)

B Talking to Maria on the telephone, you tell her about your family. Put the verbs in brackets in the correct form of the present tense.

e.g. Ich (<u>haben</u>) zwei Brüder. → Ich <u>habe</u> zwei Brüder.

Meine Familie (1)

MARIA Hast du Geschwister?

DU Ich (<u>haben</u>) zwei Brüder und eine Schwester.

MARIA Wie heißen sie?

DU Meine Brüder (<u>heißen</u>) John und Stephen. Sie (<u>sein</u>) Zwillinge. Meine Schwester (<u>heißen</u>) Jayne. Jayne (<u>sein</u>) 21.

C The conversation continues. Replace the English word in brackets with the German equivalent in the present tense.

e.g. Ich [play] gern Tennis. → Ich <u>spiele</u> gern Tennis.

Meine Familie (2)

MARIA Was sind deine Hobbys?

DU Ich [play] gern Tennis und ich [read] sehr gern und [go] gern ins Kino.

MARIA Was macht dein Vater gern in seiner Freizeit?

DU Er [listens to] sehr gern Musik und [works] jedes Wochenende im Garten.

MARIA Arbeitet deine Mutter?

DU Meine Mutter [helps] jeden Mittwoch in einem Wohltätigkeitsladen. Sie [gets] kein Geld dafür. Sie [brings] mir oft alte Taschenbücher nach Hause.

D You are packing your suitcase ready for going to Germany. You are economising so you just take one of each of the following:

e.g. ... Hose   →   eine Hose

Zum Einpacken

1 ... Hose   2 ... Jacke
3 ... Pullover   4 ... T-Shirt
5 ... Sporthemd   6 ... Paar Schuhe
7 ... Regenmantel   8 ... Schlafanzug

E You receive a postcard from the Maier family who are on an activity holiday in Austria. Unfortunately the rain has smudged some of the words. Complete the gaps in the postcard.

e.g. wir amüsieren ... hier   →   wir amüsieren uns hier

Grüße aus Österreich

Bad Gastein, 18.7.98 Grüße aus Österreich. Wir amusieren ... hier. Wir stehen jeden Tag früh ... ! Peter wäscht ... schnell und zieht ... gleich ... . Danach hat er eine Tennisstunde in die Tennishalle. Danach machen wir normalerweise einen Spaziergang. Wir fühlen ... alle sehr wohl. Eure Familie Maier	Familie XYZ 10 High St ————————

F As you leave the house to go on holiday, you are given the task of checking that the house is secure. From the German phrases given, work out which phrase matches the English. Complete the German phrase with one of these separable prefixes: **aus, ein, ab, heraus, hinaus.**

e.g. 1 Switch off the light.   →   e Schalten Sie das Licht ...   →   aus.

Vergessen Sie nicht!

1 Switch off the light.   a Ziehen Sie den Stecker des Fernsehers ...
2 Take out the rubbish.   b Schalten Sie den Sicherheitsalarm ...
3 Unplug the TV.   c Bringen Sie den Müll ...
4 Switch on the burglar alarm.   d Schließen Sie die Tür ...
5 Lock the door.   e Schalten Sie das Licht ...

CHAPTER 4   WHAT DO YOU KNOW?

A Maria describes the area where she lives, in some detail. Check the gender of the
underlined noun and then insert **einen**, **eine** or **ein** in each gap as appropriate.
e.g. Es gibt ... Tennis<u>platz</u>.   →   Es gibt <u>einen</u> Tennisplatz.

In meiner Gegend
Nicht weit von meiner Wohnung gibt es ... Einkaufs<u>zentrum</u>, ... Schwimm<u>bad</u> und
... <u>Park</u> mit Tennisplätzen. Im Einkaufszentrum gibt es ... <u>Bank</u>. Jeden Samstag gibt
es ... <u>Markt</u> auf dem Marktplatz. Es gibt ... <u>Bahnhof</u> fünf Minuten von hier entfernt.

B You write to Maria saying which of the sights in Berlin you look forward to visiting.
Again check the gender of the underlined words and then insert **den**, **die**, **das** or **die**
(plural) in the gaps as appropriate.
e.g. Ich möchte ... Kurfürstendamm sehen.
    →   Ich möchte <u>den</u> Kurfürstendamm sehen.

den 11. November

Liebe Maria,
ich freue mich schon auf meinen Besuch in Berlin. Also ich möchte ... Rote <u>Rathaus</u>, ...
Fernseh<u>turm</u> und ... Alexander<u>platz</u> sehen. Ich möchte auch ... Brandenburger <u>Tor</u>, ... <u>Reichstag</u>
und ... <u>Schloß</u> Charlottenburg besichtigen. Meine Freundin hat mir auch ... Babelsberger
Film<u>studios</u> empfohlen.

Bis bald,

_____

C At the airport you are waiting for your flight to Berlin. Look at the departure board
and read the sentences in German below. Which sentences are **richtig** (correct) and
which **falsch** (wrong)?
e.g. Die Maschine nach Paris fliegt um zwanzig Uhr fünfzehn ab.   →   richtig

LH 234	Düsseldorf	18.55	Boarding	23
LH 319	Frankfurt	19.05	Boarding	21
AF 345	Paris	20.15	Wait in hall	17
LH 567	Berlin	21.10	Wait in hall	6

Richtig oder falsch?
1 Der Abflug nach Düsseldorf ist um achtzehn Uhr fünfzig.
2 Die Maschine nach Berlin fliegt um einundzwanzig Uhr zehn ab.
3 Für den Flug nach Frankfurt bitte zum Gate dreiundzwanzig.
4 Für den Flug nach Paris gehen Sie sofort zum Gate sechs.

Accusative case

1   We saw in Chapter 1 that the German words for *the* (definite article) and *a* (indefinite article) change according to the gender of the noun. The German articles also change according to what the noun does in the sentence:

Ein Stadtplan ist nicht teuer	*A street map is not expensive*
Wir haben **einen Stadtplan**	*We have a street map*
Der Lehrer ist hier	*The teacher is here*
Er sucht **den Lehrer**	*He is looking for the teacher*

In the first sentence of each pair **Stadtplan** and **Lehrer** are the subject (doing the action or being described) and in the second sentence they are the DIRECT OBJECT (the person or thing having something done to it).

2   In German if a word is a direct object then we say it is in the ACCUSATIVE CASE (just as we say the subject is in the NOMINATIVE CASE). This only means a change to the definite and indefinite article in the masculine singular:

a   changes in the definite article:

	MASCULINE	FEMININE	NEUTER	PLURAL
NOMINATIVE	der Rock	die Bluse	das Hemd	die Kleider
ACCUSATIVE	**den** Rock	die Bluse	das Hemd	die Kleider
	the skirt	*the blouse*	*the shirt*	*the clothes*

A few other words change in the same way as the definite article. The most common are **dieser/diese/dieses** *(this)* and **jeder/jede/jedes** *(each, every).*

b   changes in the indefinite article:

	MASCULINE	FEMININE	NEUTER	PLURAL
NOMINATIVE	ein Rock	eine Bluse	ein Hemd	keine Kleider
ACCUSATIVE	**einen** Rock	eine Bluse	ein Hemd	keine Kleider
	a skirt	*a blouse*	*a shirt*	*no clothes*

3   Uses of the accusative case:

a   for a direct object:

Sie repariert **den** Wagen	*She is repairing the car*
Hast du **einen** Samstagsjob?	*Have you got a Saturday job?*

See Appendix page 144 for a further explanation of direct object/accusative case b to express duration of time:

Ich bleibe **einen Monat**   *I am staying for a month*
Ich war **einen** Tag in Köln   *I was in Cologne for a day*
Sie arbeitet **den ganzen Tag**   *She works all day long*

c with certain prepositions:

Ich arbeite **für eine** Bank   *I work for a bank*
Er schwimmt **gegen den** Strom   *He is swimming against the current*
Sie geht **durch den** Wald   *She goes through the wood*
Sie kommen **ohne ihren** Sohn   *They are coming without their son*

   See Chapter 6 for further information on the accusative after prepositions.

Telling the time

4 To express the time *at which* something happens use **um**:

Er kommt **um** vier Uhr nachmittags   *He is coming at 4 p.m.*
Die Schule beginnt **um** acht Uhr morgens *School begins at 8 a.m.*

   See Appendix pages 149–152 for more on numbers and time

5 In Germany the 24-hour clock is normally used in more formal, written German
(especially when giving opening times or times of buses and trains, or radio and
television programmes). So after midday you use:

13.00 (dreizehn Uhr)   *(1 p.m.)*   19.00 (neunzehn Uhr)   *(7 p.m.)*
14.00 (vierzehn Uhr)   *(2 p.m.)*   20.00 (zwanzig Uhr)   *(8 p.m.)*
15.00 (fünfzehn Uhr)   *(3 p.m.)*   21.00 (einundzwanzig Uhr)   *(9 p.m.)*
16.00 (sechzehn Uhr)   *(4 p.m.)*   22.00 (zweiundzwanzig Uhr)   *(10 p.m.)*
17.00 (siebzehn Uhr)   *(5 p.m.)*   23.00 (dreiundzwanzig Uhr)   *(11 p.m.)*
18.00 (achtzehn Uhr)   *(6 p.m.)*   24.00 (vierundzwanzig Uhr)   *(12 midnight)*

Der Zug fährt um **sechzehn** Uhr ab   *The train departs at 4 p.m.*

To express minutes past simply put the number after the hour (written version in
brackets):

Der Zug fährt um siebzehn Uhr **dreißig** (17.30 Uhr) ab
   The train leaves at five-thirty (5.30 p.m.)
Der Bus fährt um achtzehn Uhr **vierzig** (18.40 Uhr) ab
   The bus leaves at six-forty (6.40 p.m.)

CHAPTER 4   WHAT HAVE YOU LEARNT?

A You have prepared some questions you want to ask in the tourist office. Replace the
English word with the German equivalent.

e.g. Gibt es [a] Bus nach Dresden? → Gibt es <u>einen</u> Bus nach Dresden?

Im Verkehrsbüro

1 Gibt es [a] Ausflug nach Salzburg?
2 Gibt es denn [no] Freibad in der Nähe?
3 Ich möchte [one] Karte für [the] Stadtrundfahrt reservieren.
4 Gibt es [a] Bus nach Potsdam?
5 Kann man hier Karten für [the] Theater kaufen?
6 Ich möchte [a] Stadtplan bitte.
7 Ich möchte [the] Schloß besichtigen. Gibt es morgen [a] Führung?
8 Wo kann ich hier [a] Fahrrad mieten?

B Look at the schedule for Herr Maier's next business trip and the sentences below.
Which sentences are **richtig** and which are **falsch**? Correct those which are **falsch**.

e.g. Am Montag habe ich um 12 Uhr Konferenz mit Herrn Schmidt.

→ falsch; um zehn Uhr.

Herr Maiers Kalender

Montag	10.00	Besuch der Firma Kahl & Co.
	13.00	Mittagessen / Herr Schmidt
	15.00	Konferenz / Frau Kahl und Herr Schmidt
Dienstag	09.00	Stadtrundfahrt: Abfahrt vom Hotel
	13.00	Mittagessen / Restaurant Zum Goldenen Löwen
	18.15	Abflug nach Bremen. Übernachtung / Hotel Ritter
Mittwoch	14.00	Verabredung / Geschäftsführer der Firma Frosch

1 Also am Montag besuche ich um neun Uhr die Firma Kahl & Co.
2 Danach esse ich um 12 Uhr mit Herrn Schmidt.
3 Um 15 Uhr habe ich dann Konferenz mit Frau Kahl und Herrn Schmidt.
4 Am Dienstag mache ich eine Stadtrundfahrt.
5 Ich muß um zehn Uhr vor dem Hotel sein.
6 Um 19 Uhr esse ich im Restaurant Zum Goldenen Löwen.
7 Die Maschine nach Bremen fliegt um 17.15 Uhr ab.
8 Am Mittwoch habe ich um 14 Uhr eine Verabredung.

UNIT

2

CHAPTER 5   WHAT DO YOU KNOW?

A You are at Maria's home in Berlin watching television, but you are having problems understanding. You ask Maria to explain what's going on. In each sentence check the gender of the underlined noun and then choose either **der**, **dem** or **den** to complete the sentence.

e.g. Das Haus gehört ... Mädchen.   →   Das Haus gehört dem Mädchen.

Ich verstehe nicht
Wem gehört das Auto?
1 Das Auto gehört ... Frau.
Was macht die alte Dame?
2 Die alte Dame dankt ... Mädchen.
Was gibt sie dem Mann?
3 Sie gibt ... Mann ein Buch.
Wem hilft der Arzt?
4 Der Arzt hilft ... Studentin.
Wem folgt der Detektiv?
5 Der Detektiv folgt ... Kindern.

B Peter wants to go out so he phones his friends to see who is free.
Which of the German prepositions **nach**, **zu** or **mit** best replaces the English?
e.g. [After] dem Kino gehe ich ...   →   Nach dem Kino gehe ich ...

Hast du Lust, ins Kino zu gehen?
1 PETER   Hallo Ingrid, hier Peter. Hast du Lust, heute abend ins Kino zu gehen?
  INGRID   Tag Peter. Leider kann ich nicht. [After] der Schule gehe ich [with] meinen Freunden eislaufen.

2 PETER   Tag Max, hier Peter. Willst du heute abend [with] mir [to] dem See gehen?
  MAX   Tut mir leid. Ich gehe [with] Fredi und seinem Freund in die Disko.

3 PETER   Hallo Anja. Hast du heute abend schon etwas vor?
  ANJA   Ja, ich fahre [with] Ingrid und ihrer Mutter [to] dem Einkaufszentrum. Wir gehen einkaufen. [After] dem Abendessen muß ich unbedingt meine Hausaufgaben machen.

Dative case

1 Look at the sentence *she writes her mother a letter*. *'her mother'* is the INDIRECT OBJECT of the verb. It can often be recognised in English by the word *to* or *for* in front of the noun or pronoun.

To distinguish between the direct and indirect objects, ask first *What is she writing?* Answer: a letter, the direct object. Then ask *Who is she writing to?* Answer: her mother, the indirect object.

2 In German the indirect object is expressed by using the DATIVE CASE. We show the dative case in German by changing the article and adding -**n** to the noun in the plural:

a the definite article:

	MASCULINE	FEMININE	NEUTER	PLURAL
NOMINATIVE	**der** Rock	**die** Bluse	**das** Hemd	**die** Kleider
DATIVE	**dem** Rock	**der** Bluse	**dem** Hemd	**den** Kleidern

b the indefinite article:

	MASCULINE	FEMININE	NEUTER	PLURAL
NOMINATIVE	**ein** Rock	**eine** Bluse	**ein** Hemd	keine Kleider
DATIVE	**einem** Rock	**einer** Bluse	**einem** Hemd	keinen Kleidern

Sie bringt **einem Freund** einige Geschenke
She is bringing her boyfriend some presents/She is bringing some presents for her boyfriend
Ich schicke **einer Freundin** ein Foto von mir
I am sending my girlfriend a photo of me/I am sending a photo of me to my girlfriend

Note: the possessive adjectives mein, dein, sein, ihr, unser have the same endings as ein.

See Chapter 10.5 for more on word order with an indirect object
See Chapter 12.8 for more on possessive adjectives

Prepositions followed by the dative case

3 The dative case is also used in German after certain PREPOSITIONS, that is, words like the English *opposite, with, or from*. The following prepositions are always followed by the dative case:

aus	*out of, from*	**seit**	*since*
bei	*near; at the house of*	**von**	*from*
mit	*with*	**zu**	*to*
nach	*after*	**gegenüber**	*opposite*

Help Yourself to Essential German Grammar

Er kommt **aus** dem Haus   *He's coming **out of** the house*
Heute abend gehe ich **zu** einer Party   *This evening I'm going **to** a party*
Der Schrank ist **gegenüber** dem Bett   *The cupboard is **opposite** the bed*
Wir wohnen der Post **gegenüber**   *We live **opposite** the post office*
Note: Sometimes **gegenüber** comes after the noun it refers to.

4 In some cases (singular only) the preposition and the definite article are joined together, e.g. **zu dem Bahnhof** usually becomes **zum Bahnhof**:

beim Mittagessen (bei dem Mittagessen)   *at lunch*
am/vom/zum Bahnhof (an/von/zu dem Bahnhof)   *at/from/to the station*
im Garten (in dem Garten)   *in the garden*

Note that **zu** is the only preposition which merges with the feminine **der**:

zur Schule (zu der Schule)   *to school*

Verbs followed by the dative case

5 The dative case is used after some verbs:

a some verbs are followed by a dative object, including several where an English speaker would not expect a dative:

danken   *to thank*   **helfen**   *to help*   **folgen**   *to follow*   **passen**   *to suit, fit*

Ich danke **dem Mann** für seine Hilfe   *I thank the man for his help.*
Wir helfen **dem** Kind   *We help the child*
Folgen Sie **dem** Auto!   *Follow that car!*
Das Kleid paßt **meiner** Tochter nicht   *The dress doesn't fit my daughter*

b **gefallen** *(to please)* and **schmecken** *(to taste)* often come in constructions where English uses the German indirect object as the subject:

Das Buch gefällt **meiner** Mutter
  My mother likes the book (literally the book pleases my mother)
Der Kuchen schmeckt **dem** Kind sehr gut
  The child likes the cake very much (literally the cake tastes good to the child)

c the frequently used phrase, **es geht** + the dative of a person + adjective, indicates how someone is healthwise or more generally how things are going:

Wie geht es **dem Kanzler**?   *How is the Prime Minister?*
Es geht **meinem Freund** gut   *My friend is (doing) well*

CHAPTER 5   WHAT HAVE YOU LEARNT?

A It's nearly Christmas. Each person has told you what they will be giving and to whom. Write this out in full.

e.g. Peter / Schwester / eine CD   →   Peter gibt <u>seiner</u> Schwester eine CD.

Weihnachtsgeschenke

1 Herr Maier / Tochter / ein Buch
2 Frau Maier / Sohn / ein Paar Handschuhe
3 Peter / Vater / eine Krawatte
4 Maria / Mutter / eine Vase

B You want to go to the shopping centre but are not sure where the main buildings are. Look at Frau Maier's map and the sentences below. Which sentences are **richtig** and which are **falsch**? Correct those which are **falsch**.

e.g. Die Bank ist neben dem Kino.   →   <u>falsch</u>. Die Bank ist neben dem Kaufhaus.

Bank	Kaufhaus	Apotheke

Kino	Buchhandlung	Schuhgeschäft

Im Einkaufszentrum

1 Das Kaufhaus ist gegenüber der Apotheke.
2 Das Schuhgeschäft ist links von der Buchhandlung.
3 Die Bank ist gegenüber dem Schuhgeschäft.
4 Die Apotheke ist rechts von dem Kaufhaus.

C Look at Frau Maier's shopping list. First match what she has to do with the places she goes to. Then describe in German where she is going. Start your sentence with **Sie geht** and decide which form (**zum, zur** or **zu den**) you need to use before the place name to say 'to the'.

e.g. 1 *einen Flugschein kaufen*
   →   b Reisebüro   →   1 b, Sie geht zum Reisebüro.

Einkaufsliste

1 *einen Flugschein kaufen*   a Bibliothek
2 *Fotos holen*   b Reisebüro
3 *Bücher zurückbringen*   c Apotheke
4 *Kopfschmerztabletten kaufen*   d Fotogeschäft

Help Yourself to Essential German Grammar

UNIT

2

A You and Maria go out into the local area. Choose the right form of the article from the options given to complete each sentence.

e.g. Ich gehe zuerst in ... Kaufhaus. *das/dem*

→   Ich gehe zuerst in <u>das</u> Kaufhaus.

Wohin gehen wir?

1 Die Hauptstraße ist um ... Ecke. *die/der*
2 Wir gehen ... Weg entlang. *den/dem*
3 Ich gehe zuerst in ... Kaufhaus. *das/dem*
4 Der Eingang ist an ... Ecke. *die/der*

B You meet up with a group of friends and the conversation turns to holidays. Which word(s) should you use to say 'to'? **in die** or **nach**?

e.g. Ich fahre im Sommer ... Frankreich.   →   Ich fahre im Sommer <u>nach</u> Frankreich.

Was macht ihr in den Ferien?

1 Ich fahre im Sommer ... Spanien. Ich besuche meine Brieffreundin.
2 Wenn ich genug Geld hätte, würde ich ... Amerika fliegen.
3 Zu Weihnachten fahren wir ... Schweiz. Wir laufen gerne Ski.
4 Meine Familie kommt aus Istanbul. Wir fahren jedes Jahr in ... Türkei.

C Here's a list of words which give commands, but their meanings in English are mixed up. Can you match up the instruction in German with its correct meaning in English?

e.g. 1 Kommen Sie!   →   c Come!

Befehle

1	Kommen Sie!	a Push!
2	Gehen Sie!	b Stop!
3	Ziehen Sie!	c Come!
4	Stehen Sie auf!	d Go!
5	Drücken Sie!	e Pull!
6	Antworten Sie!	f Get up!
7	Fangen Sie an!	g Answer!
8	Hören Sie auf!	h Begin!

More on prepositions...

1   We saw in Chapter 5 that some prepositions are always followed by the dative case. Others, including **durch**, **für**, **ohne**, **gegen**, **um** and **bis**, are always followed by the ACCUSATIVE CASE.

Fahren Sie **durch** die Stadt	Go *through* the town
Sie spielt **für** eine Volleyballmannschaft	She plays *for* a volleyball team
Er geht **ohne** einen Gruß vorbei	He passes by *without* a greeting
Wir spielen **gegen** ihre Mannschaft	We are playing *against* their team
Bis nächste Woche!	*Until* next week!
Die Post ist **um** die Ecke	The post office is *round* the corner

2   **Entlang** *(along)* also takes the accusative, but it comes after the noun:

Er fährt die Straße **entlang**   *He drives **along** the street*

For lists of prepositions followed by the accusative see Appendix pages 142–143

3   A third group of prepositions is followed by *either* the accusative *or* dative:

an	*on, at*	**auf**	*on*	**hinter**	*behind*
neben	*next to*	**in**	*in, into*	**unter**	*under*
über	*over, about*	**vor**	*in front of*	**zwischen**	*between*

a   if the preposition suggests *movement*, especially *towards something or someone*, e.g. *going into a room* or *putting something somewhere*, then the preposition is followed by the accusative:

Die Katze springt **auf den** Tisch   *The cat jumps on(to) the table*
Sie setzt sich **vor den** Fernseher   *She sits down in front of the TV*

b   if the preposition shows something or someone as static or stationary, i.e. *being somewhere*, then the dative case is used after the preposition:

Die Katze liegt **auf dem** Tisch   *The cat is on the table*
Sie sitzt **vor dem** Fernseher   *She is sitting in front of the TV*

c   as with some dative prepositions, there are some merged forms with the accusative **das**. The most common is **in das** → **ins**; there is also **an das** → **ans**, **auf das** → **aufs**, and so on, which are mostly used in speech:

Gehst du oft **ins** Kino?   *Do you go to the cinema often?*
Kommen Sie bitte **ans** Telefon!   *Please come to the telephone*
Die Katze springt **aufs** Dach   *The cat jumps on the roof*

4   When **über** means *about*, it is always followed by the accusative case:

Sag mir etwas **über** deine Familie   *Tell me something about your family*

5   For travelling *to* countries use:

a   **in** followed by the accusative case with countries that include a definite article in their name:

Ich fahre **in** die USA   *I am going to the USA*
Ich fahre **in** die Schweiz   *I am going to Switzerland*

b   **nach** with all other countries:

Ich fahre **nach** Frankreich   *I am going to France*

How to tell someone what to do

6   The IMPERATIVE form of the verb is used to give orders or instructions. In the **Sie** form (polite singular and plural), the imperative is formed by turning the **Sie** and the verb round, e.g. **Sie gehen** → **Gehen Sie**:

Gehen Sie hier geradeaus!   *Go straight on here*
Nehmen Sie die dritte Straße rechts!   *Take the third street on the right*
Lesen Sie Fragen 5 bis 8!   *Read questions 5 to 8*

Note: More often than in English, an exclamation mark is still used in German, but this is becoming rarer.

7   With separable verbs the separable prefix is sent to the end of the sentence:

Füllen Sie dieses Formular **aus**   *Fill in this form*
Senden Sie es an uns **zurück**   *Send it back to us*

8   With reflexive verbs the reflexive pronoun goes to the end:

Setzen Sie sich!   *Sit down!*

For more on the imperative see section 21.4

CHAPTER 6   WHAT HAVE YOU LEARNT?

A First read Maria's diary:

Mo	14	Monika Kaufhaus
Di	15	Peter! Disko
Mi	16	Theater mit Bernd
Do	17	Tennis Michael Park
Fr	18	Max Museum 10.00
Sa	19	Sven Kino 21.00

Stefan telephones Maria to find out if she is free at all during the week. Replace the English word(s) given with the German equivalent to complete Maria's replies.
e.g. Dienstag? Wir gehen [to the] Disko.   →   Wir gehen in die Disko.

Die Wahrheit
Montag besuche ich mit Monika das Kaufhaus [next to the] Bibliothek.
Dienstag? Leider bin ich schon [with] Peter verabredet. Wir gehen [to the] Disko.
Mittwoch gehe ich [with] Bernd [to the] Theater.
Donnerstag spielen Michael und ich [in the] Park Tennis.
Freitag treffe ich Max [in front of the] Museum.
Samstag treffe ich Sven [opposite the] Kino.

B You want to call your host family to let them know you'll be late home. A passerby shows you how to use the public phone. Complete the instructions by putting the verb on the right in its imperative form.
e.g. Zuerst ... ... den Hörer ...   *abnehmen*   →   Zuerst nehmen Sie den Hörer ab.

Telefon/Fernsprecher
1 ... ... die Münzen in den Schlitz ...   *einwerfen*
2 ... ... die Nummer.   *wählen*
3 Am Ende des Telefonanrufs ... ... den Hörer ...   *auflegen*
4 ... ... auf die ungebrauchten Münzen.   *warten*

Revision test 4–6

A Whilst on holiday in Austria you feel adventurous and decide to try the public transport system. You ask for directions and how to use the local buses. Choose the appropriate word(s) from those on the right to fill the gap.

e.g. Wie komme ich ... Stadthalle? *zum   zur   zu den*
→ Wie komme ich <u>zur</u> Stadthalle?

Einmal zum Stadtzentrum bitte

1 DU   Wie komme ich am besten ... Einkaufszentrum? *zum   zur   zu den*
2 PASSANT Sie müssen entweder 20 Minuten zu Fuß gehen oder fünf Minuten mit ... Bus fahren. *dem   der   den*
3   Sie nehmen ... Linie 104. *den   die   das*
   DU   Ich fahre lieber mit dem Bus. Wo gibt es hier eine Haltestelle?
4 PASSANT Die Bushaltestelle liegt direkt vor ... Bäckerei. *dem   der   den*
   DU   Wo bekomme ich eine Busfahrkarte?
5 PASSANT ... Fahrer. *Beim   Bei der   Bei den*
   DU   Wo muß ich aussteigen?
6 PASSANT ... Rathaus. *Am   An der   An den*
   DU   Vielen Dank für Ihre Hilfe!

B You arrive successfully at the shopping centre but don't immediately see the shops and services you want. You ask a passerby for some help. Replace the English in brackets with the German equivalent.

e.g. Gibt es [a] Fotogeschäft in der Nähe?
→ Gibt es <u>ein</u> Fotogeschäft in der Nähe?

Ich suche...

DU   Gibt es [a] Bank in der Nähe?
PASSANT Die Bank ist neben [the] Bäckerei.
DU   Hat die Bank [a] Geldautomaten?
PASSANT Der Geldautomat ist in [the] Bank.
DU   Wo gibt es hier [a] Postamt?
PASSANT Das Postamt ist gegenüber [the] Markt.
DU   Gibt es hier [a] Briefkasten?
PASSANT Der Briefkasten ist vor [the] Postamt.

C Using the 24-hour clock, say what time it is in these cities.

   e.g. New York – 7 p.m.   →   Es ist <u>19</u> Uhr in New York.

   Wieviel Uhr ist es in...?

   London – 10 p.m.

   Berlin – 11 p.m.

   San Franzisco – 12 midday

   Peking – 7 a.m.

   Delhi – 3 a.m.

D You can see the cash machine inside the bank but the door appears to be locked. You ask another bank customer for help. Complete the instructions with the appropriate German equivalent of the English verb from the list provided.

   e.g. [Press] die Taste für den gewünschten Geldbetrag.

   →   Drücken Sie die Taste für den gewünschten Geldbetrag.

   Am Geldautomaten

   1 Um die Tür aufzumachen, [draw] die Bankkarte durch den Schlitz. Dann geht die Eingangstür automatisch auf.

   2 [Push] die Tür auf. [Go] hinein.

   3 Um Geld vom Automaten abzuheben, [follow] den Anweisungen.

   4 [Put in] die Karte in den Schlitz. [Choose] die gewünschte Sprache.

   5 Dann [type in] Ihre Geheimzahl, und so weiter.

   gehen   folgen   einstecken   wählen   ziehen   eintippen   drücken

E At the port in Hamburg you watch the car ferry loading and unloading. You notice the stickers which identify the countries that the cars and lorries have come from and are probably returning to.

   Gute Heimfahrt!

   Say in German where each car and lorry is driving to.

   e.g. GB   →   Er fährt nach Großbritannien.

   1 CH   2 I   3 F   4 L

   Gute Reise!

   Now say where each car and lorry has come from.

   e.g. GB   →   Er kommt aus Großbritannien.

   1 P   2 IRL   3 B   4 USA

3 Die Konsumgesellschaft

CHAPTER 7   WHAT DO YOU KNOW?

A Peter is considering how to spend the DM 50,- that he has left from his birthday money. Fill the gap with the German equivalent of the English adjective given in brackets.

e.g. Das ist nicht [cheap]. → Das ist nicht <u>billig</u>.

Was soll ich kaufen?
Eine Videokassette kostet DM 29,-. Das ist nicht [expensive].
Das T-Shirt kostet nur DM 10,-. Das ist [cheap].
Die Jeanshose kostet DM 59,-. Ich habe nur DM 50,-. Das ist nicht [enough]. Ich kaufe mir die Videokassette.

B Herr and Frau Maier discuss how to celebrate Frau Maier's birthday. Complete the adjective with the ending (**-er**, **-e** or **-es**) that matches the gender of the noun.

e.g. Das alt ... Wirtshaus. → Das alt<u>e</u> Wirtshaus.

Gehen wir ins Restaurant?
FRAU MAIER Das neu ... Restaurant in der Goethestraße soll gut sein.
HERR MAIER Gehen wir lieber zum Restaurant am See. Der schön ... Ausblick ist unübertroffen und die romantisch ... Atmosphäre gefällt mir.

Their discussion continues. Again fill in the adjective ending. You may need to check the gender of the noun this time.

e.g. Ein schön ... Theater. → Ein schön<u>es</u> Theater.

Gehen wir lieber ins Theater
FRAU MAIER Ein schön ... Ausblick nützt uns nicht, wenn wir nichts draußen sehen können.
HERR MAIER Ein voll ... Restaurant bedeutet ein gut ... Restaurant.
FRAU MAIER Ich gehe lieber ins Theater. Was spielt im Schillertheater?

C Herr Maier is doing some home repairs but needs to buy some items from the DIY store. Give the correct article (**der**, **die** or **das**) for each item.

e.g. Wandfliese → <u>die</u> Wandfliese

Im Laden
1 Steckdose   2 Glühbirne   3 Wasserhahn   4 Schraubenzieher

Describing nouns: adjectives

1   A word which describes a noun and gives us more information about it is called an
ADJECTIVE.

2   When an adjective stands alone, usually after the noun it describes, then the adjective
does not change:

Der Ausblick ist **schön**	*The view is **beautiful***
Die Straße ist **ruhig**	*The street is **quiet***
Das Restaurant ist **voll**	*The restaurant is **full***
Die Teenager sind **laut**	*The teenagers are **noisy***

3   If an adjective stands immediately before the noun then an ending is added. When
deciding which ending to add you must take into account:

- the gender of the noun
- whether it is singular or plural
- the case of the noun it describes in the sentence
- whether or not there is an article in front of the adjective.

4   In the nominative case, the adjective has the following endings:

a   after the definite article, and **dieser** *(this)* and **jeder** *(every)*:

MASCULINE	der schön**e** Ausblick	*the beautiful view*
FEMININE	die ruhig**e** Straße	*the quiet street*
NEUTER	das voll**e** Restaurant	*the full restaurant*
PLURAL	die laut**en** Teenager	*the noisy teenagers*

b   after the indefinite article, and **kein** *(no)*, **mein** *(my)*, **dein** *(your)*, etc.:

MASCULINE	ein schön**er** Ausblick	*a beautiful view*
FEMININE	eine ruhig**e** Straße	*a quiet street*
NEUTER	ein voll**es** Restaurant	*a full restaurant*
PLURAL	keine laut**en** Teenager	*no noisy teenagers*

c   if there is no article:

MASCULINE	stark**er** Wind	*strong wind*
FEMININE	leck**ere** Pizza	*delicious pizza*
NEUTER	mild**es** Wetter	*mild weather*
PLURAL	lang**e** Haare	*long hair*

Note: The plural endings are the same for all genders (masculine, feminine and
neuter).

5 The adjective endings for the accusative case are the same as for the nominative case except for the *masculine singular,* which is always **-en**:

Wir suchen eine klein**e** Wohnung	*We are looking for a small flat*
Ich habe ein rund**es** Gesicht	*I have a round face*
Sie hat lockig**e** Haare	*She has curly hair*
Wir suchen einen klein**en** Hund	*We are looking for a small dog*
Er kauft den teur**en** Wagen	*He is buying the expensive car*
Sie mögen süß**en** Wein	*They like sweet wine*

Full tables of adjective endings in every case are on Appendix pages 146–147

More about nouns...

6 In German you will often see long words consisting of two or more words put together to make one noun. These are called COMPOUND NOUNS. They always have the gender of their last part:

a   some compound nouns are two nouns put together:

| die Hausfrau | *housewife* |
| das Satellitenfernsehen | *satellite television* |

b   some are made up of a verb and a noun:

| die Fahrkarte | *ticket* | (fahren = *to travel*) |
| das Schlafzimmer | *bedroom* | (schlafen = *to sleep*) |

c   some are made up of a prefix (e.g. **unter** meaning *under*) and a noun:

die Unterschrift   *signature*   der Vorname   *first name*

7 All masculine nouns ending in **-er** which refer to people (and most of those with other endings) have a feminine form ending in **-in**. This also applies to some animals:

der Lehrer	*(male) teacher*	→	die Lehrer**in**	*(female) teacher*
der Freund	*(male) friend*	→	die Freund**in**	*(female) friend*
der Bär	*(male) bear*	→	die Bär**in**	*(female) bear*

In addition to the **-in** ending, the first vowel of some nouns takes an umlaut:

| der Arzt | *(male) doctor* | → | die Ärtz**in** | *(female) doctor* |
| der Hund | *(male) dog* | → | die Hünd**in** | *(female) dog* |

CHAPTER 7   WHAT HAVE YOU LEARNT?

A Maria has to do an essay on what she would like to be when she leaves school. She discusses it with the family. Fill the gap with the correct article.

e.g. ... Lehrerin ist sehr wichtig.   →   <u>Eine</u> Lehrerin ist sehr wichtig.

Welchen Beruf findest du am besten?

MARIA   Ich möchte Ärztin sein. Aber dann hat man ein langes Studium.

HERR MAIER ... Ärztin ist sehr wichtig. Ohne Ärzte würden wir alle krank sein.

MARIA   Ich könnte auch Krankenpflegerin sein.

OMA MAIER ... Krankenpflegerin verdient aber sehr wenig.

MARIA   Geld verdienen nur die Manager und Bankiers.

MORITZ   Bankier! Das ist ... schöner Beruf! Ich würde ... sehr schnelles Auto und ... teure Wohnung in Monaco kaufen!

B Herr Maier is looking for some garden equipment and spots some bargains. Fill in the correct ending for the adjectives.

e.g. Der weiß ... Gartentisch kostet nur DM 150,-.   →   Der weiß<u>e</u> Gartentisch ...

Alles für den Garten

1 Der grün ... Rasenmäher kostet nur DM 150,-!
2 Die groß ... Gießkanne kostet nur DM 10,-!
3 Die blau ... Blumentöpfe kosten nur DM 5,-!
4 Der bequem ... Liegestuhl kostet nur DM 75,-!
5 Die schön ... gelb ... Sonnenschirme kosten nur DM 25,-!

C You are chatting with Frau Maier about environmental issues. You describe the situation in your home town. Match the two halves of the German sentence and then say which sentence in English it corresponds to.

e.g. 1 Die Straßen sind   →   c sehr laut.   →   iii

Umweltfreundlich oder nicht?

1 Die Straßen sind   a verschmutzt.
2 Die Luft ist   b unfähig.
3 Der Verkehr in der Stadt ist c sehr laut.
4 Der Stadtrat ist   d immer stark.

  i The traffic in the town is always heavy.
 ii The town council is incompetent.
iii The streets are very noisy.
 iv The air is polluted.

UNIT

3

CHAPTER 8   WHAT DO YOU KNOW?

A You have volunteered to stay in with Moritz. You work out some puzzle sentences to keep him entertained. Beginning with the underlined word, how should he re-order the words?
e.g. gehe in Bäckerei die <u>ich</u> → ich gehe in die Bäckerei

Ein Rätsel
1 am Samstag <u>wir</u> ein müssen Sofa kaufen neues
2 Supermarkt kann im billig <u>man</u> einkaufen
3 Geschäfte am Samstag <u>die</u> sind nachmittag offen

B You and Moritz go to the shops but he never stops asking questions. You keep your calm and reply patiently. Starting each sentence with **ja**, change the word order of each question to turn it back into a statement.
e.g. Gehen wir einkaufen? → Ja, wir gehen einkaufen.

Die Plaudertasche
1 Ist das unser Bus?   2 Steigen wir hier aus?
3 Gehen wir in den Supermarkt?   4 Wollen wir Bananen?

C The Maier family discuss their plans for the day. Using the verb **wollen** in the appropriate person, complete each sentence with the suggested activity.
e.g. Frau Maier geht in die Bücherei. *einen Reiseführer kaufen*
   → Frau Maier will einen Reiseführer kaufen.

Was wollt ihr heute machen?
1 Oma Maier geht in den Supermarkt. *einkaufen*
2 Ich gehe ins Kino. *einen Film sehen*
3 Du gehst in den Park. *spazierengehen*
4 Peter und Zoran gehen in die Disko. *tanzen*

D Peter and his friends Max and Zoran discuss their plans for the evening. Put the verbs in brackets into the correct form of the present tense.
e.g. Was (<u>können</u>) ich jetzt tun? → Was <u>kann</u> ich jetzt tun?

Den muß ich sehen!
PETER   Was (<u>können</u>) wir machen?
MAX   Wann (<u>müssen</u>) ihr zu Hause sein?
PETER   Um 11 Uhr. Der neue Film mit Arnold Schwarzenegger läuft im Odeon.
MAX   Den (<u>müssen</u>) ich unbedingt sehen!

Help Yourself to Essential German Grammar

Word order

1 In German there are clear rules about the order in which words appear in a sentence. It will be helpful if you try to see a sentence in German in terms of **blocks**. The most important block is the verb.

2 In nearly all cases the verb is the second block in a sentence:

Block 1	Block 2	Block 3
SUBJECT	VERB	REST OF SENTENCE
Ich	habe	eine Schwester

I   *have*   *a sister*

3 Block 1, however, is not always the subject:

a an expression of time, for instance, can come first:

Block 1	Block 2	Block 3	Block 4
TIME EXPR	VERB	SUBJECT	REST OF SENTENCE
Morgen	geht	mein Bruder	ins Kino

Tomorrow my brother is going to the cinema

b a question word can come first:

Block 1	Block 2	Block 3	Block 4
Q/WORD	VERB	SUBJECT	REST OF SENTENCE
Wann	gehst	du	ins Kino?

When are you going to the cinema?

c In a simple question (with no question word), the verb does come first:

Block 1	Block 2	Block 3
VERB	SUBJECT	REST OF SENTENCE
Gehst	du	ins Kino?

Are you going to the cinema?

So in any question, with or without a question word, subject and verb are turned round (or inverted) with the verb before the subject.

Help Yourself to Essential German Grammar

4 As we saw in Chapter 5, where one has both an indirect and a direct object, the indirect object (dative case) is placed before the direct object (accusative case):

Block 1	Block 2	Block 3	Block 4
SUBJECT	VERB	INDIRECT OBJECT	DIRECT OBJECT
Du	schickst	deinem Freund	ein Foto
Du	schickst	ihm	ein Foto
You	*send*	*your friend/him*	*a photo*

The exception is where the direct object is a PRONOUN:

SUBJECT	VERB	DIRECT OBJECT	INDIRECT OBJECT
Du	schickst	es	ihm/der Frau
You	*send*	*it*	*to him/the woman*

For more on word order in these cases see Chapter 10

Common verbs followed by an infinitive (modal verbs)

5 The irregular verbs **wollen** *(to want to)*, **müssen** *(to have to)* and **können** *(to be able to)* are three of the so-called MODAL VERBS:

wollen	**müssen**	**können**
ich will	ich muß	ich kann
du willst	du mußt	du kannst
Sie wollen	Sie müssen	Sie können
er/sie/es will	er/sie/es muß	er/sie/es kann
wir wollen	wir müssen	wir können
ihr wollt	ihr müßt	ihr könnt
Sie wollen	Sie müssen	Sie können
sie wollen	sie müssen	sie können

6 Modal verbs are followed by an INFINITIVE which goes to the end of the sentence. All the other items in the sentence come in between:

Die Kinder **können** gut <u>schwimmen</u>   *The children can swim well*
Sie **will** mit mir Karten <u>spielen</u>   *She wants to play cards with me*
Ich **muß** heute an sie <u>schreiben</u>   *I must write to her today*
Du **mußt** jetzt früh <u>aufstehen</u>*   *You have to get up early now*

7 **Gehen** *(to go)*, which is not a modal verb, is also followed by an infinitive:

Ich **gehe** <u>tanzen</u>   *I'm going dancing*
Sie **gehen** morgen <u>eislaufen</u>   *They're going skating tomorrow*

---

*Remember the infinitive of a separable verb has the two parts in one word.

CHAPTER 8   WHAT HAVE YOU LEARNT?

A The boys catch up on each other's news. Reply to each question with **ja** or **nein**, then confirm or correct the news with the item given in brackets.

e.g. Fährt Sabine nächstes Jahr nach Amerika? (✗ *Frankreich*)

→   Nein. Sabine fährt nächstes Jahr nach Frankreich.

Was gibt's Neues?

1 Spielen wir am Mittwoch Fußball? (✓)
2 Kommen Karl und Fredi am Wochenende zum Abendessen?
   (✗ *am Montag*)
3 Gehen wir am Samstag in die neue Disko im Kurfürstendamm? (✓)
4 Kommt Philipp am Sonntag ins Schwimmbad mit? (✗ *ins Kino*)
5 Lernt Marianne jetzt Auto fahren? (✓)
6 Können wir am Samstag spät aufstehen? (✗ *Sonntag*)
7 Machen wir am Montag die Klassenfahrt? (✗ *Dienstag*)
8 Fängt der Film um 21 Uhr an? (✓)

B Peter finds in his pocket a note that he has torn up. He tries to work it out. Put the words in the correct order beginning with the underlined word.

e.g. das Buch <u>ich</u> dir gebe   →   ich gebe dir das Buch

Der Zettel

1 einen Schal schenkt <u>Manfred</u> mir
2 du ins Schwimmbad gehst <u>wann</u>
3 ins du <u>gehst</u> Kino
4 Computer ich <u>morgen</u> einen kaufe

C You work out another puzzle for Moritz to solve. You list a number of things you can do in a particular place and he has to work out where you are. Replace the verb written in English with the German equivalent and then match the place with the activity.

e.g. Man [<u>can</u>] hier Bücher lesen.

→   <u>kann</u>   →   Man kann <u>in der Bibliothek</u> Bücher lesen.

Wo bin ich?

1 Ich [<u>can</u>] hier Brötchen kaufen.   a an der Tankstelle
2 Wir [<u>must</u>] hier tanken.   b in der Apotheke
3 Vati [<u>want</u>] hier ein Glas Bier trinken.   c in der Bäckerei
4 Du [<u>can</u>] hier Medikamente kaufen.   d in der Kneipe

CHAPTER 9   WHAT DO YOU KNOW?

A At your host family's home the telephone rings. It is someone asking for Frau Maier. Link the two correct halves of the sentence and say where Frau Maier is, and why she is there using **um ... zu ...**

e.g. Sie geht in die Post,   →   d Briefmarken kaufen
    Sie geht in die Post, <u>um</u> Briefmarken <u>zu</u> kaufen.

Ist Frau Maier zu Hause?

1 Sie geht zuerst in den Supermarkt,	a eine Freundin treffen
2 Zweitens geht sie ins Blumengeschäft,	b ihr Auto holen
3 Danach geht sie ins Café,	c Blumen kaufen
4 Zuletzt geht sie in die Autowerkstatt,	d Lebensmittel kaufen

B You are in a local department store and overhear a conversation. Check the gender of the noun immediately after the adjective and then add the adjective ending (**-er**, **-e** or **-es**) as required.

e.g. Ich suche eine grün ... Jacke.   →   Ich suche eine <u>grüne</u> Jacke.

Im großen Kaufhaus

VERKÄUFER Guten Tag! Sie wünschen, bitte?

KUNDIN   Ich suche einen Pullover, Größe 42.

VERKÄUFER Die gelb ... Strickjacke ist Größe 42. Gefällt sie Ihnen?

KUNDIN   Haben Sie etwas Ähnliches in hellblau?

VERKÄUFER Der hier ist das letzt ... Modell in hellblau.

KUNDIN   Der hellblau ... Pullover sieht sehr schick aus. Welche Größe ist der?

VERKÄUFER Der ist auch Größe 42.

KUNDIN   Gut, den nehme ich.

C In the same store you then go to the electrical department to return a faulty cassette recorder. Check the gender of the noun immediately after the adjective and then add the adjective ending (**-en**, **-e** or **-es**) as required.

e.g. Wir können das alt ... Modell nicht reparieren.

    →   Wir können das <u>alte</u> Modell nicht reparieren.

Elektrowaren

VERKÄUFER Ja, Sie haben Recht. Dieses Modell hat einen eigenartig ... Fehler.
          Leider können wir hier die japanisch ... Maschinen nicht reparieren. Ich
          gebe Ihnen Ihr Geld zurück. Haben Sie die original ... Quittung dafür?
          Kommen Sie bitte mit zur Kasse.

How to say *in order to*

1 To express the idea of purpose, use **um zu** + INFINITIVE:

Ich möchte studieren, **um** Tierärztin **zu werden**
I would like to study in order to become a vet

Note: a **Zu** + INFINITIVE go to the end of the clause.
   b The two halves (or CLAUSES) of the sentence are separated by a comma. *This is compulsory in German.*

2 With a separable verb put **zu** between the prefix and the rest of the infinitive:

Ich sehe in der Zeitung nach, **um** die besten Sendungen aus**zu**suchen
I look in the paper in order to pick out the best programmes

3 Use **um zu** + INFINITIVE whenever *to* in English means *in order to*:

Sie arbeitet, **um** Geld für den Urlaub **zu verdienen**
She is working (in order) to earn some money for the holiday

The genitive case

4 The GENITIVE CASE has the basic sense *of,* and can show possession.

Der Anfang **des** Jahres	*The beginning of the year*
Das Auto **meines Bruders** steht in der Garage	*My brother's car is in the garage*
Marios* erste Fahrstunde	*Mario's first driving lesson*

The GENITIVE CASE is also used to express indefinite time:

ein**es** Tag**es**   *one day*   ein**es** Abend**s**   *one evening*

5 Here is the GENITIVE CASE of the definite and indefinite article and of **mein** (*my*) (**kein** and all the other possessive adjectives change like **mein**):

MASCULINE	FEMININE	NEUTER	PLURAL
des Lehrers	**der** Freundin	**des** Zimmers	**der** Kinder
eines Lehrers	**einer** Freundin	**eines** Zimmers	
meines Lehrers	**meiner** Freundin	**meines** Zimmers	**meiner** Kinder

Note that an **-s** (or **-es** after a short word with one syllable) is added to the noun in masculine and neuter singular:

Das Heulen **des** Babys/**des** Wind**es**   *The howling of the baby/the wind*

---

*With names possession is indicated by adding an **s** (<u>no</u> apostrophe).

Help Yourself to Essential German Grammar

More adjective endings...

6 In the GENITIVE and DATIVE cases the adjective has the following forms:

a after the definite article, **dieser** *(this)* and **jeder** *(every)*:

	GENITIVE	DATIVE	
MASCULINE	des nächst**en** Zuges	dem nächst**en** Zug	*the next train*
FEMININE	der blau**en** Tür	der blau**en** Tür	*the blue door*
NEUTER	des alt**en** Sofas	dem alt**en** Sofa	*the old sofa*
PLURAL	der meist**en** Leute	den meist**en** Leuten	*most people*

b after the indefinite article and **kein** *(no)*, **mein** *(my)*, **dein** *(your)*, etc.:

	GENITIVE	DATIVE	
MASCULINE	eines blau**en** Himmels	einem blau**en** Himmel	*a blue sky*
FEMININE	einer groß**en** Nase	einer groß**en** Nase	*a big nose*
NEUTER	eines klein**en** Hauses	einem klein**en** Haus	*a small house*
PLURAL	meiner best**en** Kleider	meinen best**en** Kleidern	*my best clothes*

c if there is no article:

	GENITIVE	DATIVE	
MASCULINE	schwarz**en** Kaffees	schwarz**em** Kaffee	*black coffee*
FEMININE	klassisch**er** Musik	klassisch**er** Musik	*classical music*
NEUTER	mild**en** Wetters	mild**em** Wetter	*mild weather*
PLURAL	lang**er** Haare	lang**en** Haaren	*long hair*

Full tables of adjective endings in every case are on Appendix pages 146–147

Prepositions with the genitive

7 There is a small group of prepositions which are always followed by the
GENITIVE CASE:

außerhalb	Er wohnt **außerhalb** der Stadt	*He lives **outside** the town*
innerhalb	**Innerhalb** eines Jahres	***Within** one year*
trotz	**Trotz** des schlechten Wetters	***In spite of** the bad weather*
wegen	**Wegen** des Verkehrs*	***Because of** the traffic*
während	**Während** der Sommerferien	***During** the summer holidays*

---

*Note that you will sometimes see **wegen** followed by the dative case.

CHAPTER 9   WHAT HAVE YOU LEARNT?

A Herr Maier gets home from work. Where is everybody? Using an **um zu** clause, tell
him where everyone is and what they are doing.
   e.g. Peter/zur Bank/Reiseschecks holen
      Peter geht zur Bank, <u>um</u> Reiseschecks <u>zu</u> holen.

Wo sind sie denn alle?
1 Maria/zur Post/einen Brief schicken
2 Frau Maier/zum Arzt/ein Rezept holen
3 Moritz/zur Schule/seine Schultasche suchen

B There has been an attempted bank robbery. Replace the underlined phrases (**von** +
dative) with the equivalent phrase using the genitive of the definite article or the
possessive adjective.
   e.g. die Scheiben <u>von dem Fenster</u>   →   die Scheiben <u>des Fensters</u>
      die Fenster <u>von meiner Bank</u>   →   die Fenster <u>meiner Bank</u>

Der Banküberfall
Das Auto <u>von den Bankräubern</u> steht immer noch vor dem Haupteingang <u>von der</u>
<u>Bank.</u> Die Fensterscheiben <u>von dem Auto</u> sind durch die Kugeln <u>von den Polizisten</u>
zersplittert.

C You are in the supermarket, helping Opa Maier with his shopping. He tells you which
items he wants. Fill in the endings of the adjectives.
   e.g. Ich esse die rot ... Tomaten.   →   Ich esse die <u>roten</u> Tomaten.

Im Supermarkt
Also zwei Kilo von den rot ... Äpfeln. Eine Tube dieser neu ... Zahnpasta. Haben sie
grün ... Bohnen? Ach ja, da, neben den groß ... Packungen Erbsen. Ich möchte eine
Dose der best ... Sardinen. Ich glaube, das war es, oder?

Now check his shopping list. Forgotten anything? Answer **ja** or **nein**.
   e.g. 1 Zahnpasta   →   Ja

1 Zahnpasta   2 Umschläge   3 grüne Bohnen
4 Sardinen 1 Dose 5 Milch 1 Liter   6 Äpfel 2 Kilo

D A consumer programme is interviewing holidaymakers about their holiday
experiences. Complete what each person says by replacing the English preposition
with the German equivalent.
   e.g. Das Hotel war [outside] der Stadt.   →   Das Hotel war <u>außerhalb</u> der Stadt.

Hat es Spaß gemacht?
1 Wir haben ein Hotel [within] der Stadt gebucht.
2 Leider war das Hotel weit [outside] des Orts.
3 [Because of] des Lärms vom Flughafen konnten wir kaum schlafen.
4 [During] der Nacht haben uns die Insekten gestochen.
5 [In spite of] dieser schlechten Erfahrungen hat es uns Spaß gemacht!

Help Yourself to Essential German Grammar

Revision test 7–9

A Your friends tell you what they think of Berlin since the dismantling of the Berlin Wall and the reunification of Germany. Replace the English adjective with the German equivalent. Choose from these adjectives: **gefährlich, voll, ruhig, teuer, bedeutend, langsam, beängstigend, laut, bezaubernd**.
e.g. Berlin ist jetzt zu [expensive]. → Berlin ist jetzt zu teuer.

Wie findest du Berlin?
1 Berlin ist jetzt zu [noisy]. Es gibt immer mehr Verkehr.
2 Es gibt zu viele Touristen. Die Straßen im Zentrum sind immer [full].
3 Die Kriminalität ist ein großes Problem. Es ist nachts [dangerous], allein mit der U-Bahn zu fahren.

a Aber früher war Berlin wie eine Insel umgeben von der DDR. Damals war das Leben in Berlin zu [quiet].
b Wir brauchen Tourismus. Berlin und Potsdam sind historisch [important]. Das Schloß Sanssouci ist [enchanting].
c Das stimmt. Die steigende Kriminalität ist [worrying].

B You have forgotten your rucksack on the bus and go to the lost property office (*das Fundbüro*) to see if it has been handed in. The official asks you to describe your rucksack and its contents. Fill in the missing adjective endings.
e.g. Sie ist eine groß ... Tasche. → Sie ist eine große Tasche.

Beschreiben Sie bitte den Rucksack
Er ist ein klein ... schwarz ... Rucksack aus Nylon. Er hat zwei Taschen vorne. In diesen klein ... Taschen sind ein blau ... Kugelschreiber und drei Postkarten. In der groß ... Tasche des Rucksacks ist mein grün ... Regenmantel.

C Look at the following signs and notices which include compound nouns. What do they mean in English?
e.g. Wegen Neujahrsferien geschlossen → Closed for New Year holiday

Schilder
1 Kinderspielplatz
2 Wartezeit 20 Minuten
3 Vorsicht Bahnübergang!
4 Kabelfernsehen
5 Mittwochs Ruhetag

D Unscramble the following sentences beginning each sentence with the underlined word. Use all the punctuation marks given for each sentence.
e.g. die ist Bushaltestelle <u>Wo</u> nächste ?   →   Wo ist die nächste Bushaltestelle?

Wortstellung!
1 ich Bahnhof <u>Wie</u> zum komme ?
2 Kino gehen um Film <u>Wir</u> morgen einen zu ins sehen , .
3 Schulhof die auf Kinder <u>Spielen</u> dem ?
4 ab nach fährt <u>Wann</u> Zug Stuttgart der ?
5 Oma <u>Nächstes</u> besuchen wir Schweiz Jahr fahren die in um zu meine , .

E You are in a shoe shop. What ending should you use for each adjective?
e.g. in einer <u>ander...</u> Farbe   →   in einer ander<u>en</u> Farbe

Im Schuhgeschäft

DU   Haben Sie diese Schuhe in einer <u>kleiner ...</u> Größe?
VERKÄUFERIN Nein, leider nicht.
DU   Vielleicht in einem <u>ähnlich ...</u> Stil?
VERKÄUFERIN Wir haben die hier. Welche Farbe möchten Sie?
DU   Ich habe sie lieber im <u>praktisch ...</u> Schwarz.
VERKÄUFERIN Ja, Schwarz ist eine <u>praktisch ...</u> Farbe. Wie finden Sie die?
DU   Plastik ist aber unangenehm bei dem <u>warm ...</u> Wetter. Haben Sie etwas Ähnliches in Leder?

F Moritz describes his family and circle. Match up the sentences with the same meaning and fill in the endings.
e.g. 1 → c → Der Name mein<u>er</u> Mutter ist Irmgard.

Die Familie Maier
1 Irmgard ist der Name von meiner Mutter.
2 Die Frau von meinem Vater heißt Irmgard.
3 Die Kinder von meinen Eltern heißen Moritz und Maria.
4 Der Leiter von unserer Schule heißt Gruber.
5 Unsere Nachbarn haben einen Sohn Klaus.

a Die Kinder mein ... Eltern heißen Moritz und Maria.
b Der Name unser ... Schulleiter ... ist Gruber.
c Der Name mein ... Mutter ist Irmgard.
d Der Sohn unser ... Nachbarn heißt Klaus.
e Die Frau mein ... Vater ... heißt Irmgard.

Freunde und Verwandte

CHAPTER 10   WHAT DO YOU KNOW?

A Frau Maier has noticed some bargains in the sales and points them out to her
husband, who just agrees. Replace the underlined words with the appropriate pronoun
for *it/they* (**er**, **sie** or **es**).
e.g. <u>Das Sofa</u> kostet DM 800.   →   Herr Maier: Ja ja. <u>Es</u> kostet DM 800.

Können wir endlich nach Hause gehen?
1 <u>Die Stühle</u> kommen aus Italien.
2 <u>Der Eßtisch</u> ist für unsere Eßecke zu groß.
3 <u>Die Einbauküche</u> ist wirklich preiswert.
4 <u>Das Kochgeschirr</u> ist aus Edelstahl.

B Peter and Zoran are also looking round the sales. Replace the underlined words
(which are in the accusative) with the correct pronoun (**ihn**, **sie** or **es**).
e.g. Wenn die Hose im Schlußverkauf ist, dann kaufe ich <u>die Hose</u>.
→   Wenn die Jeanshose im Schlußverkauf ist, dann kaufe ich <u>sie</u>.

Der Schlußverkauf
1 Wenn die Schuhe im Schlußverkauf sind, dann kaufe ich <u>die Schuhe</u>.
2 Wenn ein Pulli im Schlußverkauf ist, dann kaufe ich <u>den Pulli</u>.

C Oma Maier is doing her Christmas shopping in the sales. Replace the underlined
words (which are in the dative) with the correct pronoun (**ihm**, **ihr** or **ihnen**).
e.g. Sie schenkt <u>ihrer Tochter</u> ein Buch.   →   Sie schenkt <u>ihr</u> ein Buch.

Weihnachtsgeschenke (1)
1 Sie schenkt <u>ihrem Mann</u> eine Videokassette.
2 Sie schenkt <u>ihren Enkelkindern</u> Süßigkeiten.
3 Sie schenkt <u>ihrer Schwester</u> einen Mantel.
4 Sie schenkt <u>ihrem Sohn</u> eine Krawatte.

More presents from Oma. Replace the underlined words (dative) and the words in
bold (accusative) with the correct pronouns.
e.g. Sie gibt <u>ihrer Nachbarin</u> **eine Dose Kekse**.   →   Sie gibt **sie** <u>ihr</u>.

Weihnachtsgeschenke (2)
1 Sie gibt <u>ihrem Freund Hermann</u> **Sportstrümpfe**.
2 Sie gibt <u>ihren Kindern</u> **Weihnachtsplätzchen**.
3 Sie gibt <u>ihrer Freundin Waltraut</u> **ein Buch**.
4 Sie gibt <u>ihrem Gärtner</u> **einen Hut**.

Personal pronouns

1 PERSONAL PRONOUNS (*I, you, he, we*, etc.) change according to their function in the sentence:

NOMINATIVE	**Er** liebt Gabi	*He loves Gabi*
ACCUSATIVE	Gabi liebt **ihn**	*Gabi loves **him***
DATIVE	Sie ist immer mit **ihm**	*She is always with **him***

2 For each personal pronoun you must learn the changes which take place. Here are the personal pronouns in the three main cases you will meet:

	NOMINATIVE	ACCUSATIVE	DATIVE
I/me	ich	mich	mir
you (singular)	du	dich	dir
he/him, it	er	ihn	ihm
she/her, it	sie	sie	ihr
it	es	es	ihm
we/us	wir	uns	uns
you (plural)	ihr	euch	euch
they/them	sie	sie	ihnen
you (formal)	Sie	Sie	Ihnen

The formal *you* (**Sie**) has the same form in both singular and plural.

3 PERSONAL PRONOUNS, like nouns, are accusative or dative after prepositions depending on which preposition is used (and in some cases depending on the context – see section 6.3):

Ich weiß nichts über **sie**   *I know nothing about her*
Ich habe keine Zeit für **ihn**   *I have no time for him*
Ich gehe mit **ihr**   *I'm going with her*
Ich träume von **ihnen**   *I dream of them*

4 Be careful with *it*:

a pronouns, like nouns, can be MASCULINE, FEMININE or NEUTER. This also applies to the word for *it* in German, depending on the noun it replaces:

Der Schrank? **Er** ist teuer   *The cupboard? <u>It</u> is expensive*
Die Dusche? **Sie** ist klein   *The shower? <u>It</u> is small*
Das Schlafzimmer? **Es** ist hell   *The bedroom? <u>It</u> is bright*
Kannst du den Schrank aufmachen?   *Can you open the cupboard?*
Nein, ich kann **ihn** nicht aufmachen   *No, I can't open <u>it</u>*
Repariert er die Dusche?   *Is he repairing the shower?*
Ja, er repariert **sie**   *Yes, he is repairing <u>it</u>*

b a preposition in English followed by *it* is expressed in German by adding **da-** to the front of the preposition, or by **dar-** if the preposition begins with a vowel:

Erzählen Sie mir **davon**   *Tell me about it*
Ich weiß nicht viel **darüber**   *I don't know much about it*

5 Word order with pronouns:

a as shown in section 8.4, when you use two pronouns, one as the direct object (accusative) and one as the indirect object (dative), always put the direct object before the indirect object (as in English):

Block 1	Block 2	Block 3	Block 4	Block 5
SUBJECT	VERB	DIRECT	INDIRECT	REST OF SENTENCE
Sie	bringt	es	ihm	
She	*brings*	*it*	*to him*	

b but when you use a noun and a pronoun as the direct and indirect objects in the sentence then the *pronoun* always comes first.
Here is an example where the pronoun is the indirect object (dative case):

Block 1	Block 2	Block 3	Block 4	Block 5
SUBJECT	VERB	PRONOUN	NOUN	REST OF SENTENCE
Er	schreibt	ihr	einen Brief	
He	*writes*	*(to) her*	*a letter*	

Here is an example where the pronoun is the direct object (accusative case):

Block 1	Block 2	Block 3	Block 4	Block 5
SUBJECT	VERB	PRONOUN	NOUN	REST OF SENTENCE
Er	schreibt	ihn	der Frau	
He	*writes*	*it*	*to the woman*	

How to say what you would like

6 In Chapter 8 we saw some common verbs ('modal verbs') followed by an infinitive. The expression **ich möchte** *(I would like)* is part of the modal verb **mögen.** It is also followed by the infinitive when it means *I would like to do something,* but it can also have a direct object *(= I would like something)*:

Ich **möchte** für eine Zeitung arbeiten   *I would like to work for a paper*
Was **möchten** Sie heute machen?   *What would you like to do today?*
Möchtest du ein Eis?   *Would you like an ice?*

See Appendix page 137 for the parts of the modal verbs

CHAPTER 10   WHAT HAVE YOU LEARNT?

A What are Philipp and his friend talking about? Replace the German pronouns with the appropriate noun from the list below to make sense.

e.g. <u>Er</u> ist sehr aufregend.   *das Buch   der Film   die Fernsehsendung*

→   <u>Der Film</u> ist sehr aufregend.

Worüber sprechen sie?

1 Es ist sehr aufregend.
2 Sie ist sehr interessant.
3 Er ist weltberühmt.
4 Sie sind genau so gut wie die Bücher.

der Schriftsteller   das Buch   die Fernsehsendungen   die Geschichte

B It is Philipp's birthday. Frau Werner has asked each member of the family to buy him a present. Use the verb **schenken** and the appropriate pronouns to confirm who is giving him a particular item.

e.g. Wer gibt ihm Handschuhe? *Oma und Opa* → Oma und Opa schenken <u>sie ihm</u>.

Geburtstagsgeschenke

1 Wer gibt ihm Sportstrümpfe? *Josef*
2 Wer gibt ihm einen Tennisschläger? *Mutti*
3 Wer gibt ihm ein Stereogerät? *Vati*
4 Wer gibt ihm eine CD? *Maria*

C Oma has asked Maria for some ideas for a wedding anniversary present for her son and daughter-in-law. Give the German equivalent for the English words in brackets.

e.g. Ich kaufe [<u>him</u>] eine Flasche Wein.   →   Ich kaufe <u>ihm</u> eine Flasche Wein.

Ja, ich kaufe [<u>it</u>] ihm.   →   Ja, ich kaufe <u>sie</u> ihm (= eine Flasche Wein).

Geschenke zum Hochzeitstag

MARIA Mutti möchte Mitglied des Kinoklubs werden.

OMA   Dann kaufe ich [<u>her</u>] vielleicht eine Mitgliedskarte. Ja, ich kaufe [<u>it</u>] ihr.

MARIA Vati und Mutti möchten nächstes Jahr nach Ägypten fahren.

OMA   Vielleicht sollte ich [<u>them</u>] einen Reiseführer von Ägypten schenken.
Vielleicht kaufe ich [<u>it</u>] ihnen.

MARIA Vati arbeitet gern im Garten. Er möchte einige Bäume pflanzen.

OMA   Ich könnte [<u>him</u>] einen Apfelbaum geben. Ja, ich gebe [<u>it</u>] ihm.

Help Yourself to Essential German Grammar

UNIT

4

CHAPTER 11   WHAT DO YOU KNOW?

A You arrive at Oma and Opa Maier's flat and Oma Maier greets you. Complete each
question with the German equivalent of the bracketed English question word. Choose
one of these: **wo, warum, wann, wie**.
e.g. [Where] sind Maria und Peter?   →   Wo sind Maria und Peter?

Die Einladung
OMA Guten Tag. [How] geht es dir? Komm rein.
DU   Guten Tag Frau Maier. [Where] soll ich meinen Mantel aufhängen? Er ist
     ziemlich naß.
OMA Gib ihn mir. Ich hänge ihn im Badezimmer über die Badewanne. [When]
     triffst du Maria und Peter?
DU   Um sieben Uhr.
OMA [Why] stehst du im Flur? Komm ins Wohnzimmer in die Wärme!

B You tell Opa and Oma Maier what you have been doing during your visit to Berlin.
Replace the infinitive given with the past participle of the verb.
e.g. Am Montag habe ich Fußball (spielen).
   →   Am Montag habe ich Fußball gespielt.

Ich habe viel gemacht
1 Montagmorgen habe ich Tennis mit Maria und Peter (spielen).
2 Wir haben danach einen Ausflug nach Potsdam (machen).
3 Am Dienstag hat Peter ein Auto (kaufen).
4 Peter hat einen Ausflug in das Filmstudio (organisieren).
5 Wir haben gestern bis Mitternacht in der Disko (tanzen).
6 Ich habe erst heute Ansichtskarten nach England (schicken).

C These were Opa and Oma Maier's questions about your activities. Complete their
questions with the correct form of the verb **haben**.
e.g. Was ... du hier in Berlin gemacht?   →   Was hast du hier in Berlin gemacht?

Was hast du diese Woche gemacht?
1 Was ... du mit Peter und Maria gemacht?
2 ... Peter einen Ausflug für dich organisiert?
3 Wann ... ihr das Filmstudio besucht?
4 ... du Ansichtskarten nach England geschickt?

Asking questions

1 Here are some common QUESTION WORDS:

Wo wohnen Sie?	_Where_ do you live?
Warum wollen Sie hier arbeiten?	_Why_ do you want to work here?
Wann fährt der Zug ab?	_When_ does the train leave?
Wie viel Geld bekommen Sie?	_How much_ money do you earn?
Wer ist der Schulleiter?	_Who_ is the headmaster?
Was ist dein Lieblingsfach?	_What_ is your favourite subject?
Wie alt bist du?	_How_ old are you?

2 Notice the word order. The QUESTION WORD is the first block in the sentence, the verb comes second, and the subject comes immediately after the verb. In other words, subject and verb are turned round or 'inverted', as always in a question.

Block 1	Block 2	Block 3	Block 4
Q/WORD	VERB	SUBJECT	REST OF SENTENCE
Wo	wohnen	Sie?	

Compare this with a simple question (without a question word):

Wohnen Sie hier?   _Do you live here?_

For more ways of asking questions see Chapter 22

Saying what happened in the past: the perfect tense (weak verbs)

3 The PERFECT TENSE is used to describe an action in the past:

Ich **habe** lange genug **gewartet**	_I have waited long enough_
Er **hat** es mir **gesagt**	_He told me so_
Was **hast** du in den Ferien **gemacht**?	_What did you do in the holidays?_
Haben Sie schon hier **gearbeitet**?	_Have you ever worked here?_

Note: It can be seen that the German perfect is equivalent to several different ways of expressing the past in English (_waited, have waited, did wait_). So its use is wider than that of the English perfect (_have waited_).

4 The perfect tense is used a lot in conversation, as above. It is also used in written German, either informally, for example in a letter, or formally, for example to describe historical events:

Wir **haben** eine gute Reise nach England **gehabt**
We had a good journey to England
Picasso **hat** das Bild 1907 **gemalt**   _Picasso painted the picture in 1907_

Help Yourself to Essential German Grammar

5 As in English, the perfect tense consists of two parts. These are usually:

> PRESENT TENSE OF **HABEN** + **PAST PARTICIPLE OF THE VERB**

Here is the perfect tense of **sagen** *(to say)*, a regular weak verb:

SINGULAR			PLURAL		
ich habe	gesagt	*I said*	wir haben	gesagt	*we said*
du hast	gesagt	*you said*	ihr habt	gesagt	*you said*
Sie haben	gesagt	*you said*	Sie haben	gesagt	*you said*
er/sie/es hat	gesagt	*he/she/it said*	sie haben	gesagt	*they said*

6 This is how the PAST PARTICIPLE of weak verbs is formed:

> start with the infinitive: **machen   warten**
> remove **-en** to get the STEM: **mach   wart**
> add **ge-** to the front of the stem and **-t** to the end (or **-et** if the stem ends in a **-t**): **ge**macht **ge**wart**et**

spielen: Die Kinder haben **gespielt**   *The children played*
haben: Wir haben eine gute Reise **gehabt**   *We have had a good journey*

7 With separable verbs the prefix is attached to the past participle of the simple verb:

> <u>**aufmachen**</u> → <u>**aufgemacht**</u>

einkaufen: Wir haben in der Stadt **eingekauft**   *We shopped in town*
mitbringen: Sie hat ihn **mitgebracht**   *She brought him with her*

8 The past participles of weak verbs ending in **-ieren** in the infinitive do not start with the **ge-**, but just add a **-t** at the end:

> **telefonieren** *(to telephone)* → **telefonier<u>t</u>**

organisieren: Wir **haben** einen Besuch **organisiert**   *We organised a visit*
regieren: Die Königin **hat** lange **regiert**
              The queen ruled for a long time

See also section 12.3 for some other examples

9 Word order is important when using the perfect tense. Notice that **haben** (called the AUXILIARY VERB) is the 'working' verb which changes depending on the subject. The past participle does not change. So **haben** comes in the usual verb position, in the second block (except in simple questions – see section 8.3c). The past participle is placed *at the end* of the clause or sentence:

Block 1	Block 2	Block 3	Block 4
SUBJECT	VERB	OBJECT	PAST PARTICIPLE
Wir	**haben**	ein Zimmer	**reserviert**
VERB	SUBJECT	OBJECT	PAST PARTICIPLE
Haben	Sie	ein Zimmer	**reserviert**?

We have reserved a room. Have you reserved a room?

Help Yourself to Essential German Grammar

CHAPTER 1·1   WHAT HAVE YOU LEARNT?

A Peter has already seen the film you want to see, so he is able to answer all your questions. Complete his answers using the information in brackets.

e.g. Wer spielt die Hauptrolle? (Humphrey Bogart)

→   Humphrey Bogart <u>spielt</u> die Hauptrolle.

Fragen am Telefon

1 Wann beginnt der Film? (20.30 Uhr)

2 Was kostet es für Erwachsene? (DM 6,-)

3 Wie lange dauert der Film? (zwei Stunden)

4 Wo spielt der Film? (im Odeon)

B You have made notes in Berlin ready to write up your diary in German. Fill in the two gaps in each sentence with the correct form of the auxiliary verb **haben** in gap 1 and the past participle form of the infinitive given in gap 2.

e.g. Am Montag (1) ich Fußball (2) (<u>spielen</u>).

→   Am Montag <u>habe</u> ich Fußball <u>gespielt</u>.

Mein Tagebuch

Am Dienstag (1) Peter einen Ausflug (2) (<u>organisieren</u>).

Am Mittwoch (1) wir alle bis Mitternacht in der Disko (2) (<u>tanzen</u>).

Am Donnerstag (1) ich Oma und Opa Maier (2) (<u>besuchen</u>).

Am Freitag (1) Herr und Frau Maier bei Aldi (2) (<u>einkaufen</u>).

C You write a postcard home to a friend in German. As a joke you wrote the postcard in code. Re-order the words, beginning each sentence with the underlined word, so that the postcard makes sense.

e.g. die Karte <u>Ich</u> im Zoo habe gekauft.   →   Ich habe die Karte im Zoo gekauft.

Grüße aus Berlin!

Lieber Paul,

viel Spaß <u>Ich</u> hier gehabt habe. viel gemacht <u>Wir</u> haben.

den Reichstag <u>Wir</u> besichtigt haben. Deutsch verbessert <u>Ich</u> habe mein.

gemacht <u>Was</u> hast Du?

Bis bald,

Dein Freund _____

UNIT

4

CHAPTER 12   WHAT DO YOU KNOW?

A You describe to your friend Zoran how you spent your last Christmas holiday. Replace the English with the appropriate German past participle chosen from these: **gegessen, gelesen, verbracht, gespielt, getrunken, bekommen.**
e.g. Ich habe ein Buch [read].   →   Ich habe ein Buch <u>gelesen</u>.

Weihnachten
1 Ich habe die Weihnachtsferien bei meinen Großeltern [spent].
2 Am ersten Weihnachtsfeiertag haben wir unsere Geschenke [received].
3 Wir haben ein typisches Festessen mit Truthahn [ate].
4 Wir haben eine Flasche Wein [drank].
5 Großvater hat seine neue CD [played].

B You are feeling unwell and the family doctor asks you what you did yesterday. Replace the bracketed English with the appropriate German past participle chosen from these: **geschehen, geblieben, gegangen, geworden, gewesen.**
e.g. Wir sind im Freibad [were].   →   Wir sind im Freibad <u>gewesen</u>.

Was haben Sie gestern gemacht?
1 Ich bin mit meinen Freunden ins Schwimmbad [went].
2 Wir sind dort den ganzen Tag [stayed].
3 Ich bin schön braun [became].
4 Sonst ist nichts [happened].

C Zoran describes his favourite hobby. Replace the English possessive adjective shown in brackets with the correct German form from the options provided.
e.g. [My] Lieblingshobby ist Rad fahren.   *mein/meine*
     (Hobby is neuter, therefore:)   →   mein

In meiner Freizeit
1 [My] Lieblingssportart ist Ski laufen.   *mein/meine*
2 Jedes Jahr verbringen wir [our] Weihnachtsferien in Lech.   *unser/unsere*
3 Meine Mutter kommt auch. [Her] Familie wohnt in Lech.   *ihr/ihre*
4 Wir lachen über meinen Vater, [his] Ski laufen ist furchtbar!   *sein/seine*
5 Was ist [your] Lieblingsurlaub?   *dein/deine*

More on the perfect tense...

1 The perfect tense of STRONG VERBS is formed exactly as for weak verbs, with the auxiliary verb, usually **haben** (but see section 12.4), and the past participle. The difference is in the past participle, which is formed as follows:

ge- STEM **-en**

lesen (*to read*)	→	**gelesen**
helfen (*to help*)	→	**geholfen***
trinken (*to drink*)	→	**getrunken***

2 A number of verbs, both weak and strong, do not have **ge-** at the front of their past participle. These are verbs whose infinitive begins with **be-**, **emp-**, **ent-**, **er-** or **ver-**. These are sometimes called inseparable prefixes:

behandeln (*weak*): Der Arzt hat ihn **behandelt**   *The doctor treated him*
bekommen (*strong*): Ich habe Blumen **bekommen**   *I received flowers*

For a list of strong verbs with their past participles see Appendix pages 130–135

3 MIXED VERBS are partly like weak verbs, and partly like strong verbs. In the present tense they follow the same pattern as weak verbs (see section 1.7). Their past participle ends in **-t** like that of a weak verb, BUT the stem changes as it does in a strong verb:

INFINITIVE	PAST PARTICIPLE	INFINITIVE	PAST PARTICIPLE
kennen (*to know*)	**gekannt**	**brennen** (*to burn*)	**gebrannt**
bringen (*to bring*)	**gebracht**	**denken** (*to think*)	**gedacht**

The perfect tense with **sein**

4 For some verbs the perfect tense is formed with **sein** not **haben**:

PRESENT TENSE OF **SEIN**   **+**   **PAST PARTICIPLE OF VERB**

5 Here is the perfect tense of **kommen** (*to come*), a strong verb which takes **sein**:

SINGULAR			PLURAL		
ich bin	gekommen	*I came*	wir sind	gekommen	*we came*
du bist	gekommen	*you came*	ihr seid	gekommen	*you came*
Sie sind	gekommen	*you came*	Sie sind	gekommen	*you came*
er/sie/es ist	gekommen	*he/she/it came*	sie sind	gekommen	*they came*

Note: The word order is the same as for verbs with **haben** (section 11.9).

Wir **sind** mit dem Auto nach Berlin **gekommen**   *We came to Berlin by car*

---

*Note that in many strong verbs the stem vowel changes.

Help Yourself to Essential German Grammar

6 The following verbs take **sein** in the perfect tense:

a verbs of movement which do not take an object:

Ich **bin weggerannt**	*I made a run for it*
Wir **sind geschwommen**	*We swam*
Mein Freund **ist** vom Rad **gefallen**	*My friend fell off his bike*

b verbs showing a change of state, which do not take an object:

Er **ist gestorben**	*He has died*
Sind Sie **eingeschlafen?**	*Have you fallen asleep?*

c others such as **sein** *(to be)*, **bleiben** *(to stay)* and **geschehen** *(to happen)*:

Sind Sie im Ausland **gewesen?**	*Have you been abroad?*
Was **ist** dann **geschehen?**	*What happened then?*
Er **ist** zu Hause **geblieben**	*He stayed at home*

See Appendix pages 138–139 for a list of verbs which take **sein**

Possessive adjectives

7 POSSESSIVE ADJECTIVES (such as *my, his*) must agree with the noun they refer to, that is, have the same gender and number as it does:

Seine Freundin kann gut tanzen	*His girl friend dances well*
Ihr Zimmer ist vorne im Haus	*Her room is at the front of the house*
Deine Eltern sind auch eingeladen	*Your parents are invited too*

8 Here are the POSSESSIVE ADJECTIVES in the nominative case:

	MASCULINE	FEMININE	NEUTER	PLURAL
my	mein	meine	mein	meine
your (**du**)	dein	deine	dein	deine
his	sein	seine	sein	seine
her	ihr	ihre	ihr	ihre
its	sein	seine	sein	seine
our	unser	unsere	unser	unsere
your (**ihr**)	euer	eure	euer	eure
your (**Sie**)	Ihr	Ihre	Ihr	Ihre
their	ihr	ihre	ihr	ihre

9 POSSESSIVE ADJECTIVES add the same endings as the indefinite article in the singular, and as **keine** in the plural:

Ich habe Fotos von **einer** Stadt	*I have photos of a town*
Ich habe Fotos von **meiner** Stadt	*I have photos of my town*
Ich habe **keine** Fotos von ihr	*I have no photos of her*
Ich habe **seine** Fotos von ihr	*I have his photos of her*

CHAPTER 12   WHAT HAVE YOU LEARNT?

A Zoran tells you about his new girl friend. Complete each sentence in the perfect tense using the German verb given in brackets.

e.g. Ich ... meine neue Freundin in der Disko ...   (treffen)

→   Ich habe meine neue Freundin in der Disko getroffen.

Die neue Freundin

1 Dann ... sie mir ihre Telefonnummer ...   (geben)
2 Ich ... eine Einladung zu ihrer Geburtstagsparty ...   (bekommen)
3 Meine Schwester ... für sie ein tolles Geschenk ... (empfehlen)
4 Wir ... stundenlang am Telefon ... (sprechen)

B Philipp and Maria arrive. Philipp is annoyed and limping. What has happened? Complete each sentence with the appropriate form of the auxiliary **sein** and the past participle of the verb given in brackets.

e.g. Ich ... zur Bushaltestelle (gehen).   →   Ich bin zur Bushaltestelle gegangen.

Was ist passiert?

1 Der Bus ... nie (kommen).
2 Ich ... schließlich mit Maria zur U-Bahn-Station (laufen).
3 Wir ... mit der U-Bahn (fahren)!
4 Was ... denn hier ... (geschehen)?

C As you all go into a local sports centre you hear an announcement. Re-word it, changing the underlined pronouns and possessive adjectives into the more common formal **Sie** pronoun and **Ihr** possessive adjective forms. You will need to change the verb endings to match the change in pronoun.

e.g. Ihr seid herzlich willkommen.   →   Sie sind herzlich willkommen.

Liebe Gäste

Liebe Gäste, ihr seid herzlich willkommen. Wir bitten euch, auf euren Besitz aufzupassen, und empfehlen euch, daß ihr die Schließfächer für eure Wertsachen benutzt.

D You are all waiting for Maria to come out of the changing room. What is she doing? Complete the sentence with the appropriate German definite article.

e.g. I'm drying my face: Ich trockne mir ... Gesicht.

→   Ich trockne mir das Gesicht.

Moment mal!

I washed my hair: Ich habe mir ... Haare gewaschen.

I'm putting my T-shirt on: Ich ziehe mir ... T-Shirt an.

Revision test 10–12

A Stefan has been to the cinema. He tells his mother about the film. Replace the underlined nouns with one of these pronouns: **er**, **sie**, **es** or **sie** *(pl)*.
e.g. <u>Die Leinwand</u> ist riesig. → <u>Sie</u> ist riesig.

Der Sci-fi-Film (1)
<u>Der Film</u> ist fantastisch! <u>Das Kino</u> hat eine enorme Leinwand. <u>Die Spezialeffekte</u> sind so realistisch. <u>Das Raumschiff</u> sieht toll aus.

In this next text, replace the personal pronouns underlined with one of the nouns below. Remember to adjust the word order as necessary.
e.g. Vati schenkt es mir. → Vati schenkt mir das Modell.

Der Sci-fi-Film (2)
Moritz schenkt <u>es</u> mir zum Geburtstag. Ich schenke <u>ihn</u> ihm. Mutti, kannst du <u>sie</u> mir kaufen?

den Raumkämpfer   die Videokassette   das Modell

B Stefan has come home from school with a number of borrowed items in his school bag. He tells his mother who they belong to. Replace the name underlined with a personal pronoun. NB **Gehören** takes the dative.
e.g. Der Taschenrechner gehört <u>Maria</u>. → Der Taschenrechner gehört **ihr**.

Was hast du denn hier?
Das Buch gehört <u>Susanne</u>. Das Lineal gehört <u>Philipp</u>. Die Bleistifte gehören <u>Kamal und Gürkan</u>.

C Stefan is trying to plan his birthday party with Moritz and Philipp, but each of his guests wants to do something different. Complete each sentence with **möchte**, **möchten**, etc.
e.g. Er … ins Theater gehen. → Er möchte ins Theater gehen.

Meine Geburtstagsparty
Ich … ins Kino gehen. Susanne … in den Zoo. Mutti und Vati … hier zu Hause feiern. Moritz und Philipp, ihr … eislaufen gehen.

D Stefan decides to go ice-skating with his friends. Complete each question with the German question word that fits the English in brackets.
e.g. [<u>When</u>] treffen wir uns? → <u>Wann</u> treffen wir uns?

Wir gehen eislaufen
[<u>Where</u>] treffen wir uns? [<u>How</u>] fahren wir dorthin? [<u>How much</u>] kostet es?
[<u>Why</u>] kommt Sabine erst um sechs Uhr? [<u>When</u>] kommen wir nach Hause?

E You write a postcard to your German penfriend describing your holiday. Write each
sentence in the perfect using the verb given in brackets.
e.g. Wir … einen guten Flug (haben). → Wir haben einen guten Flug gehabt.

Eine Postkarte aus Spanien

Grüße aus Spanien! Ich … einen guten Flug nach Malaga … (haben). Wir … für die
Ferien viel … (organisieren). Jeden Tag … ich Tennis … (spielen). Meine Freundin
… windsurfen … (lernen). Heute morgen … wir ein Boot … (mieten). Kristel …
jeden Tag im Supermarkt … (einkaufen).

F You receive a postcard from your penfriend in which he uses a number of mixed or
strong (irregular) verbs. From the past participle underlined, give the infinitive of the
verb concerned and give its meaning in English.
e.g. mitgebracht → mitbringen → to bring with you

Grüße aus Holland

Ich habe zwei Wochen in Holland verbracht. Nach der Reise sind wir alle müde
gewesen. Wir sind aber sofort ausgegangen. Ich habe natürlich meinen Reiseführer
mitgenommen. Wir haben gefunden, daß Amsterdam viel kleiner als Berlin ist.

G You write to your penfriend describing an accident. In each case decide which
auxiliary verb you should use (**haben** or **sein**) and which part of it.
e.g. gestern … ich gegangen → gestern bin ich gegangen

Ein Unfall

Gestern … ich mit dem Fahrrad in die Stadt gefahren. Ich … das Fahrrad zum
Geburtstag bekommen. Plötzlich … ich vom Rad gefallen. Ein Autofahrer … mich
ins Krankenhaus gebracht. Mein Kopf … mir weh getan.
Der Arzt … sehr freundlich gewesen. Glücklicherweise … ich nur leichte Schäden
am Fahrrad gehabt.

H At the airport there has been a mix-up with the luggage. Each passenger identifies his
or her luggage. Replace the English possessive with the correct German possessive
adjective in the appropriate case.
e.g. Das ist [my] Koffer. → Das ist mein Koffer.

Am Gepäckfließband

Ich habe schon [my] Koffer. Wo ist [your : *familiar singular*] Reisetasche?
Ich sehe das Etikett von [our] Skiern. Hat Stefan [his] Rucksack gefunden?
Wo sind Herr und Frau Braun? Ich habe [their] Kinderwagen gerade gesehen. Kinder,
da kommen endlich [your: *familiar plural*] Taschen.

CHAPTER 13   WHAT DO YOU KNOW?

A With your German friends you compare Great Britain with Germany. Replace the
English adjective in brackets with the German equivalent (not forgetting an ending if
needed). Choose from: **größer, größte, höher, höchste, schöner, schönste.**
e.g. London ist [bigger] als Berlin.   →   London ist <u>größer</u> als Berlin.

Im Vergleich zu

1 Die Bundesrepublik ist [bigger] als Großbritannien.
2 Der Zugspitze ist [higher] als Snowdon.
3 Schottland ist [more beautiful] als England.
4 Ben Nevis ist der [highest] Berg Großbritanniens.
5 Die [most beautiful] Stadt Deutschlands ist Quedlinburg.
6 Deutschland ist aber das [biggest] Land.

B You have been feeling unwell but you do not like the doctor's advice. Match the
(female) doctor's recommendations with your replies.
e.g. 1   →   b

Ratschläge

Die Ärztin:

1 Das Beste ist, Sie schwimmen im Hallenbad.
2 Das Beste ist, Sie sitzen im Schatten.
3 Das Beste ist, Sie bleiben morgen zu Hause.
4 Das Beste ist, Sie nehmen diese Tabletten.

Du:

a Aber ich gehe gern mit meinen Freunden aus.
b Aber ich schwimme gern im Freibad.
c Aber ich nehme nicht gerne Medikamente.
d Aber ich sitze gern in der Sonne.

C The doctor recommends you stay out of the sun for a few days. Your host family ask
what you would enjoy doing. Replace the English word in each sentence with the
equivalent German word chosen from this list: **gern, lieber, am liebsten.**
e.g. Was machst du in deiner Freizeit? [like]
   →   Was machst du <u>gern</u> in deiner Freizeit?

Interessen

1 Was für Filme siehst du? [most like]
2 Was für Bücher liest du? [prefer]

Comparative/superlative of adjectives °

1 COMPARATIVE FORMS of adjectives say one thing or person has more of a particular characteristic than something or someone else:

Wer ist **schlanker**? Peter oder Paul? *Who is **thinner**? Peter or Paul?*

2 To form the comparative in German add **-er** to the end of the adjective:

interessant (*interesting*) → interessant**er** (*more interesting*)
klein (*small*) → klein**er** (*smaller*)

Some common adjectives of one syllable also add an umlaut to their stem vowel (**a, o** or **u**) in the comparative:

alt (*old*)	→	**älter** (*older*)	groß (*large*)	—	**größer** (*larger*)
stark (*strong*)	→	**stärker** (*stronger*)	hoch (*high*)	→	**höher** (*higher*)
dumm (*stupid*)	→	**dümmer** (*more stupid*)	kurz (*short*)	→	**kürzer** (*shorter*)

3 The German for *than* after a comparative is **als**:

Jutta ist **älter als** Jürgen *Jutta is older **than** Jürgen*

4 The SUPERLATIVE FORM of the adjective says one thing or person has the *most* of a particular characteristic. In German it is formed:

a by adding **-ste** to the adjective in the nominative, or **-este** if the adjective ends in **-t**, **-s**, **-sch** or **-z**:

Sie ist das klein**ste** Mädchen   *She is the **smallest** girl*
Was ist der wichtig**ste** Unterschied?   *What is the **most important** difference?*
Die ält**este** Burg Deutschlands   *Germany's **oldest** castle*

Note: The adjectives which have an umlaut in the comparative also have one in the superlative. See the list above in section 13.2.

b by using the form **am ... sten** if the adjective stands alone after **ist, sind**, etc. and there is no noun to give us the gender. But if there is a noun or a name in the sentence, **der/die/das ... ste** should be used:

Wer ist **am** klüg**sten** von ihnen?   *Who is the **cleverest** of them?*
Sie ist **die** klein**ste** (von den Schwestern)   *She is the **smallest** (of the sisters)*

am ... sten is also used where there is no *the* in front of the adjective in English and the sense is *at its/their most ...*:

Die Stadt ist **am** schön**sten** bei Nacht   *The town is most beautiful at night*

5 Two adjectives have very irregular comparative and superlative forms:

gut (*good*)   → besser (*better*)   →   am besten (*best*)
viel (*much, many*) → mehr (*more*)   →   am meisten (*most*)

6 As with all adjectives, the comparative or superlative adjective must change its ending if it comes before a noun:

Ich brauche eine **bessere** Qualifikation   *I need a better qualification*
Beschreibe den **besten** Tag!   *Describe the best day*
Sie trägt ihr schön**stes** Kleid   *She is wearing her most beautiful dress*

See Chapter 7, Chapter 9 and Appendix pages 146–147 for the adjective endings

How to say that you like doing something

7 To say that you like doing something you can use **gern** with most verbs:

Thomas geht **gern** in die Schule   *Thomas likes going to school*
Ißt du **gern** Tomaten?   *Do **you** like (eating) tomatoes?*
Wir essen **gern** Tomaten   ***We** like eating tomatoes*

The **gern** does not change: it is the verb which changes according to the person who is doing the action.
Note that **gern** should be placed as soon after the verb as possible, but not between verb and the subject.

8 To say you *like doing something better* or *prefer doing something* use **lieber** (i.e. the COMPARATIVE form of **gern**). To say you *like doing something best* use **am liebsten** (which is the SUPERLATIVE form of **gern**):

Ich wohne **lieber** in der Stadt   *I prefer living in the town*
Wo kaufst du **lieber** Brot?   *Where do you prefer to buy bread?*
Was machst du **am liebsten**?   *What do you like doing best?*
Ich sehe **am liebsten** fern   *I like watching television best*

9 The following IMPERSONAL EXPRESSION can also be used to say you like doing something:

ES GEFÄLLT ✚ PRONOUN IN DATIVE, ZU ✚ INFINITIVE

Es gefällt <u>ihm</u>, in der Stadt **zu** wohnen.   *He likes living in the town*
Es gefällt <u>meiner Mutter</u>, hier **zu** arbeiten   *My mother likes working here*

*See section 5.5b for the use of **gefallen** with a noun as subject*
See section 10.6 for how to say you <u>would</u> like to do something

CHAPTER 13   WHAT HAVE YOU LEARNT?

A Peter is showing you and your other German friends his new car. Whatever anyone suggests, his car is bigger and better! Complete the comparative adjective.
e.g. Der Opel ist <u>schön</u>. Mein Auto ist …   →   Mein Auto ist <u>schöner</u>.

Größer, besser, schneller (1)
1 Der BMW ist <u>schnell</u>. Mein Auto ist …
2 Der Mercedes ist <u>groß</u>. Mein Auto ist …
3 Der Audi ist <u>bequem</u>. Mein Auto ist …

B Peter continues praising his wonderful car. Complete the comparative adjective with the correct adjectival agreement where needed.
e.g. Der Corsa hat einen <u>niedrigen</u> Benzinverbrauch.
      Mein Auto hat einen … Benzinverbrauch.
   →   Mein Auto hat einen <u>niedrigeren</u> Benzinverbrauch.

Größer, besser, schneller (2)
1 Der BMW hat ein gutes Stereo. Mein Auto hat ein … Stereo.
2 Der Jaguar hat eine hohe Leistung. Mein Auto hat eine … Leistung.
3 Der Mercedes hat viel Platz. Mein Auto hat … Platz.

C Maria likes detective novels and classical music.
Peter likes detective films and historical novels.
Philipp likes action films and enjoys reading detective stories.

Match each sentence with who likes what and how much. Complete each sentence with **gern, lieber** or **am liebsten** as appropriate.
e.g. Ich sehe … Krimis [<u>like</u>].   →   Peter: Ich sehe gern Krimis.

Filme, Musik, Bücher
1 Ich höre … klassische Musik [<u>like</u>].
2 … sehe ich Krimis [<u>most like</u>].
3 Ich lese … Krimis [<u>prefer</u>].
4 Actionfilme sehe ich … [<u>most like</u>].
5 Ich lese … geschichtliche Romane [<u>prefer</u>].
6 Die Musik von Beethoven höre ich … [<u>most like</u>].

UNIT 5

A Moritz asks for help with his homework. He has to join together two short sentences using a conjunction (linking word) to make one sentence. Join the two short sentences using the German word given. Will you need a comma?

   e.g. Ich heiße Moritz. Ich bin 13 Jahre alt.   *und*

   → Ich heiße Moritz und ich bin 13 Jahre alt.

   *(Conjunction is **und** and same subject in both clauses therefore **no comma**)*

Die Hausaufgabe

   1 Ich schreibe meine Hausaufgaben. Ich möchte eine gute Note.   *denn*
   2 Ich wohne in einer Wohnung. Meine Großeltern wohnen in einem Haus.   *aber*
   3 Meine Mutter ist Lehrerin. Mein Vater ist Kaufmann.   *und*
   4 Zum Frühstück esse ich ein Butterbrot. Ich trinke ein Glas Milch.   *oder*

B Moritz asks Maria to check some further sentences he has written. He is not sure when to use the word **sondern** and when to use the word **aber** when he wants to say *but*. Complete each sentence with either **sondern** or **aber**.

   e.g. Ich lerne nicht Englisch ... Deutsch.

   → Ich lerne nicht Englisch <u>sondern</u> Deutsch.

Sondern oder aber?

   1 Ich fahre nicht mit dem Bus zur Schule, ... gehe zu Fuß.
   2 Peter ist mein Bruder, ... er wohnt nicht bei uns.
   3 Maria ist meine Schwester, ... sie ist eine Nervensäge!
   4 Ich bekomme keine schlechte Note, ... eine gute.

C Fill in the gaps with the appropriate **da-** or **dar-** plus preposition forms.

   e.g. Er spricht von seiner Familie. Er spricht gern <u>davon</u>.

Worauf wartest du?

   1 Ich warte auf einen Telefonanruf. Ich warte schon lange ...
   2 Sie lacht über diese Fernsehsendung. Sie lacht oft ...
   3 Er fragt nach der Zeit. Er fragt immer wieder ...
   4 Ich denke an deine Gesundheit. Du solltest auch ... denken.

Conjunctions

1 Linking words called CONJUNCTIONS are used to join two sentences:

Meine Freunde gehen reiten, **und** ich sitze zu Hause
*My friends go riding **and** I stay at home*

2 **Und** *(and)*, **oder** *(or)*, **aber** *(but)*, **sondern** *(but* after a negative) and **denn** *(for, as)*
are called CO-ORDINATING CONJUNCTIONS because they join sentences or clauses which
are seen as equally important and the same type:

a **und** *(and)* and **oder** *(or)*:

Ich lese gern und (**ich**) gehe oft ins Kino
*I like reading **and** (I) often go to the cinema*

In the example above, the subject is the same (**ich**) in both parts of the sentence,
and it can even be left out, both in English and in German, after the conjunction.
You therefore do not need a comma in German. This rule also applies to **oder**:

Wir spielen abends Tennis oder (**wir**) bleiben zu Hause
*We play tennis in the evenings or (**we**) stay at home*

However if there is a CHANGE OF SUBJECT a comma separates the two clauses:

Meine Mutter ist Lehrerin, und **mein Vater** ist Mechaniker
My mother is a teacher and my father is a mechanic

b with **aber** *(but)*, **sondern** *(but, on the contrary)* and **denn** *(for, as)*, there is usually
a comma whether there is a change of subject or not:

Er soll mich anrufen, **aber** er muß vor sieben anrufen
He is to ring me, but he must ring before seven
Ich bade nicht, **sondern** ich dusche
I don't have a bath but a shower
Ich konnte nicht gehen, **denn** ich war krank
I couldn't go as I was ill

c **aber** and **sondern** both mean *but,* but are used differently. In most cases **aber** is
used, but if something is said to *correct* a statement *(not a* but *b)* then it must be
sondern. Here we have the same negative statement twice. In the first case the
clause with **aber** does not correct the statement; the clause with **sondern** does:

Er ist jetzt nicht im Büro, **aber** er ruft später zurück
He's not in the office at the moment, but he will ring back later
Er ist jetzt nicht im Büro, **sondern** zu Hause
He's not in the office at the moment, but at home

Verbs with prepositions

3 As in English, many verbs are followed by a particular PREPOSITION before a noun or a pronoun. The most common are:

bitten **um** (+ ACCUSATIVE) *to ask for*	Ich bitte dich **um** Rat *I am asking you for advice*
denken **an** (+ ACCUSATIVE) *to think about*	Wir müssen mehr **an** die Umwelt denken *We must think more about the environment*
sich erinnern **an** (+ ACCUSATIVE) *to remember**	Erinnerst du dich **an** meinen Freund? *Do you remember my friend?*
sich freuen **auf** (+ ACCUSATIVE) *to look forward to*	Wir freuen uns sehr **auf** dein Kommen *We are looking forward to your arrival*
erzählen **von** (+ DATIVE) *to tell about*	Erzähl mir **von** deiner Familie *Tell me about your family*
warten **auf** (+ ACCUSATIVE) *to wait for*	Wir warten **auf** ihn *We are waiting for him*

See Appendix pages 141–142 for a list of verbs followed by prepositions

4 As with all prepositions, use **da-** or **dar-** in front of the preposition to express *it*:

Ich freue mich **darauf**   *I am looking forward to it*

Sie erinnert sich nicht **daran**   *She doesn't remember it*

5 If the verb + preposition introduces another verb, there are two possible constructions, both of which need the **da-** or **dar-** before the preposition:

a if the two clauses have the *same subject*, **zu** + THE INFINITIVE can be used:

Ich freue mich **darauf**, dahin **zu fahren**
  I am looking forward to going there
Er erinnert sich **daran**, Sie **getroffen zu haben**
  He remembers meeting you

b if the two clauses have *different subjects*, a **daß** clause can be used:

Ich freue mich **darauf, daß** sie zu uns kommt
  I am looking forward to her coming to see us
Sie wartet **darauf, daß** er in den Ruhestand geht
  She is waiting for him to retire

---

*Note that the German verb needs a preposition, while the English does not. Some English verbs need a preposition, while their German equivalents do not:

Sie sucht einen Polizisten   *She is looking for a policeman*

Help Yourself to Essential German Grammar

CHAPTER 14   WHAT HAVE YOU LEARNT?

A Herr Maier telephones a local restaurant to book a table for six people for next
Saturday. The waiter dealing with the call makes several mistakes. Replace the words
in English with the equivalent German conjunction.
e.g. Nicht Freitag, [but] Samstag.   →   Nicht Freitag, <u>sondern</u> Samstag.

Der unerfahrene Kellner

KELLNER   Einen Tisch für acht Personen.

HERR MAIER Nein, nicht acht Personen, [but] sechs Personen. Für nächsten Samstag.

KELLNER   Es tut mir leid, [but] wir haben am Samstag nichts frei.

B Moritz asks you how his homework can be improved. You suggest he links his
sentences to make longer sentences. Rewrite the sentences using the German
equivalent of the English conjunction given in brackets.
e.g. Ich habe Musik gehört. [and] Ich habe ferngesehen.
  →   Ich habe Musik gehört <u>und</u> ich habe ferngesehen.

Mein Wochenende

Letzten Samstag bin ich schwimmen gegangen. [as] Das Wetter war schön. Am
Abend bin ich zu Hause geblieben. [but] Mein Bruder und meine Schwester sind
ausgegangen. Meine Eltern sind ins Kino gegangen. [and] Ich habe mir eine
Videokassette angesehen.

C You've missed the first part of the TV programme and you ask Moritz what has
happened so far. Fill in each gap with the missing preposition (**an**, **auf**, **um** or **von**).
e.g. Sie hat ... den Mann gewartet.   →   Sie hat <u>auf</u> den Mann gewartet.

Was ist bis jetzt passiert?

1 Der Mann hat ein paar Minuten ... die blonde Dame gewartet.
2 Sie ist ins Zimmer gekommen. Sie hat ... ihrer Tochter gesprochen.
3 Sie hat ihn ... Hilfe gebeten. Ich weiß nicht warum.
4 Sie hat ... einer Antwort bestanden und jetzt streiten sie.
5 Ich freue mich schon ... die Werbung!

UNIT

5

CHAPTER 15   WHAT DO YOU KNOW?

A Philipp and his friend Zoran are on the phone. From their conversation find the
equivalent German phrases to match the English below.
e.g. How are you? → Wie geht's?

Wie geht's?
PHILIPP Wie geht's?
ZORAN   Es geht mir gut. Und dir?
PHILIPP Es geht mir schlecht. Es ist mir schwindelig.
ZORAN   Es tut mir leid. Was ist mit dir los?

1 I'm sorry.
2 I'm not well.
3 I feel dizzy.
4 I'm well.

B For her homework, Maria has had to find out people's opinions about particular jobs
and professions. She looks at her notes and forms them into sentences using the
conjunction **daß**, and remembering to place the verb in the **daß** clause at the end.
e.g. Mein Vater denkt/Ärzte sind sehr wichtig
→ Mein Vater denkt, <u>daß</u> Ärzte sehr wichtig <u>sind</u>.

Meinungen
1 Meine Oma findet/Fußballspieler bekommen zu viel Geld
2 Meine Mutter denkt/Hausfrauen sind am wichtigsten
3 Mein Opa findet/Rentner brauchen mehr Geld

C Herr Maier has returned home late. Beginning with the phrase **Ich habe den Zug
verpaßt, weil ...**, complete each sentence with the reasons for his delay listed below.
Remember the main verb in the **weil** clause (which is underlined), should be moved
to the end of the clause.
e.g. Der Aufzug im Büro <u>funktioniert</u> nicht.
→ Ich habe den Zug verpaßt, <u>weil</u> der Aufzug im Büro nicht <u>funktioniert</u>.

Ein schrecklicher Tag
1 Die Ampel vor dem Büro <u>ist</u> kaputt.
2 Die Rolltreppe zu den Gleisen <u>ist</u> wegen Reparatur ausgeschaltet.
3 Es <u>gibt</u> jeden Abend einen Stau auf der Hauptstraße.

Impersonal expressions

1 Some verb expressions are IMPERSONAL. This means that the subject of the verb is always **es** (*it*).
   Many common impersonal expressions are about the weather:
   Es regnet   *It is raining*   **Es** schneit   *It is snowing*

2 **Es gibt** *(there is/are)* and **es geht mir** … *(I am or I feel …)* are two very common impersonal expressions:
   Es gibt in London viel zu sehen   *There is a lot to see in London*
   Es gibt sehr wenige davon   *There are very few of them*
   Wie **geht es** Ihnen? **Es geht** mir gut   *How are you? I am/I feel fine*

3 You say *who* you are talking about in impersonal expressions like the ones below by using the dative case of a noun or pronoun:

   ES   +   VERB   +   DATIVE NOUN OR PRONOUN

   Es tut **mir** leid   *I am sorry*
   Es tut **meinem Bruder** leid   *My brother is sorry*
   Es geht **meinem Vater** sehr schlecht   *My father is very ill*
   Es gefällt **dem Kind**   *The child likes it*

   For a list of impersonal expressions see Appendix pages 139–140

More on conjunctions…

4 In Chapter 14 you saw some conjunctions (so-called CO-ORDINATING CONJUNCTIONS). SUBORDINATING CONJUNCTIONS are different because they change the word order. **Weil** *(because)* and **daß** *(that)* are two of the most common subordinating conjunctions:
   Er will keine Fabrikarbeit. Es ist zu langweilig   →
   Er will keine Fabrikarbeit, **weil** es zu langweilig ist
      He doesn't want factory work because it is too boring
   Ich habe so viel Arbeit. Ich habe sehr wenig Freizeit   →
   Ich habe so viel Arbeit, **daß** ich sehr wenig Freizeit habe
      I have so much work that I have very little free time

   For more on subordinating conjunctions see sections 16.1–4

5 As you see, the difference is the position of the verb in the clause after one of these conjunctions (the SUBORDINATE CLAUSE). The verb always goes to the end of the clause:

a   here is an example where there is a single verb in the subordinate clause:

Block 1	Block 2	Block 3		Block 1	Block 2	Block 3
SUBJECT	VERB	REST OF MAIN CLAUSE		SUBJECT	REST OF SUB CLAUSE	VERB
Ich	habe	so viel Arbeit	, **daß**	ich	sehr wenig Freizeit	**habe**

I have so much work   *that*   *I have very little free time*

b   when the subordinate clause has a two-verb construction (e.g. an infinitive and a 'working' verb) in it, put the working verb at the end:

Block 1	Block 2	Block 3		Block 1	Block 2	Block 3
SUBJECT	VERB	REST OF MAIN CLAUSE		SUBJECT	REST OF SUB CLAUSE	VERB
Sie	hat	so viel im Koffer	, **daß**	sie	ihn nicht tragen	**kann**

She has so much in the suitcase   *that*   *she cannot carry it*

c   if the verb in the subordinate clause is in the perfect tense, put the auxiliary (**haben** or **sein**) to the end as the 'working' verb:

Block 1	Block 2	Block 3		Block 1	Block 2	Block 3
SUBJECT	VERB	REST OF MAIN CLAUSE		SUBJECT	REST OF SUB CLAUSE	VERB
Wir	gehen	ins Krankenhaus	, **weil**	mein Freund	sich verletzt	hat

We are going to the hospital   *because*   *my friend has injured himself*

Note: In each case you must use a comma to separate the two clauses.

6   As in English, the subordinate clause can come at the beginning of the sentence:

Weil ich so viel Arbeit habe, **habe ich** sehr wenig Freizeit
Because I have so much work, I have very little free time

The subordinate clause is unchanged, with its verb at the end. BUT the subject and verb in the main clause are turned round or 'inverted'. This is because the whole subordinate clause is seen as being the first block, and the second block in the sentence has to be the main verb:

Block 1		Block 2	Block 3	Block 4
SUBORDINATE CLAUSE		VERB	SUBJECT	REST OF SENTENCE
Weil ich so viel Arbeit habe	,	**habe**	ich	sehr wenig Freizeit

CHAPTER 15   WHAT HAVE YOU LEARNT?

A Moritz wants to know the plot of the Shakespeare play *Macbeth*. Maria gives a brief description. Fill in the gaps with the appropriate impersonal phrase.
e.g. (<u>gehen</u>) ihm am Anfang gut.   →   <u>Es geht</u> ihm am Anfang gut.

Macbeth
Macbeth trifft drei Hexen. (<u>regnen</u>). (<u>donnern</u>). (<u>blitzen</u>). Die Frau von Macbeth ermordet den König Malcolm. (<u>gehen</u>) Macbeths Frau immer schlechter. Ganz am Ende (<u>geben</u>) eine große Schlacht und Macbeth stirbt.

B Moritz arrives home late. Frau Maier is worried and asks why he is so late. Link each excuse to the preceding sentence with **weil**.
e.g. Ich komme spät nach Hause – Ich habe Herrn Eilers getroffen.
   →   Ich komme spät nach Hause, <u>weil</u> ich Herrn Eilers getroffen habe.

Warum kommst du so spät nach Hause?
1 Ich habe die Schule spät verlassen.
2 Meine Klassenlehrerin hat mit mir gesprochen.
3 Sie ist mit meiner Arbeit nicht zufrieden.
4 Ich habe zu viele Fehler in meiner Klassenarbeit gemacht.

C The Maiers express their opinions about the cinema and give their reasons. Put each opinion and explanation together in one sentence beginning with **Ich finde, daß** for the opinion and using **weil** for the reasons.
e.g. Frau Maier: Die alten Western sind unrealistisch. Wir wissen jetzt mehr über die Geschichte der Zeit.
   →   <u>Ich finde, daß</u> die alten Western unrealistisch sind, <u>weil</u> wir jetzt mehr über die Geschichte der Zeit wissen.

Die alten Filme sind besser gewesen
1 OMA MAIER   Die neuesten Krimis sind entsetzlich. Sie verherrlichen die Kriminalität.
2 HERR MAIER   Die alten Liebesgeschichten sind schöner. Sie bringen nicht so viel Sex.
3 MARIA   Die modernen Actionfilme sind blöd. Sie zeigen keine normalen Menschen.

Revision test 13–15

A Read the descriptions of Stefan and Moritz:

Moritz ist 13 Jahre alt.   Stefan ist 12.
Moritz ist 1,50 m groß.   Stefan ist 1,60 m groß.

Now answer these questions in German with comparisons between them.
e.g. Wer ist älter?   →   Moritz ist älter als Stefan.

Zwei Jungen
1 Wer ist jünger?
2 Wer ist größer?
3 Wer ist kleiner?

B Stefan, Moritz, Birgit and Yasmin are in the same class at school. Read the following personal details:

Moritz: Alter 13   Größe 1,50   Stefan: Alter 12   Größe 1,60
Birgit: Alter 13   Größe 1,45   Yasmin: Alter 14   Größe 1,55

Now answer the questions in German using the superlative form.
e.g. Wer ist am größten?   →   Stefan ist der größte.

Vier Schüler
1 Wer ist am größten?
2 Wer ist am kleinsten?
3 Wer ist am jüngsten?
4 Wer ist am ältesten?

C The class teacher describes his pupils. Complete the ending of the comparative and superlative adjectives.

Gute Noten
1 Stefan braucht eine besser … Note, wenn er an der Uni studieren will.
2 Moritz schreibt immer einen länger … Aufsatz als Stefan.
3 Yasmin hat immer die best … Noten in der Klasse.
4 Stefan ist der best … Schüler in der Klasse.
5 Moritz bekommt immer das schlechtest … Zeugnis.
6 Birgit ist die ruhigst … Schülerin.

D The students express their feelings about the new teacher. Replace the underlined pronoun (in the 1st person) with the appropriate pronoun in the 3rd person.
e.g. Kirsten: Es gefällt <u>mir</u>, wie er aussieht.   → Es gefällt ihr, wie er aussieht.

Der neue Lehrer
STEFAN   Es gefällt <u>mir</u>, wie er die Klasse behandelt.
YASMIN   Es gefällt <u>mir</u>, wie er spricht.
MORITZ UND BIRGIT Es gefällt <u>uns</u>, wie er alles erklärt.

E The class teacher writes the report for Stefan. Complete the report with the German equivalent of the bracketed English conjunction.

Das Schulzeugnis
Stefan liest sehr gern [and] schreibt gern Aufsätze. Leider schwätzt er zu viel [or] konzentriert sich nicht gut. Er muß bessere Noten kriegen, [for] er möchte weiter studieren. Er soll nicht mehr, [but] besser arbeiten.

F The class teacher talks with his colleagues. Complete each sentence with a definite article in the appropriate case.
e.g. Ich interessiere mich für … Theater.   → Ich interessiere mich für <u>das</u> Theater.

Die Sommerferien
Ich freue mich schon auf … Ferien. Wir interessieren uns für … Türkei. Erinnert ihr euch an … letzten Sommerferien? Meine Freundin erzählt mir viel von … Türkei. Wir warten auf … Prospekt vom Reisebüro.

G Frau Schmidt is the school matron. She tells the class teacher why each child has come to her. Fill in the missing personal pronoun.
e.g. Ich habe Bauchschmerzen. Es geht … schlecht.   → Es geht <u>mir</u> schlecht.

Mir geht's schlecht
1 Philipp hat Kopfschmerzen. Es geht … nicht gut.
2 Susanne hat Ohrenschmerzen. Die Ohren tun … weh.
3 Stefan und Birgit haben Zahnschmerzen. Die Zähne tun … weh.
4 Yasmin hat eine Erkältung. Es geht … schlecht.

H Stefan explains why he did not go to the cinema. Starting with **Er hat gesagt, daß…** repeat Stefan's excuses, changing each sentence as needed.
e.g. Ich habe keine Zeit gehabt.   → Er hat gesagt, daß er keine Zeit gehabt hat.

Ich habe den Film schon gesehen
1 Ich habe den Film in England schon gesehen.
2 Ich bin lieber schwimmen gegangen.
3 Ich habe zu viel Hausaufgaben gehabt.
4 Ich bin lieber mit Yasmin in die Disko gegangen.

6 Im Familienkreis

A You are discussing with your host family the things you should do before you go home. Replace the English word in each sentence with the appropriate German conjunction. Choose from: **da**, **bevor**, **obgleich**.

e.g. [before] du nach Hause fährst...   →   <u>Bevor</u> du nach Hause fährst...

Du mußt noch...

[before] ich Berlin verlasse, möchte ich euch zum Essen im Restaurant einladen.

[although] Samstag mein letzter Tag ist, habe ich mittags Zeit, [as] mein Zug erst um 21 Uhr abfährt.

B Your host family asks you what you would like to do on Saturday, but you don't know what the options are. Beginning each reply with **Ich weiß nicht**, answer the questions re-using all the words in the original question but in the new word order required.

e.g. Was läuft im Kino?   →   Ich weiß nicht, was <u>im Kino läuft</u>.

Ich weiß nicht

1 Wie ist die Wettervorhersage für Samstag?
2 Wann hat die neue Eishalle auf?
3 Wer spielt im Fußballstadion?
4 Was für Musik gibt es in der Disko?
5 Warum kommt Peter nicht mit?

C You consider what you still have to do before you leave for home. For each sentence decide if you must use the word **zu**. Answer **ja** if you think you must use **zu**, and complete the sentence. Answer **nein** if you do not have to use **zu**.

e.g. Ich muß meinen Fotoapparat in meinem Rucksack ... einpacken.   →   <u>nein</u>

Ich muß noch

1 Ich habe vergessen, Daniela ihr Buch ... geben.
2 Ich muß Peter ... anrufen, bevor ich abfahre.
3 Ich soll Marias Großeltern ... besuchen.
4 Ich brauche Geschenke für meine Eltern ... kaufen.
5 Ich freue mich darauf, meine Familie wieder ... sehen.

More on subordinating conjunctions...

1 Here are some more common subordinating conjunctions that behave like **weil** and **daß**:

bevor *before*	**Bevor** wir nach Hause fahren, müssen wir Geld wechseln *Before we go home we have to change some money*
nachdem *after*	**Nachdem** ich aufgestanden bin, mache ich das Frühstück *After getting up I get breakfast*
bis *until*	Ich werde arbeiten, **bis** die Schule wieder anfängt *I will work until school begins again*
ob *whether*	Fragen Sie, **ob** Sie helfen können *Ask whether you can help*
obgleich, **obwohl** *although*	Maria steht früh auf, **obgleich/obwohl** es Sonntag ist *Maria is getting up early although it is Sunday*
während *while*	**Während** meine Mutter arbeitet, lese ich die Zeitung *While my mother is working I read the paper*

For information on word order see section 15.5

2 There are two conjunctions meaning *since* in German: **seitdem** *(since referring to time)* and **da** *(since, as, giving a reason)*:

Seitdem es das Satellitenfernsehen gibt, sehe ich mehr fern
   Since satellite TV arrived, I watch more TV
Wir standen eine halbe Stunde, **da** es einen Unfall gab
   We were stuck for half an hour, as there was an accident

3 All the common QUESTION WORDS can be used as conjunctions, as in English, but they then behave like subordinating conjunctions and send the verb to the end of the sentence or clause:

Was machen Sie da?   →   Er fragt, **was** Sie da **machen**
   What are you doing there? → *He is asking what you are doing there*
Warum antworten Sie nicht? →   Sie will wissen, **warum** Sie nicht **antworten**
   Why don't you answer? → *She wants to know why you don't answer*

4 In German a question word or conjunction can also be formed by placing **wo-** in front of a preposition (or **wor-** if the preposition starts with a vowel). The **wo(r)-** has the sense of *what*:

Worauf wartet er?   →   Ich weiß nicht, **worauf** er wartet
   What is he waiting for? → *I don't know what he's waiting for*
Wovon spricht er?   →   Ich habe keine Ahnung, **wovon** er spricht
   What is he talking about? → *I have no idea what he's talking about*

*See also sections 17.1–45 on the subordinating conjunction for **when***

Help Yourself to Essential German Grammar

The infinitive with **zu**

5   Most VERBS which are followed by the infinitive (apart from modal verbs *see chapter 8* and verbs of movement *see Appendix page 140*) need **zu** in front of the infinitive. The **zu + INFINITIVE** then goes to the end of the sentence or clause:

Ich hoffe immer, nette Leute **zu treffen**   *I always hope to meet nice people*

Note: There is a comma before the infinitive clause, which consists of the infinitive and its object (if it has one) and any other words that belong to it.

Common verbs of this type are **helfen** *(to help)*, **hoffen** *(to hope)*, **bitten** *(to ask)*, and **brauchen** *(to need)*. **Brauchen** is unusual: there is no comma after it:

Sie **brauchen** nicht sofort **zu** bezahlen   *You don't have to pay right away*
Ich habe ihr **geholfen**, den Koffer **zu** tragen   *I helped her carry her suitcase*

With separable verbs the **zu** is placed between the prefix and the infinitive:

Er freut sich darauf, seinen Freund wieder**zu**sehen
   He is looking forward to seeing his friend again

> *For verb plus preposition phrases with the infinitive see section 14.5*
> *For a fuller list of verbs followed by* ***zu*** *+ infinitive see Appendix page 140*

6   Other expressions which are followed by **zu** + infinitive are:

a   **es ist** + adjective *(it is + adjective)*:

Es ist nicht teuer, ein Fahrrad **zu** mieten   *It is not expensive to hire a bike*
Es ist verboten, hier **zu** rauchen   *It is forbidden to smoke here*

b   **ohne zu** ... *(without ... ing)* and **anstatt zu** ... *(instead of ... ing)*:

Er geht vorbei, **ohne** mich **zu** sehen   *He walks past without seeing me*
Anstatt zu warten, ging sie nach Hause   *Instead of waiting, she went home*

c   usually with **ist**, **war**, etc. to express *to be* sold, etc:

Es ist **zu erwarten**, daß er stirbt   *It is to be expected that he will die*
Das Haus ist **zu verkaufen**   *The house is to be sold/for sale*
Jede Woche ein Auto **zu gewinnen**!   *Every week a car to be won!*

d   after **etwas** *(something)*, **nichts** *(nothing)* and **viel** *(a lot)*:

Sollen wir **etwas zu essen** mitnehmen?   *Should we take something to eat?*

Note: In this case the infinitive follows immediately and does not go to the end of the clause or sentence.

CHAPTER 16   WHAT HAVE YOU LEARNT?

A You are going out with the Maiers for the evening. There are a number of things to
do before you leave. Replace the English words in brackets with the appropriate
German conjunctions and then join the two sentences together.
e.g. [before] wir gehen ins Theater. Moritz muß den Müll hinausbringen.
  → Bevor wir ins Theater gehen, muß Moritz den Müll hinausbringen.

Wir gehen ins Theater
1 [although] Das Wetter ist sehr gut. Wir müssen alle Fenster zumachen.
2 Die Katze will bestimmt hereinkommen. [after] Wir sind ausgegangen.
3 Ich muß meine Schlüssel finden. [before] Wir fahren ab.
4 [since] Ich habe die Karten gekauft. Das Theater ist ganz ausgebucht.
5 Wir brauchen nicht in der Schlange zu stehen. [as] Wir haben schon Karten.

B Peter phones home on his mobile. However, the line is very poor. Frau Maier
becomes very exasperated. Combine the two sentences using the question word as a
conjunction.
e.g. Ich verstehe nicht! Was sagt er? → Ich verstehe nicht, was er sagt.

Die Verbindung ist schlecht
1 Ich habe keine Ahnung! Wovon sprichst du?
2 Ich will wissen! Warum funktioniert dein Telefon nicht?
3 Ich habe nicht gehört! Wann kommst du zurück?

C You thank your host family for their hospitality and invite them to visit you.
Complete each sentence with one of these German verbs in the infinitive: **begrüßen,
weinen, besuchen, verabschieden, danken**.
Decide whether or not you need to use **zu** before the infinitive.
e.g. Ich möchte euch für einen wunderschönen Aufenthalt [to thank].
  → Ich möchte euch für einen wunderschönen Aufenthalt danken.

Eine Einladung
DU   Ich lade euch ein, nächstes Jahr meine Familie und mich [to visit].
HERR MAIER Nichts danke. Es war für uns ein Vergnügen, dich bei uns [to
            welcome].
FRAU MAIER Moritz! Maria! Ihr müßt euch [to say goodbye]. Ach nein. Ihr könnt
            euch nie verabschieden, ohne [to cry]!

UNIT

6

A You are about to leave for home after your holiday in Germany. Frau Maier is seeing you off. Fill in each gap with the right German word for *when*. Use either **wenn** *(whenever, when, if)* or **wann** *(at what time, when)*.

e.g. ... fährt dein Zug?   →   Wann fährt dein Zug?

Wann fährt dein Zug?

1 Auf der Fähre, ... das Wetter schön ist, kannst du draußen sitzen.
2 Weißt du, ... du in London ankommst?
3 ... du in London ankommst, grüße deine Eltern recht schön von uns.
4 Wir kommen dich besuchen, aber ich bin nicht sicher, ...

B You can't find the house key Frau Maier lent you. You try to remember where you last saw it. Separate the long sentence linked with the conjunction **als** into the original two short sentences.

e.g. Als wir vom Kino zurückgekommen sind, war der Schlüssel auf dem Schlüsselbund.
   →   Wir sind vom Kino zurückgekommen.
   Der Schlüssel war auf dem Schlüsselbund.

Wo ist der Schlüssel?

1 Als ich das Licht angeschaltet habe, habe ich den Schlüssel in der Hand gehabt.
2 Als Peter eine Tasse Kaffee gemacht hat, habe ich das Schlüsselbund auf den Tisch gelegt.
3 Als ich ins Wohnzimmer gegangen bin, habe ich den Schlüssel nicht mehr gehabt.

C Herr Maier has won some money on the lottery. He dreams of what the family will do with the money. Fill in the gap in each sentence with the appropriate form of **werden**.

e.g. Ich ... Millionär!   →   Ich werde Millionär!

Die Millionäre

1 Meine Eltern ... eine Villa in Italien kaufen!
2 Kinder, ihr ... eure Lieblingspopstars treffen!
3 Meine Frau ... einen neuen Mercedes fahren!
4 Wir ... eine Weltreise machen!

Help Yourself to Essential German Grammar

How to say *when*

1 There are three ways of saying *when* in German: **wann**, **wenn** and **als**:

Wann kommst du?
***When** are you coming?*
Wenn meine Schwester kommt, geben Sie ihr dieses Buch
***When** my sister comes, give her this book*
Als wir herauskamen, waren wir in der Fußgängerzone
***When** we came out, we were in the pedestrian precinct*

2 Use **wann**:
  a with direct questions, as a question word:

    Wann ist der Zug gefahren?   *When did the train go?*

  b with indirect questions, as a conjunction:

    Ich weiß nicht, **wann** der Zug gefahren ist   *I don't know when the train went*

3 Use **wenn**:
  a with present and future tenses to express *upon doing something*:

    Wenn du ins Zimmer gehst, ist der Fernseher gleich da
    When you go into the room, the TV is right there
    Wenn ich ihn sehe, werde ich es ihm geben
    When I see him, I shall give it to him

  b to express habitual action *(= whenever)* in the present or past:

    Wenn das Wetter schön ist, frühstückt sie im Garten
    When(ever) the weather is nice she has breakfast in the garden
    Wenn das Wetter schön war, frühstückte sie im Garten
    When(ever) the weather was nice she had breakfast in the garden

  c to express *when* in the sense of *if:*

    Wenn man ein Paket aufgeben will, geht man zur Post
    When/If you want to post a parcel, you go to the post office
    Wenn ich den Brief morgen bekomme, werde ich dich anrufen
    When/If I get the letter tomorrow I will give you a ring

            See Chapter 23 for more on clauses with if

4 Use **als** with past tenses to express *upon doing something*:

    Als ich angekommen bin, war er nicht da *When I arrived he was not there*
    Ich war dabei, **als** er das sagte   *I was present when he said that*

5 The word order and use of commas with **wenn** and **als** (and **wann** as a conjunction) is the same as for all subordinating conjunctions (*see sections 15.4–6*).

The future tense

6 The FUTURE TENSE says what is going to happen e.g. they **will survive**. In German it is formed by the present tense of **werden** + infinitive, the equivalent of *will* + verb in English:

Ich **werde** einen Job **suchen**   *I will look for a job*
Wir **werden** dich vom Flughafen **abholen**   *We will pick you up at the airport*

Note that the infinitive goes to the end of the clause or sentence.

7 Here is the present tense of **werden**:

SINGULAR	PLURAL
ich werde	wir werden
du wirst	ihr werdet
Sie werden	Sie werden
er/sie/es wird	sie werden

8 Notice that **er/sie will** (which comes from **wollen** meaning *to want*) is used to express a wish or desire, and **er/sie wird** (which comes from **werden**) is used to express a future fact:

Diana **will** ihn heiraten   *Diana wants to marry him (wish)*
Diana **wird** ihn heiraten   *Diana will/is going to marry him (fact)*

9 The PRESENT TENSE is often used in German to express the future. Particularly with a word or expression to indicate time (see section 2.6) it is equivalent to the English *am/is/are ... ing* form of the present:

Ich **fahre** heute nachmittag in die Stadt   *I am going into town this afternoon*
Sie **gehen** morgen schwimmen   *They are going swimming tomorrow*

However, sometimes German uses the present where English can only use the future. For instance, in the **wenn** clauses given above in sections 17.3a and 17.3c, one can also say in German:

Wenn ich ihn sehe, **gebe** ich es ihm   *When I see him, I will give it to him*
Wenn ich den Brief morgen bekomme, **rufe** ich dich an
   When I get the letter tomorrow, I will call you

CHAPTER 17   WHAT HAVE YOU LEARNT?

A   The Maier family plan an outing and mention the various possibilities, which depend on the weather. Link the two sentences using **wenn**.
e.g. Das Wetter ist schön. Wir machen gewöhnlich eine Schiffahrt.
   → <u>Wenn</u> das Wetter schön <u>ist, machen wir</u> gewöhnlich eine Schiffahrt.

Ausflüge
1   Das Wetter ist schlecht. Wir besuchen das Schloß Charlottenburg.
2   Die Sonne scheint. Die Familie macht einen Spaziergang durch den Wald.
3   Es regnet sehr stark. Wir fahren irgendwohin essen.
4   Es ist sehr warm. Die Jungen können ins Freibad gehen.

B   The Maiers remember a terrible outing they once made. Complete the description with the correct German for the English *when*.
e.g. ... wir diese Schiffahrt gemacht haben, war das Wetter furchtbar.
   → <u>Als</u> wir diese Schiffahrt gemacht haben, war das Wetter furchtbar.

Der Ausflug war ein Alptraum!
Ich erinnere mich nicht genau, ... das Schiff abgefahren ist. Wahrscheinlich am frühen Nachmittag. ... wir sonntags einen Ausflug machen, gehen wir gewöhnlich nach dem Mittagessen.
... das Schiff mitten auf dem See war, hat es einen schrecklichen Sturm gegeben. Wir waren alle seekrank.
Jetzt ... wir ausgehen, passen wir immer auf das Wetter auf!

C   Each member of the Maier family has their dream about what life will be like when they win the lottery. Put each sentence in the future tense.
e.g. Moritz: Ich verbringe jeden Sommer in Griechenland.
   → Moritz <u>wird</u> jeden Sommer in Griechenland <u>verbringen</u>.

Träume
1   Frau Maier: Ich fahre jeden Winter in Gstaad Ski.
2   Oma und Opa Maier: Wir kaufen ein dickes Auto.
3   Herr Maier: Ich kaufe mir ein Haus in Spanien.
4   Maria: Ich gehe in alle Konzerte der Berliner Philharmoniker.

Help Yourself to Essential German Grammar

UNIT

6

A Moritz has just received his (not very good) school report. He promises his mother to
do better. Complete each sentence with one of the following German adverbs to
match the English word in brackets: **regelmäßig**, **viel**, **gut**.
e.g. Ich werde [regularly] meine Hausaufgaben machen.
   → Ich werde regelmäßig meine Hausaufgaben machen.

Das Schulzeugnis
1 Ich werde [well] lernen.
2 Ich werde [a lot] arbeiten.
3 Ich werde nicht so [much] plaudern.

B The class teacher points out how much better he works when he is sitting by himself.
Complete each sentence with one of the following German adverbs in the
comparative: **mehr**, **schneller**, **weniger**, **besser**.
e.g. Er arbeitet [quicker], wenn er allein sitzt.
   → Er arbeitet schneller, wenn er allein sitzt.

Am Elternabend (1)
1 Er lernt [more].
2 Er plaudert [less].
3 Er kann sich [better] konzentrieren.

C Complete the teacher's comments with the following adverbs in the superlative form:
am schnellsten, **am wenigsten**, **am besten**, **am fleißigsten**, **am meisten**.
e.g. Moritz arbeitet [fastest], wenn er allein sitzt.
   → Moritz arbeitet am schnellsten, wenn er allein sitzt.

Am Elternabend (2)
Moritz lernt [most diligently] und [the most], plaudert [least] und konzentriert sich
[best] von der ganzen Klasse, wenn er allein sitzt.

D Maria's father asks her why she isn't going to the cinema. Combine the two halves of
the German sentence and give the meaning.
e.g. 1 → b → I have saved for four weeks.

Gehst du denn nicht ins Kino?
1 Ich habe vier   a der Film nicht mehr!
2 Ich arbeite seit   b Wochen gespart.
3 Am Samstag läuft   c einem Monat in der Bäckerei.

Adverbs

1 ADVERBS describe how something is done or happens, or when, or where:

Er fährt **schnell**	He drives _quickly_
Es regnet **sehr stark**	It's raining _very hard_
Sie kommt **heute**	She's coming _today_
Er wohnt **anderswo**	He lives _somewhere else_

Adverbs are said to qualify the verb, just as the adjective qualifies the noun.

2 In German most adjectives can be used as ADVERBS without alteration:

ADJECTIVE	Stefan ist **gut** im Sport	Stefan is _good_ at sport
ADVERB	Stefan tanzt **gut**	Stefan dances _well_

Note that adverbs, unlike adjectives, are INVARIABLE – they do not add endings.

3 In addition to using the basic form of an adjective as an adverb, you can add **-weise** to some nouns and **-erweise** to some adjectives to make adverbs:

-weise	der **Versuch** (trial)	**versuchsweise** (on a trial basis)
	der **Liter** (litre)	**literweise** (by the litre)
-erweise	**normal** (normal)	**normalerweise** (normally)

4 An adverb often comes at the beginning of a sentence. When this happens, the subject and the verb are turned round to allow the verb to be in the second block of the sentence. This is called inversion (see Chapter 8 for another example):

Morgen nehmen wir den Bus   _Tomorrow we are taking the bus_

5 Where there are a number of adverbs in a sentence, the order in which they are placed normally follows the order TIME – MANNER – PLACE:

	TIME	MANNER	PLACE	
Er ist	**um drei Uhr**	**schnell**	**nach Hause**	gefahren

He drove home quickly at three o'clock

Comparative and superlative of adverbs

6 The COMPARATIVE ADVERB is exactly the same in form as the adjective, you simply add **-er**:

schnell _(quick, quickly)_   →   schnell**er** _(quicker, more quickly)_

The comparative adverb is used to say something is done or happens _more_ in a particular way:

Ich werde **langsamer** sprechen	_I shall speak _more slowly__
Es regnet **stärker**	_It is raining _harder__

7 The SUPERLATIVE ADVERB is made in the same way as the superlative adjective in its second form (see section 13.4b): **am** + ADVERB + **sten**:

> schnell *(quickly, fast)*   →   **am** schnell**sten** *(most quickly, fastest)*

8 Use the superlative form to say something is done or happens *the most* in a particular way:

Hanna fährt **am** sicher**sten**   *Hanna drives the most safely*
Sie sind **am** früh**esten** gekommen   *They came (the) earliest*

9 The following adverbs have irregular comparative and superlative forms:

gern *(gladly)*	lieber *(more gladly)*	am liebsten *(most gladly)*
gut *(well)*	besser *(better)*	am besten *(best)*
viel *(a lot, much)*	mehr *(more)*	am meisten *(most)*

Das Wetter in Spanien gefällt mir **besser**   *I like the weather in Spain better*

Expressions of time

10 In German there are three ways to express *for* in time expressions:

a with a completed action, use the ACCUSATIVE CASE for the length of time:

Sie haben **zwei Wochen** bei einer Firma gearbeitet
They worked in a firm for two weeks

b to express continuing action *(has/have been … ing)* use **seit** + DATIVE CASE:

Sie arbeitet **seit einem Monat** in der Jugendherberge
She has been working in the youth hostel for a month

Note that German uses the PRESENT TENSE here, and English the perfect.

c to express future plans use **für** + ACCUSATIVE CASE:

Morgen fahre ich **für zwei Wochen** nach Bonn
Tomorrow I will be going to Bonn for two weeks

11 To express a specific day or date on which something happens use **am (= an dem)**:

am Samstag   *on Saturday*
am Samstag **den** 3. Mai   *on Saturday May 3rd*

See sections 4.4–5 for how to tell the time

CHAPTER 18   WHAT HAVE YOU LEARNT?

A Frau Maier wants someone to telephone Canterbury to get information for the
family's visit to England. She tries to persuade Peter to make the call. Put the adverb
in brackets in its comparative form.
e.g. Frau Maier: Du sprichst es (gut) als ich.   →   Du sprichst es besser als ich.

Ein Telefonanruf nach England

PETER   Du sprichst Englisch genauso gut wie ich.

FRAU MAIER Aber du sprichst es (deutlich) aus. Am Telefon ist das wichtig.

PETER   Du hast dein Englisch (viel) geübt.

FRAU MAIER Ich telefoniere (gern) heute abend. Ja, ich rufe (spät) an.

PETER   Es wird heute abend zu spät sein. Gib mir das Telefon!

FRAU MAIER OK. Aber es ist (gut), wenn ich dir die Fragen aufschreibe.

B Frau Maier says where and how they want to go. Put the adverb in brackets in its
superlative form.
e.g. Wir fahren (schnell) über die Autobahn.
   →   Wir fahren am schnellsten über die Autobahn.

Reisepläne

1 Wir fahren (schnell) durch den Tunnel.
2 (Gut) übernachten wir auf einem Campingplatz in der Nähe von Canterbury.
3 Wir kommen (gern) am 20. Juli in Canterbury an.
4 (Spät) fahren wir am 25. Juli ab.
5 Wir kommen (früh) am 31. Juli nach Berlin zurück.

C When confirming the travel details the tourist information officer repeats the
information Peter gives him. Is the word order correct? Answer **richtig** or **falsch**.
Correct those sentences you think are **falsch**.
e.g. Sie fahren von Deutschland nach Großbritannnien mit dem Auto.
   →   **falsch**   →   Sie fahren mit dem Auto von Deutschland nach Großbritannien.

Ja, ich spreche Deutsch

1 Die Familie fährt mit dem Zug durch den Tunnel.
2 Sie kommen in Canterbury am 20. Juli an.
3 Die Familie möchte auf einem Campingplatz fünf Nächte bleiben.
4 Die Familie fährt nach fünf Tagen in Canterbury weiter.

Revision test 16–18

A Oma Müller, a widow in an old people's home, talks about her plans. Replace the English word with the equivalent German conjunction.

e.g. [time since] ich hier wohne, sehe ich mehr fern.

→ Seitdem ich hier wohne, sehe ich mehr fern.

Mein Freund und ich
1 [before] wir heiraten, müssen wir warten.
2 Wir warten, [until] wir das Geld für ein Haus gespart haben.
3 Meine Kinder haben gefragt, [whether] sie uns helfen können.
4 [although] wir warten müssen, macht es uns keine Sorgen.
5 [while] wir sparen, wohnen mein Freund und ich hier im Altersheim.
6 [time since] es Satellitenfernsehen hier gibt, schauen wir mehr Sport.

B Opa Heinrich is becoming slightly hard of hearing. The assistant in the old people's home asks him some questions which Oma Müller has to repeat for him. Reconstruct the original questions using the formal **Sie** form.

e.g. Sie fragt, warum deine Tochter heute nicht kommt.

→ Warum kommt Ihre Tochter heute nicht?

Was hat sie gesagt?
1 Sie fragt, wann wir essen möchten.
2 Sie will wissen, wo du die Zeitung gelassen hast.
3 Sie möchte wissen, warum dein Sohn ein neues Auto gekauft hat.
4 Sie fragt, wie wir nach Hause gefahren sind.

C In the old people's home there are a number of rules and regulations. Decide whether or not the final infinitive needs **zu** in front of it. Answer **ja** or **nein**.

e.g. Sie werden gebeten, Besucher nicht selbst herein … lassen.

→ ja. Sie werden gebeten, Besucher nicht selbst hereinzulassen.

Hausvorschriften
1 Es ist verboten, im Altersheim … rauchen.
2 Wir bitten unsere Gäste, die Bibliothek morgens … benutzen.
3 Wir empfehlen unseren Gästen, ihre Wertsachen im Safe … lassen.
4 Bitte, verlassen Sie das Altersheim nicht, ohne das Personal … informieren.

D Oma Müller gives more information about herself. Fill in the gaps with the appropriate German word for *when*.

e.g. … ich ins Altersheim gekommen bin, habe ich niemand gekannt.

→   <u>Als</u> ich ins Altersheim gekommen bin, habe ich niemand gekannt.

Oma Müller

… mein Mann gestorben ist, war ich ganz allein zu Hause. Meine Tochter kommt heute nachmittag, aber ich weiß nicht, … sie ankommt. … ich sie wiedersehe, werde ich mich freuen. Ich war sehr froh, … ich Herrn Heinrich kennengelernt habe.

E Moritz writes an essay on life in the future. Complete his essay with the appropriate part of **werden**.

e.g. Alles … elektronisch funktionieren.   →   Alles <u>wird</u> elektronisch funktionieren.

Das Jahr 2030

Wir besuchen das Jahr 2030. Der Supermarkt … ganz anders aussehen. Die Kunden … von zu Hause aus alles durch das Internet bestellen. Es … kein Plastik mehr geben, sondern nur wiederverwendbare Stoffe. Ich … in einem umweltfreundlichen Haus wohnen.

F Moritz complains to his mother that Yasmin is better at everything at school. Change each adverb used into its comparative form.

e.g. Sie paßt <u>gut</u> auf.   →   Sie paßt <u>besser</u> auf.

Besser

Yasmin schreibt <u>gut</u>. Sie arbeitet <u>langsam</u> aber <u>genau</u>. Sie tanzt <u>schön</u> und läuft <u>schnell</u>.

G Frau Maier tells Moritz what he's best at. Complete what she says by giving the German for the English superlative adverbs.

e.g. Du ißt [<u>fastest</u>].   →   Du ißt <u>am schnellsten</u>.

Am besten

1 Du stehst [<u>slowest</u>] auf.
2 Du läufst [<u>fastest</u>] nach der Schule nach Hause.
3 Du singst [<u>most beautifully</u>] in der Badewanne.
4 Du spielst [<u>best</u>] auf dem Computer.

H For your homework your German teacher has asked you to identify in each sentence the Time phrase, the Manner phrase and/or the Place phrase.

e.g. jeden Abend   →   Time phrase

Wortstellung

1 Er ist jeden Abend mit dem Bus nach Hause gefahren.
2 Max macht seit einem Jahr Teilzeitarbeit in der Jugendherberge.
3 Ich habe am Wochenende Tennis mit meinen Freunden im Park gespielt.

Help Yourself to Essential German Grammar

Die Arbeitswelt

A Each student has to prepare a CV to apply for jobs when their apprenticeship finishes. Zoran describes his school career. Put the weak verb in brackets in the imperfect tense.

e.g. Ich (besuchen) eine Grundschule in Kroatien.
   →   Ich besuchte eine Grundschule in Kroatien.

Mein Lebenslauf
Von 1992 bis 1997 (besuchen) ich eine Gesamtschule in Berlin. Ich (absolvieren) 1997 meine Schulbildung mit dem Realschulabschluß.

B Clive describes his school career. Put the strong verb in brackets into the imperfect tense. Choose from the following: **bestand, half, ging, beschloß**.

e.g. Er (bestehen) sein Abitur.   →   Er bestand sein Abitur.

Die Lehrzeit
Ab dem Alter von 12 Jahren (gehen) ich in ein Gymnasium. Obwohl ich mein Abitur (bestehen), (beschließen) ich trotzdem eine Lehrzeit als Automechaniker zu machen. Ich (helfen) meinem Onkel jedes Wochenende in seiner Autowerkstatt.

C Clive describes which qualities are important in his work. For each noun that is underlined, state the adjective that it is formed from.

e.g. Sauberkeit finde ich unwichtig.   →   sauber

Mein Beruf
1 Die größte Schwierigkeit war, eine Lehrzeit zu finden.
2 Gute Gesundheit ist für diesen Beruf am wichtigsten.
3 Müdigkeit ist immer ein Problem.
4 Meiner Meinung nach habe ich die Fähigkeit mit Maschinen zu arbeiten.

The imperfect tense

1   The IMPERFECT TENSE in German is the simple past tense. It is used particularly when telling a story, describing *what happened:*

> Stefan **lief** hinaus, **kam** wieder zurück und **sprang** schnell auf seinen Platz
> *Stefan ran out, came back again, and jumped quickly into his seat*

The PERFECT TENSE also tells what happened in the past. It is used to refer to the more recent past, so often occurs in conversation and letters, but can also refer to any single completed event, even in history (see sections 11.3–5). The IMPERFECT on the other hand, as well as telling a story, describes a continuing action or state, as well as a repeated action in the past (see sections 20.1–4).

> *See sections 20.1–4 for more uses of the imperfect tense*

2   To form the imperfect tense of WEAK VERBS, add the endings shown below to the stem. Here is the imperfect tense of **wohnen** *(to live)*:

SINGULAR		PLURAL	
ich wohn**te**	*I lived*	wir wohn**ten**	*we lived*
du wohn**test**	*you lived*	ihr wohn**tet**	*you lived*
Sie wohn**ten**	*you lived*	Sie wohn**ten**	*you lived*
er/sie/es wohn**te**	*he/she/it lived*	sie wohn**ten**	*they lived*

3   The imperfect tenses of STRONG VERBS have changes to the stem vowel and slightly different endings. Here is the imperfect tense of **geben** *(to give)*:

SINGULAR		PLURAL	
ich **gab**	*I gave*	wir **gaben**	*we gave*
du **gabst**	*you gave*	ihr **gabt**	*you gave*
Sie **gaben**	*you gave*	Sie **gaben**	*you gave*
er/sie/es **gab**	*he/she/it gave*	sie **gaben**	*they gave*

> *See Appendix pages 130–135 for a list of strong verbs and their stem changes*

4   MIXED VERBS also have a vowel change in the imperfect, but use the same endings as the weak verbs. Here is the imperfect tense of **kennen** *(to know)*:

SINGULAR		PLURAL	
ich kann**te**	*I knew*	wir kann**ten**	*we knew*
du kann**test**	*you knew*	ihr kann**tet**	*you knew*
Sie kann**ten**	*you knew*	Sie kann**ten**	*you knew*
er/sie/es kann**te**	*he/she/it knew*	sie kann**ten**	*they knew*

The other important basic imperfect forms are:

brennen	→	**brannte**
bringen	→	**brachte**
denken	→	**dachte**

> *See Appendix pages 129–130 for a fuller list of mixed verb forms*

Help Yourself to Essential German Grammar

Nouns from adjectives

5 ADJECTIVAL NOUNS are adjectives used as nouns.

> alt *(old)* → der Alte *(the old man)*

Their endings change in the same way as those of ordinary adjectives (see sections 7.4–5 and 9.6).

Here is the singular of an ADJECTIVAL NOUN in all cases, masculine and feminine:

	the stranger	*a stranger*
NOMINATIVE	der Fremde/die Fremde	ein Fremder/eine Fremde
ACCUSATIVE	den Fremden/die Fremde	einen Fremden/eine Fremde
GENITIVE	des Fremden/der Fremden	eines Fremden/einer Fremden
DATIVE	dem Fremden/der Fremden	einem Fremden/einer Fremden

The plural form is **Fremden** in all cases after the definite article, and where there is no article **Fremde** for the nominative and accusative, **Fremder** for the genitive, and **Fremden** for the dative:

> Sie haben **den Fremden/die Fremde** freundlich aufgenommen
> *They received the stranger in a friendly way*

Note: a   The adjectival noun always has a capital letter.

b   The singular form depends on whether the person is male or female.

6 After **etwas** *(something)*, **viel** *(a lot)*, **wenig** *(few)*, **nichts** *(nothing)*, **allerlei** *(all sorts of)*, the adjectival noun has the neuter endings of an adjective with no article in front of it:

NOMINATIVE	nichts Neues
ACCUSATIVE	nichts Neues
GENITIVE	nichts Neuen
DATIVE	nichts Neuem

7 Many NOUNS describing a state or characteristic ('abstract nouns') are formed from adjectives with the ending **-heit** or **-keit** (all are feminine):

traurig *(sad)*	die Traurigkeit *(sadness)*
schwierig *(difficult)*	die Schwierigkeit *(difficulty)*
gesund *(healthy)*	die Gesundheit *(health)*
krank *(ill)*	die Krankheit *(illness)*
verschieden *(different)*	die Verschiedenheit *(difference)*

8 INFINITIVES can also be used as NOUNS. All are neuter and start with a capital:

> **Das Lernen** macht mir Spaß   *Learning is fun*

Help Yourself to Essential German Grammar

CHAPTER 19   WHAT HAVE YOU LEARNT?

A The students take part in mock job interviews, describing their school career and giving other relevant information. Replace the English verb with the appropriate German verb from those given, in the imperfect tense.

e.g. Meine Familie [lived] zu der Zeit in Spanien. *arbeiten   wohnen*
   → Meine Familie <u>wohnte</u> zu der Zeit in Spanien.

Das Interview

SABINE   Früher [lived] meine Familie in Duisburg. Ich [went to] am Anfang ein Gymnasium. Wegen meiner schlechten Noten in Mathe [changed] ich meine Schule.   *wechseln   wohnen   besuchen*

ZORAN   Ich [began] eine Lehrzeit als Tischler, aber die Firma hat bankrott gemacht. Danach [decided] ich, einen Beruf mit besseren Aussichten zu lernen.

entscheiden   beginnen

B The students discuss their feelings about the mock interviews. Replace the German adjective in brackets with the adjectival noun formed from it.

e.g. Ich habe nichts (<u>neu</u>) gelernt.   →   Ich habe nichts Neues gelernt.

Die Diskussion

1 Ich habe viel (<u>interessant</u>) gelernt.
2 Ich habe allerlei (<u>blöd</u>) gesagt.
3 Wir möchten nächste Woche etwas (<u>ähnlich</u>) machen.

C The students express their opinions about the Berufsschule. Fill in each gap with the appropriate definite article **der**, **die** or **das**.

e.g. ... Studieren macht mir viel Spaß.   →   Das Studieren macht mir viel Spaß.

In der Kantine

1 ... einzige Schwierigkeit für mich ist die Fahrt hierher.
2 ... Kochen ist ein großes Vergnügen.
3 ... Verschiedenheit der Fächer gefällt mir.
4 Ich finde ... Lernen der vielen Tatsachen sehr schwierig.

UNIT

7

CHAPTER 20   WHAT DO YOU KNOW?

A Herr Dietrich asks Zoran why Manfred, a student, has been absent from college recently. Replace the English verb with one of the following: **hatte**, **hatten**, **war**, **waren**.

e.g. Die alte Oma [was] allein in Köln.   →   Die alte Oma <u>war</u> allein in Köln.

Die Familie ist nach Köln umgezogen

1 Manfred [had] keine Wahl, seine Familie ist nach Köln umgezogen.
2 Sein Vater [was] arbeitslos und konnte keine Arbeitsstelle finden.
3 Seine Brüder [had] auch in der Schule Schwierigkeiten.
4 Sie [were] beide unartig.

B At college, Zoran is looking for his friend Peter. Match up the two halves of the sentence to make a sentence that is the equivalent of the English below.

e.g. 1 b i Als ich hinkam, saß er in der Ecke.

Hast du Peter gesehen?

1 Als ich hinkam,   a als ich ihn sah.
2 Seitdem du hier bist,   b saß er in der Ecke.
3 Er wartete im Flur,   c habe ich ihn nicht gesehen.
 i When I got there he was sitting in the corner.
 ii Since you've been here I haven't seen him.
 iii He was waiting in the corridor when I saw him.

C Zoran contradicts everything Peter says. Look at what Peter says and turn each sentence into the negative by adding **nicht** or by replacing the underlined words with **noch nicht** (not yet) or **nichts** (nothing) as appropriate.

e.g. Das glaube ich.   →   Das glaube ich nicht.
   Sie weiß <u>alles</u>.   →   Sie weiß nichts.

Ein Widerspruch!

1 Sabine hat die Hausaufgaben <u>schon</u> gemacht.
2 Es geht dem Lehrer gut.
3 Stefan versteht <u>alles</u>, was der Lehrer sagt.
4 Der Lehrer hat uns die Arbeit <u>schon</u> erklärt.
5 Sie hat ihn <u>gut</u> verstanden.

· More on the imperfect tense...

1 The IMPERFECT TENSE, as well as saying what happened in the past (see section 19.1), also describes a state, the way things were in the past:

Ich **war** dieses Jahr zwei Wochen in Spanien
I was in Spain for two weeks this year
Mein Zimmer **war** winzig und **hatte** weder Bad noch Dusche
My room was tiny, and didn't have a bath or a shower
Ich **hatte** ein Telefon, aber der Farbfernseher **war** kaputt
I had a telephone, but the colour TV was broken

2 The imperfect tenses of **sein** *(to be)* and **haben** *(to have)* are irregular:

SINGULAR	PLURAL	SINGULAR	PLURAL
ich war	wir war**en**	ich hat**te**	wir hat**ten**
du war**st**	ihr war**t**	du hat**test**	ihr hat**tet**
Sie war**en**	Sie war**en**	Sie hat**ten**	Sie hat**ten**
er/sie/es war	sie war**en**	er/sie/es hat**te**	sie hat**ten**

3 The imperfect tense is used to express a continuing action, for instance what was happening in the background when another action took place:

Als ich zurückkam, **saß** er immer noch da
*When I came back he **was** still **sitting** there*
Seitdem du das letzte Mal hier **warst**, ist nicht viel passiert
*Since you **were** last here not much has happened*
Wie alt **waren** Sie, als Sie mit dem Autorennen angefangen haben?
*How old **were** you when you began car racing?*

4 **Seit** *(since)* + imperfect tense expresses the idea that something *had been* going on for some time (and still was), just as **seit** + present expresses something that *has been* going on (and still is):

Er **arbeitete seit** zwei Wochen hier   *He **had been** working here for two weeks*
Er **arbeitet seit** zwei Wochen hier   *He **has been** working here for two weeks*

Negatives

5 The usual way to say something is not the case is to use **nicht**:

Das glaube ich **nicht**!   *I don't believe that!*
Es geht mir **nicht** gut   *I am not well*
Ich wußte **nicht**, was ich machen sollte   *I did not know what I should do*

Nicht is placed either at the end of a sentence, if the sentence is very short, or immediately before the word it is referring to (or 'negating').

6 *Not a/no* in German is expressed by **kein**:

Ich habe **keine** Geschwister	*I have **no**/I haven't any brothers or sisters*
Man versteht wirklich **kein** Wort	*You really **can't** understand **a** word*
Kein Problem!	***No** problem!*

In the above examples **kein** is an adjective and has the same endings as the INDEFINITE ARTICLE (**ein**) (see sections 2.1 and 4.2).

7 To express *no one* or *nobody* you can use **keiner/keine** as well as **niemand**:

Ich habe Angst davor, daß mich **keiner/niemand** akzeptiert
*I am afraid that **no one** will accept me*
Keine spielt die Rolle besser als sie
***No one** plays the part better than she does*
Sie wollte mit **keinem** anderen/mit **niemand** anderem gehen
*She did **not** want to go **with anybody** else*

Note that while **keiner** has different endings, **niemand** is invariable.

8 Where a negative statement is corrected by a statement starting with *but*, the word for *but* is **sondern** (see section 14.2):

Es gibt dort **kein** Hotel, **sondern** nur eine Pension
*There **isn't** a hotel there, **but** only a guesthouse*
Er machte es **nicht** aus Interesse, **sondern** weil es nicht anders ging
*He did **not** do it out of interest, **but** because there was no other way*

Sondern is also used in translating the expression *not only but also*:

Sie helfen uns, **nicht nur** die Sprache **sondern auch** die Leute kennenzulernen
*They help us to get to know **not only** the language, **but also** the people*

9 Other negative words which it is useful to know:

Mein Zimmer hatte **weder** Bad **noch** Dusche
*My room had **neither** a bath **nor** a shower*

Ich kann ihn **nirgends** finden	*I cannot find him **anywhere***
Sie sind **nie** gekommen	*They **never** came*
Ich war **noch nie** in Indien	*I've **never** been to India*
Ich weiß **nichts** davon	*I know **nothing** about it*
Mir geht's **gar nicht** gut	*I am **not at all** well*
Sie hat die Arbeit **noch nicht** gemacht	*She has **not** done the work **yet***
Er ist **nicht mehr** hier	*He is **no longer** here*

CHAPTER 20   WHAT HAVE YOU LEARNT?

A Peter talks about a holiday job he had in Italy. At first the conditions of work and his accommodation were not what he expected. Put **haben** and **sein** into the correct form of the imperfect.

e.g. Ich (sein) letztes Jahr in Italien. → Ich war letztes Jahr in Italien.

Der Ferienjob (1)

Ich (haben) eine Stelle in einem Restaurant in Florenz. Die Arbeitsstunden (sein) viel länger als erwartet. Mein Zimmer (sein) winzig und (haben) keinen Fernseher.

B Peter explains how he improved conditions. Fill the gap with the verb provided in the imperfect tense.

e.g. Als ich hinkam, ... es keinen Fernseher. *geben*

→ Als ich hinkam, gab es keinen Fernseher.

Der Ferienjob (2)

1 Als ich mit ihm die Arbeitsbedingungen besprochen habe, ... der Chef sehr nett zu mir. *sein*
2 Während ich in dem Zimmer ... , hat er mir einen Farbfernseher geliehen. *wohnen*
3 Obwohl ich im Restaurant gern ... , war ich froh zurück nach Deutschland zu kommen. *arbeiten*

C All in all, Peter found working abroad a useful experience. Change the following summary from the negative to the positive.

e.g. Ich fand es nicht interessant. → Ich fand es interessant.

Im Rückblick

1 Im Rückblick fand ich die ganze Erfahrung nicht interessant.
2 Ich habe keine gute Erinnerung an meine Zeit in Italien.
3 Ich bin alles in allem keiner, der gerne im Ausland arbeitet.
4 Ich würde nicht gerne wieder im Ausland arbeiten.

D Zoran has also worked abroad. He describes his job and accommodation. Use the construction **weder ... noch ...** to replace the **kein** phrases.

e.g. Die Wohnung hatte kein Bad und keine Dusche.

→ Die Wohnung hatte weder Bad noch Dusche.

Ferienjob mit Unterkunft

1 Das Wohnzimmer hatte keine Vorhänge und keinen Teppich.
2 Die küche hatte kein Feuster und keinen Ventilator.
3 Das Büro hatte keinen Computer und kein Faxgerät.
4 Die Arbeitskollegen hatten keine Zeit und keine Lust, mir zu helfen.

Help Yourself to Essential German Grammar

UNIT

7

A Zoran originally wanted to learn to be a carpenter. Put the auxiliary (or working) verb in brackets in the correct form to give the pluperfect tense so that Zoran describes what <u>had</u> happened to make him change his career goals.

e.g. Ich (haben) eine Lehrzeit begonnen. → Ich hatte eine Lehrzeit begonnen.

Eine neue Karriere

1 Ich (haben) vor einem Jahr eine Lehrstelle als Tischler gefunden.
2 Lange Zeit (haben) die Firma finanzielle Probleme gehabt.
3 Nachdem die Firma bankrott gemacht (haben), mußte ich eine neue Stelle finden.
4 Meine Eltern (sein) sowieso mit der Firma enttäuscht gewesen.

B Zoran's family originally came from Croatia. He explains why the family decided to move to Germany and how his parents first met. Link the two sentences with the conjunction provided, remembering to move the auxiliary verb (underlined) to the end of the subordinate clause.

e.g. Seit 1993 wohnt die Familie in Bonn.
   Meine Mutter <u>hatte</u> dort eine Wohnung gefunden. *weil*
   → Seit 1993 wohnt die Familie in Bonn, weil meine Mutter dort eine Wohung gefunden <u>hatte</u>.

Meine Familie stammt aus Kroatien

1 Seit 1973 wohnt meine Familie in Deutschland.
   Mein Vater <u>hatte</u> damals Arbeit in Berlin gefunden. *da*
2 Meine Mutter arbeitete zu der Zeit in seiner Firma.
   Ihre Eltern <u>waren</u> nach Berlin umgezogen. *weil*

C At work Zoran and the other apprentices are often given instructions on what to do. Match up the informal form of the Imperative with the more formal **Sie** version.

e.g. 1 → c

Befehle

1 Mach die Tür zu!   a Schreiben Sie das Menü auf!
2 Seid leise!   b Hören Sie auf zu schwatzen!
3 Gib mir bitte das Papier!   c Machen Sie die Tür zu!
4 Hört auf zu schwatzen!   d Geben Sie mir bitte das Papier!
5 Schreib das Menü auf!   e Seien Sie leise!

Using the pluperfect tense

1 The PLUPERFECT TENSE describes what someone *had* done or what *had* taken place:

Ein Gewitter **hatte eingesetzt**, und ich konnte nicht schlafen.
*A storm **had set in**, and I couldn't sleep*
Alle unsere Sachen **waren** im Regen naß **geworden**
*All our things **had got** wet in the rain*

2 The PLUPERFECT TENSE consists of:

IMPERFECT TENSE OF **HABEN** OR **SEIN**   +   PAST PARTICIPLE OF THE VERB

Verbs which take **sein** in the PERFECT TENSE (see section 12.6) also take **sein** with the PLUPERFECT TENSE:

For the formation of the past participle see sections 11.6–8 and 12.1–3

a here is the pluperfect tense of **sagen** *(to say)*, a verb which takes **haben**:

SINGULAR			PLURAL		
ich hatte	**gesagt**	*I had said*	**wir hatten**	**gesagt**	*we had said*
du hattest	**gesagt**	*you had said*	**ihr hattet**	**gesagt**	*you had said*
Sie hatten	**gesagt**	*you had said*	**Sie hatten**	**gesagt**	*you had said*
er/sie/es hat	**gesagt**	*he/she/it had said*	**sie hatten**	**gesagt**	*they had said*

b here is the pluperfect tense of **gehen** *(to go)*, a verb which takes **sein**:

SINGULAR			PLURAL		
ich war	**gegangen**	*I had gone*	**wir waren**	**gegangen**	*we had gone*
du warst	**gegangen**	*you had gone*	**ihr wart**	**gegangen**	*you had gone*
Sie waren	**gegangen**	*you had gone*	**Sie waren**	**gegangen**	*you had gone*
er/sie/es		*he/she/it*	**sie waren**	**gegangen**	*they had gone*
war	**gegangen**	*had gone*			

3 The word order when using the pluperfect tense is the same as for the perfect:

a the past participle goes to the end of the clause (see section 11.9):

Frau Brandt hatte Kaffee **gekocht**   *Frau Brandt had made coffee*

b in subordinate clauses the past participle *and* the auxiliary verb (**haben** or **sein**) go to the end of the clause, with the auxiliary verb coming last (see section 15.5c):

Ich wohnte in Deutschland, da mein Vater Arbeit in Frankfurt **gefunden hatte**
I was living in Germany as my father had found work in Frankfurt

c the pluperfect is often used in a main clause after an **als** clause, because the event in the main clause had occurred earlier. In this case the subject and verb of the main clause are turned round (see section 15.6):

Als ich nach Österreich kam, **war er** schon **gestorben**
When I reached Austria he had already died

Giving commands

4 In Chapter 6 we saw how to tell someone to do something using the polite form of
   the verb – the **Sie** form. To give an order to someone in the familiar form, there is
   a singular form (when you are talking to one person), and a plural form (when you
   are talking to more than one person).

   a here is the SINGULAR form:

   > Weak verbs and strong verbs with no change of stem in the present:
   > add **-e** to the stem
   > e.g. kaufen: **Kaufe*!** *Buy!*   schreiben: **Schreibe*!** *Write!*
   >
   > Strong verbs with a change of stem in the present:
   > drop **-st** from the **du** form:
   > e.g. sprechen: **Sprich!** *Talk!*

   Schreib bald wieder!   *Write back soon!*

   b the PLURAL form is the **ihr** form of the present tense without the pronoun:

   ihr lauft   *you run*   →   **Lauft!**   *Run!*

   c to suggest to a group that *we* do something, use the present tense, placing the
      SUBJECT after the VERB, i.e. inverting the subject and the verb:

   Wir gehen nach Hause   *We are going home*
   →   **Gehen wir** nach Hause!   *Let's go home!*

---

*The final **-e** is usually dropped in colloquial speech and letters.

Help Yourself to Essential German Grammar

CHAPTER 21   WHAT HAVE YOU LEARNT?

A Herr Maier talks about jobs that he has had in the past. Decide whether you should use **haben** or **sein** and complete the sentences in the pluperfect.

e.g. Die erste Firma ... immer mehr Arbeiter aus Westdeutschland angestellt.   →
   Die erste Firma <u>hatte</u> immer mehr Arbeiter aus Westdeutschland <u>angestellt</u>.

Arbeitserfahrungen

1 Der erste Chef ... früher Probleme mit Lehrlingen gehabt.
2 Die nächste Firma ... von Stuttgart nach Berlin umgezogen.
3 Die Fahrt zu der dritten Firma ... zu gefährlich geworden.

B Herr Maier explains why he left his past jobs. Link what happened to his reasons for leaving each job using the conjunction indicated.

e.g. Ich wollte nach Berlin umziehen.
   Die Gehälter waren hier höher geworden.   *da*
   → Ich wollte nach Berlin umziehen, <u>da</u> die Gehälter hier höher geworden waren.

Kündigung

1 Die erste Firma hat mich entlassen.
   Sie hatte mehr Arbeitnehmer angeworben.   *obwohl*
2 Ich habe der nächsten Firma gekündigt.
   Die Arbeit war zu langweilig geworden.   *weil*
3 Die Arbeitsstunden gefielen mir nicht bei der dritten Firma.
   Ich hatte bei den anderen Firmen mehr Freizeit gehabt.   *da*

C Zoran and his friends meet up after work. They discuss how they can spend their evening. Replace the English imperative with the German equivalent. Choose from the following: **geh, geht, gehen wir/Sie; spiel, spielt, spielen wir/Sie; gib, gebt, geben wir/Sie**.

e.g. Zoran: [Let's go] ins Kino!   →   Gehen wir ins Kino!

Was machen wir denn?

PETER   Nein. [Let's play] lieber Basketball auf dem Hof!
MICHAEL   [Give: singular] mir die Zeitung!
SABINE   [Let's go] in die Disko.
ZORAN   Peter, [go] schnell nach Hause und hol dein Auto!

Revision test 19–21

A   Oma Maier tells you about her youth. Change what she says from the perfect to the imperfect tense.
e.g. Als ich ein Kind gewesen bin...   →   Als ich ein Kind war...

In meiner Jugend
Als ich ein Kind gewesen bin, habe ich eine Grundschule in Neukölln besucht. Die Lehrer sind sehr streng gewesen. Alle Kinder haben eine Schuluniform getragen. Wir haben viele Hausaufgaben gehabt. Nach der Schule habe ich eine Lehre als Bäckerin gemacht. Ich habe nur zwei Jahre lang gearbeitet, dann habe ich Opa Maier getroffen.

B   Oma Maier describes her work as a baker. Change the adjective provided into the noun derived from it to complete what Oma Maier says.
e.g. (sauber) war die Hauptsache.   →   Sauberkeit war die Hauptsache.

In der Bäckerei
(sauber) war die Hauptsache. Zu der Zeit gab es eine furchtbare (krank). Ein Freund ist viele Jahre später daran gestorben. Das war sehr traurig.
Ich kann mich genau an die (schön) des Schaufensters erinnern. Die (verschieden) der Brotsorten war erstaunlich.

C   Herr Maier has arrived home from work. Frau Maier asks how his day was. Complete their dialogue with the correct form of the adjectival noun.
e.g. Ich habe etwas (besondere) getan.   →   Ich habe etwas Besonderes getan.

Wie war dein Tag?
FRAU MAIER   Hast du heute etwas (interessant) gemacht?
HERR MAIER   Nein. Nichts (neu). Nur viel (langweilig). Wie war dein Tag?
FRAU MAIER   Ich habe allerlei (verschieden) getan.

D   Frau Maier tells her husband the arrangements for a coach trip. Change the following sentences into the past using the imperfect of the underlined verbs.

Die Konferenz (1)
Wir treffen uns am Rudower S-Bahnhof. Dann fahren wir zum Busbahnhof. Wir nehmen den Reisebus vom Busbahnhof nach Stuttgart. Dort müssen wir mit der Straßenbahn ins Zentrum fahren.

E Frau Maier has returned from the Stuttgart conference. She was very disappointed.
Change the positive description of events below into a negative description.
e.g. Ich hatte eine schöne Aussicht. → Ich hatte keine schöne Aussicht.

Die Konferenz (2)
1 Das war ein gutes Hotel.
2 Ich hatte ein Einzelzimmer mit Dusche und WC.
3 Ich konnte meine Kollegen überall finden.
4 Jemand hat den Direktor getroffen.

F Herr Maier tells Frau Maier what happened whilst she was away. Insert the
appropriate pluperfect form of the verb given on the right.
e.g. Er ... keine Zeit ... (<u>haben</u>). → Er hatte keine Zeit gehabt.

Als du in Stuttgart warst
1 Ich ... um 17 Uhr von der Arbeit ... (<u>kommen</u>).
2 Die Kinder ... etwas früher nach Hause ... (<u>kommen</u>).
3 Frau Rust ... an die Tür ... (<u>klopfen</u>).
4 Ihre Waschmaschine ... am Morgen nicht richtig ... (<u>funktionieren</u>).
5 Sie ... sofort zum Hausmeister ... (<u>gehen</u>).
6 Leider ... er keine Zeit ... (<u>haben</u>).

G In the canteen, Peter tells Zoran and Michael what to get for him. Fill in the informal
imperative form of the verb indicated.
e.g. ... mir was zu essen! *kaufen (plural)* → Kauft mir was zu essen!

In der Kantine (1)
1 Zoran, ... mir bitte eine Flasche Cola. *bringen (singular)*
2 ... mir Messer und Gabel. *holen (plural)*
3 Michael, ... nicht Salz und Pfeffer. *vergessen (singular)*
4 ... schnell, ihr beiden, ich verhungere! *machen (plural)*

H Zoran and Michael discuss what to buy. Change the verb shown into the 'Let's...'
form.
e.g. ... ... etwas zu trinken. *kaufen* → <u>Kaufen wir</u> etwas zu trinken.

In der Kantine (2)
1 ... ... Hamburger mit Pommes! *essen*
2 ... ... lieber Milch! *trinken*
3 ... ... einige Süßigkeiten! *kaufen*
4 ... ... einen Moment auf Peter! *warten*

In den Nachrichten

A In the car the Maier family are listening to the news on the radio. Frau Maier is concentrating on driving and asks the others what they have heard. Complete her questions with the appropriate word for *which*: **welcher, welche** or **welches**.

   e.g. ... Präsident besucht Deutschland?   →   Welcher Präsident besucht Deutschland?

   Was hat er gesagt?
   1 ... Königin besucht Großbritannien?
   2 ... Parlament diskutiert Terrorismus?
   3 ... Minister ist in einen Skandal verwickelt?
   4 ... Sportlerin hat einen neuen Rekord erzielt?

B Frau Maier asks further questions. Match the German with the English translation.

   e.g. 1 → c

   Was sagt sie?
   1 Welche Politik beschreibt sie?   a Which politician is she talking about?
   2 Von welchem Politiker spricht sie?   b Which politician are they arguing about?
   3 Über welchen Politiker streiten sie?   c Which policy is she describing?

C The news report continues with an account of a state visit to Berlin. This time Herr Maier asks for the details to be repeated. Choose the correct reply to each of his questions.

   e.g. 1 → c

   Ein Staatsbesuch
   1 Wen besucht der Kaiser von Japan?   a Mit dem Finanzminister.
   2 Mit wem wird er sprechen?   b Der Präsident.
   3 Wer fliegt nach Amerika zurück?   c Den Bundeskanzler.

D Herr Maier suggests what each of the family would do if they were politicians. Complete each sentence with the correct translation of *would*: **würde, würdest, würden** or **würdet**.

   e.g. Irmgard, du ... eine Frau zum Bundeskanzler wählen.
      → Du würdest eine Frau zum Bundeskanzler wählen.

   Meine Politik
   1 Moritz ... die Preise für Süßigkeiten reduzieren.
   2 Meine Eltern ... die Renten erhöhen.
   3 Ich ... mehr Arbeitsplätze schaffen.

More on asking questions...

1 In German **welcher/welche/welches** *(which)* is an INTERROGATIVE ADJECTIVE – a question word which comes before a noun:

Welcher Sohn ist der klügste?   *Which son is the cleverest?*
Welche Rechnung ist richtig?   *Which bill is right?*
Welches Kleid willst du tragen?   *Which dress do you want to wear?*

2 **Welcher** has the same endings as **dieser**, and changes according to the gender, number (singular or plural), and case of the noun it is with:

	MASCULINE	FEMININE	NEUTER	PLURAL
N.	welcher Stock	welche Rechnung	welches Kleid	welche Probleme
A.	welchen Stock	welche Rechnung	welches Kleid	welche Probleme
G.	welches Stocks	welcher Rechnung	welches Kleides	welcher Probleme
D.	welchem Stock	welcher Rechnung	welchem Kleid	welchen Problemen

3 The interrogative adjective will normally be the first word in the sentence except where there is a preposition in front of it:

Welchen Zug nimmst du?   *Which train are you catching?*
Von **welchem** Film spricht er?   *Which film is he talking about?*
In **welchen** Stock gehst du?   *Which floor are you going to?*

4 The question word for *who* in German is **wer**. **Wer** also has different forms for the different cases:

NOMINATIVE	ACCUSATIVE	GENITIVE	DATIVE
wer	**wen**	**wessen**	**wem**

Wer kommt heute abend?   *Who is coming this evening?*
Wen sehen Sie?   *Who can you see?*
Wessen Sohn ist das?   *Whose son is that?*
Wem schickt sie einen Brief?   *Who is she sending a letter to?*

Note that there is no gender or number. The same form is used for masculine and feminine, singular and plural.

5 If there is a preposition in front of **wer**, you must remember to put **wer** into the case which normally follows the preposition:

Auf **wen** wartet sie?   *Who is she waiting for?*
Mit **wem** gehst du meistens?   *Who do you usually go with?*

6 The question word for *what* is **was**, which is invariable (it never changes):

   Was machst du?   *What are you doing?*
   Was ist in dem Paket?   *What is in the parcel?*

   Note: **Was** does not usually occur with a preposition. Instead, there are the forms beginning with **wo-** (or **wor-** before a vowel):

   Womit kann ich dir helfen?   *What can I help you with?*
   Worauf wartet sie?   *What is she waiting for?*

7 A common phrase asking for confirmation is **nicht wahr**, added at the end of a statement:

   Es ist heiß, **nicht wahr**?   *It's hot, isn't it?*
   Du hast ihn gesehen, **nicht wahr**? *You've seen him, haven't you?*
   Du kennst ihn, **nicht wahr**?   *You know him, don't you?*

   Note that **nicht wahr** is INVARIABLE.

The conditional tense

8 The CONDITIONAL TENSE is used to express what someone *would* do in certain conditions or in a hypothetical situation:

   An deiner Stelle **würde** ich meine Hausaufgaben machen
   If I were you, I would do my homework
   Was **würdest** du in diesem Fall machen?
   What would you do in this case?

9 The CONDITIONAL TENSE is formed as follows:

   würde, würdest, würden, würdet* + INFINITIVE

   Here is the conditional tense of **gehen** *(to go)*:

SINGULAR			PLURAL		
ich würde	gehen	*I would go*	**wir würden**	gehen	*we would go*
du würdest	gehen	*you would go*	**ihr würdet**	gehen	*you would go*
Sie würden	gehen	*you would go*	**Sie würden**	gehen	*you would go*
er/sie/es würde	gehen	*he/she/it would go*	**sie würden**	gehen	*they would go*

---

*This form of **werden** is called the imperfect subjunctive (see chapters 23 and 25).

CHAPTER 22   WHAT HAVE YOU LEARNT?

A Frau Maier is trying to read the newspaper. Moritz however wants to see the sports
pages. Complete his questions with the correct form of **welcher**.
e.g. ... Fußballmannschaft spielt heute abend?
  → Welche Fußballmannschaft spielt heute abend?

Sportreportage
1 ... Tennisspieler hat die APT Meisterschaften gewonnen?
2 Über ... Athletin schreibt man hier?
3 Von ... Pferd spricht der Reporter?

B Herr Maier wants to read the political news, but Frau Maier has not finished with the
paper. He asks her a number of questions. Complete his questions with the correct
form of **wer: wer, wen** or **wem**.
e.g. ... hat im Bundestag gesprochen?   →   Wer hat im Bundestag gesprochen?

Politik
1 ... hat der Bundeskanzler angekündigt?
2 ... gibt der König einen Preis?
3 Mit ... fährt der Präsident nach Italien?

C Moritz makes some disparaging remarks about photos of people in the newspaper.
Turn his statements into a question by adding **nicht wahr**.
e.g. Der sieht häßlich aus.   →   Der sieht häßlich aus, nicht wahr?

Nicht wahr?
1 Der Tennisspieler sieht dick aus.
2 Man kann ihn kaum erkennen.
3 Der Minister hat ein Doppelkinn.
4 Der Filmstar trägt zu viel Make-up.

D Frau Maier says what she would do to solve the problem of the daily fight for the
newspaper. Fill in the gap in each sentence with the appropriate form of the
conditional, and replace the English word with one of the following infinitives:
lassen, lesen or **sein**.
e.g. Ich ... lieber eine Zeitschrift [read].   →   Ich würde lieber eine Zeitschrift lesen.

Probleme lösen
1 Dann ... meine Kinder mich morgens in Ruhe [leave].
2 Mein Mann ... auch froh [be], seine eigene Zeitung zu lesen.
3 Ich ... gerne jeden Morgen die Zeitung [read].

UNIT

8

CHAPTER 23   WHAT DO YOU KNOW?

A The reports in the newspaper suggest an element of doubt. Replace the underlined verb with its matching form in the present indicative to make each sentence a fact. Choose from the following: **ist**, **sind**, **hat**.

e.g. Der Kaiser <u>sei</u> wieder gesund.   →   Der Kaiser ist wieder gesund.

Zeitungsberichte

1 Der Präsident <u>sei</u> bereit, mit den Oppositionsparteien zu verhandeln.
2 Die Gewerkschaften <u>seien</u> mit den Arbeitsbedingungen zufrieden.
3 Der Koalitionspartner <u>habe</u> finanzielle Schwierigkeiten.
4 Der Vaten <u>sei</u> des Mords schuldig.

B A politician describes the possible advantages of a new treaty. Replace the English words with the equivalent German verb. Choose from the following: **müßten**, **könnten**, **dürften**.

e.g. Arbeiter [would be able to] ohne Erlaubnis arbeiten.
   →   Arbeiter könnten ohne Erlaubnis arbeiten.

Der Vertrag

1 Ausländische Arbeiter [would be allowed to] ohne Arbeitserlaubnis arbeiten.
2 Studenten [would be able to] im Ausland arbeiten.
3 Reisende [would have to] keinen Paß an der Grenze zeigen.

C There is an item in the news about the latest lottery winner.

Ich habe immer davon geträumt, was ich machen würde, wenn ich viel Geld hätte. Ich würde jeden Tag spät aufstehen. Ich wäre echt faul! Ich hätte mindestens vier Autos. Die Familie würde eine Villa in Frankreich kaufen. Wir wären alle reich und glücklich. Das Leben wäre perfekt!

From the German text, select phrases to match the English sentences below.

e.g. if I had a lot of money   →   wenn ich viel Geld hätte

Der Lottogewinner

1 I would be really lazy!
2 We would all be rich.
3 I would get up late every day.
4 I would have at least four cars.
5 The family would buy a villa in France.
6 Life would be perfect!

The subjunctive

1 The SUBJUNCTIVE 'mood' of the verb expresses something unreal or hypothetical, a possibility rather than a fact. The INDICATIVE on the other hand (which is all the 'usual' tenses we have met so far) deals with facts:

FACT (INDICATIVE)	Bruno ist hier *Bruno is here*
VERY PROBABLE (INDICATIVE)	Wenn Bruno hier ist, dann kannst du ihn treffen *If Bruno is here, you can meet him*
NOT LIKELY (SUBJUNCTIVE)	Wenn Bruno hier **wäre**, dann **könntest** du ihn treffen *If Bruno were here, you could meet him*

2 In German, the forms of the present and imperfect subjunctive for WEAK VERBS are almost all the same as the usual (indicative) tenses. The one different form you will meet is the third person singular of the present:

kaufen: PRESENT   er/sie/es **kauft**   →   PRESENT SUBJUNCTIVE er/sie/es **kaufe**

See Chapter 25 for the use of the present subjunctive

3 The subjunctive forms most often found are those of these STRONG VERBS:

a **sein** *(to be)* in the present and imperfect tenses:

PRESENT SUBJUNCTIVE				IMPERFECT SUBJUNCTIVE			
ich	sei	wir	seien	ich	wäre	wir	wären
du	sei(e)st	ihr	seit	du	wärst	ihr	wärt
Sie	seien	Sie	seien	Sie	wären	Sie	wären
er/sie/es	sei	sie	seien	er/sie/es	wäre	sie	wären

b **haben** *(to have)* is the same as a weak verb in the present, the one form to note being the third person singular:

PRESENT SUBJUNCTIVE				IMPERFECT SUBJUNCTIVE			
ich	habe	wir	haben	ich	hätte	wir	hätten
du	habest	ihr	habet	du	hättest	ihr	hättet
Sie	haben	Sie	haben	Sie	hätten	Sie	hätten
er/sie/es	habe	sie	haben	er/sie/es	hätte	sie	hätten

c some MODAL VERBS (see section 8.5) are also irregular in the imperfect subjunctive. In the subjunctive **können**, **müssen** and **dürfen** add an Umlaut to their usual imperfect forms, so that:

konnte → könnte mußte → müßte durfte → dürfte

Here is the imperfect subjunctive of **können** *(to be able)*:

SINGULAR		PLURAL	
ich	könnte	wir	könnten
du	könntest	ihr	könntet
Sie	könnten	Sie	könnten
er/sie/es	könnte	sie	könnten

4   There is no direct translation in English of the subjunctive, although the imperfect subjunctive can often be translated as *would*:

Wenn du mich besuchen **könntest, wäre** es schön
If you could visit me, it would be nice

5   For verbs other than **sein, haben** and the modals, the function of the imperfect subjunctive is often taken by **ich würde** + infinitive (see section 22.8), which is of course also the conditional:

Wenn du viel Geld **hättest**, was **würdest** du **kaufen**?
If you had a lot of money what would you buy?
Wenn Sie weniger **rauchen würden, wären** Sie gesünder
If you smoked less you would be healthier

wenn *(if)* clauses

6   Clauses beginning with **wenn** meaning *if* are known as CONDITIONAL CLAUSES, because they express a condition. What is stated in the main clause can only happen where the condition is fulfilled:

Er fährt nach Italien, **wenn** es nicht zu teuer ist
*He is going to Italy **if** it is not too expensive*
Sie wird morgen kommen, **wenn** sie Zeit hat
*She will come tomorrow **if** she has time*

These are simple cases where if one thing happens, the other will follow. The present tense is used in both clauses in German and English (the future is also possible in the main clause as in the second example).

7   However, where the **wenn** clause expresses some distant possibility, something unlikely or even impossible, rather than a fact, then its verb should be in the IMPERFECT SUBJUNCTIVE (we have already had some examples above). The verb in the main clause is effectively conditional (**würde** + infinitive except for **sein, haben** and the modals):

Wenn ich nicht arbeiten **müßte, würde** ich spät **aufstehen**
If I didn't have to work, I would get up late
Wenn ich nicht arbeiten **würde, wäre** es langweilig
If I didn't work it would be boring

CHAPTER 23   WHAT HAVE YOU LEARNT?

A Some holidaymakers are asked where they would go if money were no object. Replace the English verb in brackets with one of these German verbs in the imperfect subjunctive/conditional: **wäre**, **wären**, **hätte**, **hätten**, **würde**, **würden**, **würdest**, **wärst**.

e.g. Wenn wir viel Geld [had]...   →   Wenn wir viel Geld <u>hätten</u>...

Traumferien

1 Wenn ich viel Geld [<u>had</u>], [<u>would</u>] ich eine Weltreise machen.

2 Wenn wir reich [<u>were</u>], [<u>would</u>] wir China besuchen.

3 Wenn mein Vater ein Millionär [<u>were</u>], [<u>would</u>] er uns auf einer Kreuzfahrt mitnehmen.

4 Wenn Peter DM 1000,- [<u>had</u>], [<u>would</u>] er seine Ferien in Spanien verbringen.

5 Manfred, du [<u>would</u>] lieber zu Hause bleiben, auch wenn du reich [<u>were</u>].

6 Ich [<u>would</u>] an einem Sprachkurs in England teilnehmen.

B The newspaper agony aunt gives help and advice to various readers. Put the verb given in brackets in its imperfect subjunctive form.

e.g. Wenn die Kinder später ins Bett gehen [<u>dürfen</u>], hätten Sie abends keine Freizeit
→   Wenn die Kinder später ins Bett gehen <u>dürften</u>, hätten Sie abends keine Freizeit.

Leserbriefe–Eva Martins antwortet

1 Sicher [<u>dürfen</u>] Sie allein mit dem Auto einkaufen gehen.

2 Ich [<u>werden</u>] einmal versuchen, in Ruhe mit ihr Ihre Probleme zu besprechen.

3 Wenn Sie Ihre Eltern öfter besuchen [<u>können</u>], wäre es schön.

4 Ihr Mann wäre bestimmt glücklicher, wenn er jedes Wochenende nicht arbeiten [<u>müssen</u>].

5 Ihr Sohn [<u>werden</u>] lieber mit seinen Freunden in Urlaub fahren.

6 Wenn Sie nicht arbeiten [<u>müssen</u>], hätten Sie mehr Zeit für die Kinder.

UNIT

8

A Look at what Frau Maier says and separate each sentence into two short sentences. Replace the underlined word with the appropriate subject pronoun (**er**, **sie** or **es**).
e.g. Hier ist die Tankstelle, <u>die</u> Dieselöl verkauft.
→   Hier ist die Tankstelle. Sie verkauft Dieselöl.

An der Raststätte

1 Hier ist die Raststätte, <u>die</u> in der Nähe von Köln liegt.
2 Das war das Auto, <u>das</u> schnell vorbeigefahren ist.
3 Wo sind die Toiletten, <u>die</u> am nächsten sind?

B Herr Maier comments to his wife on the radio traffic report. Read the sentences below and match up the beginning of each sentence with the appropriate ending to produce the German equivalent of the English.
e.g. 1   →   b Das ist die Autobahn, auf der ich fahren wollte.

Der Verkehrsbericht

1 Das ist die Autobahn,   a der wir folgen müssen?
2 Hier ist der Bericht,   b auf der ich fahren wollte.
3 Gibt es eine Umleitung,   c an der wir tanken können.
4 Hier ist die Raststätte,   d auf den ich wartete.

  i That is the motorway that I wanted to drive on.
 ii Here is the report I was waiting for.
iii Is there a detour that we must follow?
 iv Here are the services we can fill up at.

C Frau Maier discusses with her husband the latest news report. Complete what she says with the German word for *whose*. You should choose between: **dessen** (masculine/neuter) and **deren** (feminine/plural). To help you decide, the noun that the relative pronoun is referring back to has been underlined.
e.g. Dieser Fußballspieler hat <u>einen Freund</u>, ... Frau drogensüchtig ist.
→   hat einen Freund, <u>dessen</u> Frau drogensüchtig ist. *(Freund is masculine)*

Skandalös

1 Die Politiker haben <u>Freunde</u>, ... Kollegen skrupellos sind.
2 Das ist <u>das Kind</u>, ... Eltern im Fernsehen waren.
3 Der Parteichef hat <u>eine Kollegin</u>, ... Vater berühmter Schauspieler ist.
4 Die Königin spricht mit <u>dem Soldaten</u>, ... Hand verletzt wurde.

Relative pronouns

1   *Who, what, whom, which* and *that,* when used in the middle of a sentence to join two
clauses together, are RELATIVE PRONOUNS. In German they are *all* translated by **der,
die, das** (see section 24.2 below for forms):

> Ich arbeite in einem Laden, **der** Produkte aus der Dritten Welt verkauft
> *I work in a shop **which** sells products from the Third World*
> Ich habe einige Kunden, **die** zu mir kommen
> *I have a few customers **who** come to me*

Note: There is always a comma between the two clauses, before the relative pronoun.

2   The RELATIVE PRONOUN has the same form as the definite article, *except* in the
accusative (masculine singular), in the genitive (singular and plural), and the dative
(singular and plural):

	MASCULINE	FEMININE	NEUTER	PLURAL
NOMINATIVE	der	die	das	die
ACCUSATIVE	**den**	die	das	die
GENITIVE	**dessen**	**deren**	**dessen**	**deren**
DATIVE	**dem**	**der**	**dem**	**denen**

Here are examples of a relative pronoun in all its cases, singular and plural:

NOMINATIVE	Er hat einen Freund, Er hat Freunde, *He has a friend/friends*	**der** kein Taschengeld bekommt **die** kein Taschengeld bekommen *who gets/who get no pocket money*
ACCUSATIVE	Er hat einen Freund, Er hat Freunde, *He has a friend/friends*	**den** er in England besucht hat **die** er in England besucht hat *whom he visited in England*
GENITIVE	Er hat einen Freund, Er hat Freunde, *He has a friend/friends*	**dessen** Vater arbeitslos ist **deren** Vater arbeitslos ist *whose father is unemployed*
DATIVE	Er hat einen Freund, Er hat Freunde, *He has a friend/friends*	**dem** er einen Brief geschickt hat **denen** er einen Brief geschickt hat. *to whom he sent a letter*

3   The German relative pronoun must have the same number (singular or plural) and the
same gender (masculine, feminine or neuter) in the singular as the noun it refers back to:

> Hier ist **der Brief, der** heute gekommen ist
> *Here is the letter which arrived today*
> Hier ist **die Sendung, die** die Familie erhalten hat
> *Here is the packet which the family received*
> Hier ist **das Paket, das** ich geschickt habe   *Here is the parcel which I sent*
> Hier sind **die Briefe, die** gekommen sind   *Here are the letters which have come*

Help Yourself to Essential German Grammar

4 To decide THE CASE of the relative pronoun (whether it is nominative, accusative, genitive or dative) you must look at its function in the sentence:

> Hier ist der Brief, **der** heute gekommen ist

The relative pronoun **der** is the SUBJECT of its clause *(which came today)*, so nominative case.

> Hier ist der Brief, **den** die Familie erhalten hat

The relative pronoun **den** is the OBJECT of its clause *(which the family received)*, so accusative case.

> Hier ist der Brief, **dem** ich geantwortet habe

The relative pronoun **dem** is the INDIRECT OBJECT of its clause *(to which I replied)*, so dative case.

5 The genitive pronouns **dessen** and **deren** always come before the subject of the clause, like the English *whose*, but they also refer to things:

> Der Brief, **dessen** Anfang ich gelesen hatte, lag auf dem Tisch
> *The letter, the beginning of which I had read, was on the table*

6 If there is a PREPOSITION before the relative pronoun, the relative pronoun is in the case required by the preposition:

> Er hat einen englischen Freund, **an den** er regelmäßig schreibt
> *He has an English friend to whom he writes regularly*

This does not apply to **dessen** and **deren**, which always remain the same:

> Sie hat einen Freund, **mit dessen Vater** sie schlecht auskommt
> *She has a boyfriend, with whose father she does not get on well*

With things, instead of using the preposition + **der**, **die**, **das**, you can use the preposition with **wo-** (or **wor-** before a vowel) such as **womit**, **wovor**, **worauf**:

> Das ist ein Tag, **an den** *or* **woran** ich mich gern erinnere
> *That is a day which I remember with pleasure*
> Das Einzige, **wovor** ich mich fürchte,* ist ein Erdbeben
> *The only thing of which I am afraid is an earthquake*

> *For **was** as a relative pronoun see sections 25.7–10*

---

*Note the two commas which enclose the relative clause when it is in the middle of the sentence.

CHAPTER 24   WHAT HAVE YOU LEARNT?

A A famous actress is talking about her early career. Complete her account with the appropriate relative pronoun in the nominative case only.

e.g. Ich arbeitete mit Kollegen, … sehr nett waren.

→ … Kollegen, die sehr nett waren.

Meine Karriere

1 Ich arbeitete an einem Theater, … in der Karl-Marx Straße liegt.
2 Tagsüber arbeitete ich auf einem Markt, … nicht mehr da ist.
3 Ich hatte damals eine sehr gute Freundin, … jetzt sehr berühmt ist.
4 Alle diese Autos, … hier im Foto sind, gehörten meinem dritten Mann.

B The actress continues. Again complete her account by inserting the correct relative pronoun, this time in the accusative case only.

e.g. Hier ist der Brief, … ich von Hollywood bekam.

→ Hier ist der Brief, den ich von Hollywood bekam.

Hollywood

1 Dürrenmatt war ein guter Freund, … ich oft besuchte.
2 Hier ist ein Bild von dem Haus, … ich 1937 in Hollywood kaufte.
3 Hier sind die Schuhe, … ich in meinem berühmtesten Film trug.
4 Meine Tochter, … ich 1939 bekam, lebt mit mir in Genf.

C Herr Maier reminisces about the old Hollywood films. Fill the gaps with the appropriate relative pronouns and prepositions.

e.g. Das ist ein Film, … … ich mich gern erinnere.

→ … ein Film, an den ich mich gern erinnere.

In der guten alten Zeit

1 Ich mag die alten Western, … … John Wayne spielt.
2 Das war der Film, … … sie einen Oscar bekommen hat.
3 Richard Tauber war der Sänger, … Stimme ich immer gern hatte.
4 Ich erinnere mich an die Freundinnen, … … ich ins Kino ging.

Revision test 22–24

A Michael and Sabine discuss the latest results in the Olympic games. Complete each question with the appropriate form of **welcher** *(which)*.
e.g. ... Land hat die meisten Goldmedaillen gewonnen?
→ <u>Welches</u> Land hat die meisten Goldmedaillen gewonnen?

Die Olympiade
1 ... Athlet hat den Hürdenlauf gewonnen?
2 ... Mannschaft hat einen neuen Weltrekord?
3 Der Favorit spielt gegen ... Spieler?
4 Die Resultate sind in ... Zeitung?

B Their discussion continues. Complete each question with the correct form of **wer** *(who)*.
e.g. ... spielt jetzt?   → <u>Wer</u> spielt jetzt?

Die Olympischen Spiele
1 ... gewinnt?
2 Er spielt gegen ... ?
3 Mit ... trainiert er?

C Herr and Frau Maier talk about the latest state visit to the UK. Change the questions in the conversation into a statement.
e.g. Ist der Kanzler mit seiner Frau gefahren?
→ Der Kanzler ist mit seiner Frau gefahren.

Der Staatsbesuch
1 Ist der Kanzler schon nach London abgefahren?
2 Er fliegt mit Lufthansa, nicht wahr?
3 Trägt die Königin immer eine Handtasche?
4 Sie hat nichts darin, nicht wahr?

D The conversation turns to wider issues. Complete the dialogue with the German equivalent of the English word in brackets.
e.g. Der Kanzler [wants to] Argentinien besuchen.
→ Der Kanzler <u>will</u> Argentinien besuchen.

Südafrika
1 Der Präsident [wants to] nächstes Jahr Südafrika besuchen.
2 Er [would like to] Nelson Mandela wieder treffen.
3 Wenn möglich, [would] er auch Namibia besuchen.

E The ADAC* have re-opened the motorail service from Berlin to Hannover. A radio interviewer asks passengers why they have decided to take the motorail train. Complete their replies with the definite article in the genitive.

e.g. Außerhalb ... Hauptreisezeit ist das Fahren auf der Autobahn angenehmer.

→   Außerhalb <u>der</u> Hauptreisezeit ...

Der Autoreisezug

1 Während ... Weihnachtsferien gibt es immer viel Verkehr auf der Autobahn nach Hannover.
2 Wegen ... Verkehrs fahren wir lieber mit dem Zug.
3 Obwohl unsere Verwandten innerhalb ... Orts wohnen, nehmen wir lieber das Auto mit.
4 Trotz ... guten Autobahnen gibt es zu Weihnachten lange Staus.

F During a discussion between Michael and Sabine a number of opinions are given. Give the appropriate form of **haben** or **sein** in the imperfect subjunctive to match the English.

e.g. Wenn sie intelligent [was], würde sie mich verstehen.

→   Wenn sie intelligent wäre, würde sie mich verstehen.

Meinungen

1 Wenn du intelligent [were], würdest du meinen Standpunkt verstehen.
2 Wenn Peter Lust [had], könnte er gut singen.
3 Wenn ich älter [was], [would have] du mehr Respekt.
4 Ich [would have] Angst, da allein zu sein.
5 Wir [would be] froh, hier zu wohnen.

G Stephanie shows you an article in the local newspaper. Complete each sentence with the relative pronoun.

e.g. Das ist der Minister, ... die Firma besucht hat.

→   Das ist der Minister, der die Firma besucht hat.

In der Zeitung

1 Frau Müller zeigt ihm das Büro, in ... ich arbeite.
2 Da sind meine Kollegen, von ... ich oft spreche.
3 Hinter ihnen ist mein Freund, ... Mutter neben uns wohnt.
4 Auf der linken Seite sind meine Freundinnen Kirstin und Bärbel, mit ... ich zur Firma fahre.
5 Sie können im Foto den Pullover sehen, ... du mir zum Geburtstag geschenkt hast.

---

*ADAC = Allgemeiner Deutscher Automobilclub (the German Automobile Association).

Die internationale Welt

A Zoran and Peter consider where to go on holiday. For each underlined verb, give the infinitive that it comes from. Choose from: **können, geben, haben, sein, liegen, sprechen, legen.**

e.g. Peter: Meine Traumreise <u>wäre</u> nach Namibia zu reisen.   →   <u>sein</u>

Hier spricht man Deutsch

ZORAN Namibia? Wieso? Namibia <u>liegt</u> in Südafrika, nicht wahr?

PETER Ja. Stimmt. Wir <u>könnten</u> die Raubtiere sehen. Löwen, Nashörner.

ZORAN Aber was <u>spricht</u> man dort? Englisch? Da <u>hätten</u> wir Probleme.

PETER   Es <u>gibt</u> immer noch eine deutschsprachige Bevölkerung in Namibia.

B Zoran and Peter still have not chosen their holiday destination. Say which of their statements express uncertainty or just a possibility, and which express a fact or a certainty.

e.g. Wir hätten nicht genug Geld dafür.   →   uncertainty

Hätten wir genug Geld dafür?

1 Ich hätte Probleme, genug Geld dafür zu sparen.
2 Es gibt in Südafrika eine Menge zu tun, und zu sehen.
3 Wenn Michael hier wäre, dann könnten wir ihn fragen.

C Zoran has spoken to Michael on the phone. He tells Peter what Michael said. On the left are Michael's actual words, followed by the way Zoran reported them. Fill in the verbs in the present subjunctive.

e.g. „Ich schreibe an meinen Onkel."   →   Er sagte, daß er an seinen Onkel schreibe.

Was hat er gesagt?

1 „Wir können Geld dafür sparen." Er sagte, daß wir Geld dafür sparen …
2 „Ich hole Prospekte vom Reisebüro." Er sagte, daß er Prospekte vom Reisebüro …
3 „Südafrika ist sehr interessant." Er sagte, daß Südafrika sehr interessant …

D Zoran and Peter agree that what Michael says makes sense. Complete their remarks by translating the English with **alles, nichts** or **etwas.**

e.g. Ich habe [something] gesehen, was unmöglich ist.

  →   Ich habe <u>etwas</u> gesehen, was unmöglich ist.

Michael hat recht

[Everything], was er sagt ist richtig. [Nothing], was er sagt ist falsch. Er hat [something] darüber gelesen, was er uns zeigen wird.

Other uses of the subjunctive

1 In Chapter 23 we saw the SUBJUNCTIVE being used in **wenn** clauses. The imperfect subjunctive is also more generally used when expressing a hypothetical idea, something that could or might happen:

> Mein Traum für die Zukunft **wäre**, eine Boutique aufzumachen
> *My dream for the future would be to open a shop*
> Ich **hätte** keine Probleme, hier einen Arbeitsplatz zu finden
> *I would have no problem finding a job here*
> Sie **könnte** schon dort sein   *She could be there by now*

2 There are three specific areas for this use:

a wishes:

> **Hätte** ich ihm nur geglaubt!   *If only I had believed him!*
> Ich **wäre** lieber in Italien   *I would rather be in Italy*
> Ich wünschte, ich **hätte** mehr Geld   *I wish I had more money*

b requests (very polite):

> **Würden** Sie bitte die Tür zumachen?   *Would you please close the door?*

c doubt (past tenses):

> Ich war unsicher, ob er stark genug **wäre**
> *I wasn't sure whether he was strong enough*

3 The subjunctive is also used (mostly in written language) in INDIRECT SPEECH. The tense here depends on what was originally said. If it was in the present, as in most cases, the present subjunctive is used, if it was in the past, the perfect subjunctive is used, *regardless of the tense of the main verb*:

> Sie meinten, die Sendungen **seien** interessant
> *They thought the programmes **were** interesting*
> Er sagte, daß er es schon gehört **habe**   *He said he **had** already heard it*

In English we change the tense of the reported speech depending on that of the main verb, in German the tense of the reported speech remains the same:

> Sie **fragt**, ob er ihn **kenne**   *She is asking if he knows him*
> Sie **fragte**, ob er ihn **kenne**   *She asked if he knew him*

4 The PERFECT and PLUPERFECT SUBJUNCTIVE are formed as follows:

PRESENT/IMPERFECT SUBJUNCTIVE OF **SEIN** OR **HABEN** **+** THE PAST PARTICIPLE

> Perfect: **er sei gekommen**   **er habe geglaubt**
> Pluperfect: **er wäre gekommen**   **er hätte geglaubt**

5 The perfect subjunctive, like the present, is mainly used in indirect speech. If the original statement is in the perfect tense, then the subjunctive in the indirect statement will also be perfect:

Der Polizist fragte „Haben Sie die Ampel nicht gesehen?"
The policeman asked "Didn't you see the traffic lights?"
Der Polizist fragte, ob er die Ampel nicht **gesehen habe**
The policeman asked if he hadn't seen the traffic lights

Note: **Gesehen hätte** would also be possible in this case, giving the statement a more tentative sense.

6 The pluperfect subjunctive is used in the same contexts as the imperfect, such as **wenn** clauses and the other cases given above in sections 25.1 and 25.2:

Wenn ich das **gewußt hätte**, **wäre** ich nicht **hingegangen**
*If I **had known** that, I **would** not **have gone***

was as a relative pronoun

7 *Which* as a relative pronoun does not always refer back to a specific noun or pronoun, but to an idea. In these cases, German uses **was**:

Anna hat uns eingeladen, **was** wir sehr nett gefunden haben
Anna has invited us, which we found very nice

8 Sometimes there will be no word in German which **was** refers back to, and sometimes **was** is short for **das** (*that which, what*):

Ich wiederhole nochmal **(das)**, **was** ich schon gesagt habe
I will repeat once more what I have already said
Man muß **das** machen, **was** die Lehrer sagen
You have to do what the teachers tell you

9 **Was** also refers back to an indefinite pronoun like **alles** *(everything)*, **nichts** *(nothing)* or **etwas** *(something)*:

Alles, **was** auf der Speisekarte steht, ist zu teuer
Everything (which is) on the menu is too dear
Sie kann **nichts** essen, **was** Tomaten enthält
She can't eat anything which contains tomatoes
Ich habe **etwas** gegessen, **was** mich krank gemacht hat
I have eaten something which has made me ill

10 **Was** is also used to refer back to a superlative adjective:

Es ist **das Beste**, **was** wir haben   *It is the best (that) we have*

CHAPTER 25   WHAT HAVE YOU LEARNT?

A Peter has gone to a travel agency to find out more about holidays abroad. He tells
Zoran what happened. Fill in the gap with the auxiliary (**sein** or **haben**) in the correct
form to make with the past participle (underlined) the pluperfect subjunctive.
e.g. Wenn ich schon im Ausland <u>gewesen</u> ...
  → Wenn ich schon im Ausland <u>gewesen wäre</u>...

Im Reisebüro
Wenn wir letztes Jahr dorthin <u>gefahren</u> ... , ... wir die Flugtickets billiger
<u>bekommen</u>. Er hat mir erzählt, daß du schon öfters in dem Reisebüro gewesen bist.
Du ... mir sagen <u>können</u>, daß du schon dort warst!

B The students in the vocational college (<u>die Berufsschule</u>) are collecting opinions
about the canteen. Zoran summarises his findings. Change the second clause in each
sentence from the subjunctive to a **daß** clause with the verb in the indicative. The
tense may need changing.
e.g. 50% der Studenten meinten, das Essen sei langweilig.
  → 50% der Studenten meinten, daß das Essen langweilig war.

Eine Umfrage
1 20% sagen, die Kantine sei schmutzig.
2 Ein Mädchen sagte, die internationalen Gerichte seien interessant.
3 Ein Lehrer behauptet, das Essen sei immer kalt.
4 Viele Studenten behaupteten, die Kantine sei preisgünstig.

C Herr and Frau Maier have been invited to the International Evening at Moritz's
school. She comments upon this to her neighbour. Replace the English word in
brackets with the German relative pronoun.
e.g. Der Direktor hat etwas gesagt, [<u>which</u>] wir nicht verstanden haben.
  → Der Direktor hat etwas gesagt, <u>was</u> wir nicht verstanden haben.

Der internationale Abend
Der Direktor hat uns eingeladen, [<u>which</u>] wir sehr nett finden. Die Eltern müssen
[<u>that</u>] mitbringen, [<u>which</u>] auf der Liste steht. Alles, [<u>which</u>] auf dem Menü ist,
kommt aus einem anderen Land.

Help Yourself to Essential German Grammar

UNIT

9

CHAPTER 26   WHAT DO YOU KNOW?

A An item in the newspaper tells of an abandoned baby. State whether each sentence is in the present tense or the past tense.

e.g. Ein Mann wird gesucht.   →   present

In der Zeitung

1 Ein Baby wurde um zwei Uhr morgens im Stadtpark von einem Passanten gefunden.

2 Das etwa sechsmonatige Kind war in einer hellblauen Wolldecke eingewickelt und unter einem Busch versteckt worden.

3 Die Mutter wird von der Polizei gesucht.

4 Das Baby wurde zur Polizeiwache in Wedding gebracht.

B Zoran reads aloud the item about the abandoned baby to Peter. Say whether each question Peter asks uses the passive (i.e. the action is/was *being done to* someone) or the active (i.e. the action is/was *done by* someone).

e.g. Wo wurde das Baby versteckt?   →   passive

Unglaublich!

1 Was wurde gefunden?

2 Wer hat das Kind gefunden?

3 Wen sucht die Polizei?

4 Worin ist das Kind eingewickelt worden?

C The newspaper item gives more details. Complete the item with **von** + dative and the indefinite article **einem** (masculine and neuter) or **einer** (feminine).

e.g. Es konnte von ... Frau identifiziert werden.

   →   Es konnte von <u>einer</u> Frau identifiziert werden.

Wer ist das Kind?

1 Das Kind konnte von ... Arzt identifiziert werden.

2 Die Mutter wird von ... Sozialarbeiterin beraten.

3 Das Kind wurde von ... Frau ausgesetzt.

4 Das Baby wird von ... Familie in Wedding versorgt.

The passive

1 The passive is used to describe an action *being done to* someone or something. You may or may not know who or what is doing the action:

> Die Handtasche **wurde** in einem Busch **gefunden**
> *The handbag was found in a bush*

2 The passive is formed as follows:

APPROPRIATE TENSE OF **WERDEN** + PAST PARTICIPLE OF THE VERB

The tense of **werden** will determine the tense of the passive:

PRESENT TENSE	Die Handtasche **wird** in einem Busch **gefunden** *The handbag is found in a bush*

IMPERFECT TENSE (SIMPLE PAST)	Die Handtasche **wurde** in einem Busch **gefunden** *The handbag was found in a bush*

PERFECT TENSE	Die Handtasche **ist** in einem Busch **gefunden worden*** *The handbag has been found in a bush*

*For the full forms of **werden** see Appendix page 129*

3 In order to express the person or thing which causes the action, **von** + the dative is usually used:

> Sie wurde **von einem Auto** überfahren   *She was run over **by a car***
> Er konnte **von seiner Frau** identifiziert werden
>   *He could be identified **by his wife***

However **durch** + the accusative is also used, especially where something more general or abstract is concerned:

> Die Tiere wurden **durch den** Lärm gestört
>   *The animals were disturbed **by the noise***
> Das kann nur **durch Ausdauer** erzielt werden
>   *This can only be achieved **by persistence***

4 The passive can also be used impersonally, using the construction **es wird, es wurde**, etc. + past participle:

> **Es wird** getanzt und gesungen   *There is singing and dancing*
> **Es wurde** zu Mittag gegessen   *Lunch was taken*

---

*Note that the past participle of **werden** (which is usually **geworden**) drops the **ge-** when used in the passive.

Help Yourself to Essential German Grammar

5 The passive, which can be cumbersome, is avoided by using **man** *(one)*:

Man hat die Handtasche in einem Busch **gefunden**
The handbag was found in a bush
Man gab ihnen zu essen   *They were given something to eat*

This is in fact the only possibility if a verb is followed by the dative:

Man hat mir gesagt, daß ...   *I was told that ...*

More on pronouns and adjectives...

6 There are a few important pronouns and adjectives to learn:

a   to express *some* or *a few,* use **ein paar** or **einige***:

Sonntags kommen **ein paar** Besucher   *A few visitors come on Sundays*
Note that **ein paar** never changes – it is INVARIABLE.

Er trank mit **einigen** Freunden   *He was drinking with some friends*

b   to express *each* or *every,* use **jeder**. On its own it can mean *everyone:*

Fast **jedes** Mädchen und **jeder** Junge   *Almost every girl and every boy*
Jeder denkt nur an sich   *Everyone thinks only of himself*

Note that **jeder** has the same endings as **dieser** (see Appendix page 145).

c   to express *both,* use **beide***:

Wir wollten **beide** Automechaniker werden
We both wanted to become car mechanics
Es ist für uns **beide** wichtig   *It is important for both of us*

d   to express *everything,* use **alles**:

Sie kauft **alles** im Supermarkt   *She buys everything in the supermarket*
Er ist mit **allem** zufrieden   *He is satisfied with everything*

There is no genitive, but the dative is used in some expressions instead:

trotz allem   *in spite of everything*

e   to express *everybody,* use **alle***:

Wir sind eine Schule für **alle**   *We are a school for everybody*

---

*Note that **alle**, **beide** and **einige** are always plural and have the same endings as an adjective with no article in front of it (**-e, -e, -er, -en**).

Help Yourself to Essential German Grammar

CHAPTER 26   WHAT HAVE YOU LEARNT?

A You read in the newspaper about the assassination of a leading political figure. Complete each sentence with the verb in the passive form, by putting in gap 1 the appropriate part of **werden** in the imperfect and in gap 2 one of the following past participles: **erschoßen, gefunden, beobachtet, gesehen**.

e.g. Ein Mann (1) um Mitternacht (2). [was seen]
   → Ein Mann *wurde* um Mitternacht *gesehen*.

Das Attentat
1 Die Leiche von dem Präsidenten (1) im Badezimmer (2). [was found]
2 Er (1) fünfmal mit einem Revolver (2). [had been shot]
3 Zwei Frauen (1) von einem Dienstmädchen (2). [were observed]

B This event reminds you of a film and you tell the story. Again, complete each sentence with the appropriate part of **werden**, this time in the present tense, and the past participle of the verb given.

e.g. Ein Mann ... um Mitternacht ... (sehen).
   → Ein Mann wird um Mitternacht gesehen.

Der Krimi
1 Eine Frau ... sechsmal mit einem Revolver ... (erschießen).
2 Der Präsident ... von Agenten vom Geheimdienst ... (beobachten).
3 Die Leiche der Frau ... im Schlafzimmer des Präsidenten ... (finden).

C Peter tells Zoran of an incident in a football match. Match up the statements in the original account which is in the active (sentences 1–4) with sentences a–d which are in the passive.

e.g. 1 → d

Das Fußballspiel
1 Der Tormann kickt den Ball.
2 Ein Verteidiger geht den Stürmer an.
3 Er wirft den Stürmer um.
4 Der Schiedsrichter gibt einen Elfmeter.

a Der Stürmer wird von einem Verteidiger angegangen.
b Ein Elfmeter wird vom Schiedsrichter gegeben.
c Der Stürmer wird von ihm umgeworfen.
d Der Ball wird vom Tormann gekickt.

UNIT

9

CHAPTER 27   WHAT DO YOU KNOW?

A Herr and Frau Braun prefer to holiday in German-speaking countries. An interviewer discusses their reasons with them. Select from the interview the phrases that match the English.

e.g. 1 How is that then?   →   Wieso denn?

Wir sprechen nur Deutsch
Sie fahren lieber in deutschsprachige Länder in Urlaub. Wieso denn?
Es ist ja blöd, aber wir sprechen keine Fremdsprachen.
Haben Sie denn keine Fremdsprache in der Schule gelernt?
Doch, aber mit Fremdsprachen hatten wir immer Schwierigkeiten.
Es gefällt Ihnen sicher in Österreich.
Ja. Wir sind schon öfters in Österreich gewesen.

1 How is that then?
2 Yes, we did.
3 It <u>is</u> stupid.
4 Didn't you learn a foreign language at school then?
5 You like it in Austria, I'm sure.

B Frau Braun is planning a holiday in Scotland with her husband. Fill in the gaps with the appropriate part of the verb **sollen** *(be supposed to, should)*. Choose from: **soll, sollst, sollen**.

e.g. Die Stadt … interessant sein.   →   Die Stadt soll interessant sein.

Reisepläne
Wir … Edinburgh besuchen. Die Burg … sehr schön sein. Dann … du deine Freundin in Glasgow sehen. Die hast du seit Jahren nicht gesehen. Ich … eine Landkarte kaufen, damit wir unsere Reise besser planen können. Die Polizisten in Großbritannien … Touristen gegenüber sehr freundlich sein.

C Herr and Frau Braun are now learning English at the local adult education centre (<u>die Volkshochschule</u>). Herr Braun explains why. Replace the English word in each sentence with one of the following: **können, dürfen, sollen, müssen**.

e.g. Wir [should] Französisch lernen.   →   Wir <u>sollen</u> Französisch lernen.

Wir lernen Englisch
Unsere Tochter hat uns gesagt, daß wir Englisch lernen [should], damit wir in andere Länder fahren [can]. Wir [must] viel lernen. Wir [are allowed to] im Unterricht kein Deutsch sprechen!

Particles

1 PARTICLES are small words which are often not translatable, but which are used a lot in spoken German giving it its typical flavour. The most common are:

a **denn**, when used in a question, makes the question less abrupt:

Wieso **denn**?   *How come?*   Was ist **denn** los?   *What's the matter then?*

b **doch** is used when you correct a wrong, usually negative statement. In other words, someone says something is not the case, and you say it is:

Sie waren nicht zu Hause? **Doch.**   *They weren't at home? Yes, they were.*

c **ja** answering a question means *yes*. But it can reinforce a verb or adjective:

Es ist **ja** schwer, aber…   *It is difficult, but…*

d **mal** reinforces a verb, especially an imperative:

Sehen Sie **mal** hier!   *Just look over here!*
Moment **mal**!   *Just a minute!*
Kommen Sie **mal** vorbei!   *Look in sometime*
Na hören Sie **mal**!   *Now look here!*

e **schon** as an adverb means *already*, but is often used to add reassurance that something will happen or to reinforce the verb:

Sie wird **schon** kommen   *She'll come, don't worry*
Das stimmt **schon**   *That's quite true*

f **wohl** as an adverb usually means *well,* but as a particle can mean *probably*:

Er ist **wohl** schon dort   *He is probably there by now*

Weak masculine nouns

2 WEAK MASCULINE NOUNS add endings, rather as if they were adjectives:

NOMINATIVE	der Präsident der Herr
ACCUSATIVE	den Präsident**en** den Herr**n**
GENITIVE	des Präsident**en** des Herr**n**
DATIVE	dem Präsident**en** dem Herr**n**
PLURAL	die Präsident**en** die Herr**en**

Die Königin begrüßte **den** Präsident**en**   *The queen welcomed the president*
Der Hund folgte **seinem** Herr**n**   *The dog followed his master*

More modals

3   In Chapter 8 you saw three of the most common MODAL VERBS. Here are the other three in the present tense, **sollen** *(be supposed to, should)*, **dürfen** *(be allowed to/may)* and **mögen** *(like/want to, may)*:

sollen	**dürfen**	**mögen**
ich soll	ich darf	ich mag
du sollst	du darfst	du magst
Sie sollen	Sie dürfen	Sie mögen
er/sie/es soll	er/sie/es darf	er/sie/es mag
wir sollen	wir dürfen	wir mögen
ihr sollt	ihr dürft	ihr mögt
Sie sollen	Sie dürfen	Sie mögen
sie sollen	sie dürfen	sie mögen

4   As with the other modal verbs they are followed by an infinitive which goes to the end of the clause.

Er **soll** sehr reich **sein**	*He is supposed to be very rich*
Sie **sollen** zu mir **kommen**	*They are to come to me*
Hier **darfst** du **rauchen**	*You are allowed to smoke here*
Ich **mag** kein Fleisch essen	*I don't like/want to eat meat*
Das **mag** wohl sein	*That may well be so*

5   When trying to say *must not* in German, remember that **nicht müssen** means there is no compulsion to do something, not a ban on it:

Sie **müssen** nicht im Gras sitzen   *You don't have to sit on the grass*
BUT
Sie **dürfen** nicht im Gras sitzen   *You mustn't (aren't allowed to) sit on the grass*

6   The verb **lassen** can be used as a modal verb with the sense *to let*. It can also mean *to have something done:*

Laß mich sehen!	*Let me see!*
Sie **läßt** sich die Haare schneiden	*She is having her hair cut*
Ich **ließ** meinen Wecker reparieren	*I had my alarm clock repaired*

7   Modal verbs have two PAST PARTICIPLES. The first is formed following the normal pattern (**ge-** + STEM + **-t**):

Sie hat das Buch **gewollt**   *She wanted the book*

The second is identical to the infinitive:

Sie hat das Buch lesen **wollen**   *She wanted to read the book*

This second form is used when the modal verb is used with another verb in the infinitive.

CHAPTER 27   WHAT HAVE YOU LEARNT?

A A group of friends discuss Kamal's absence in the canteen at the Volkshochschule.
Complete their dialogue with the most suitable particle chosen from the following:
denn, doch, ja, mal, schon.
e.g. Er wird … rechtzeitig erscheinen.
  →   Er wird schon rechtzeitig erscheinen.

Die Volkshochschüler

YUNG SU Wo ist Kamal? Was ist … mit ihm los?
AYSCHA Er wird … kommen.
GÜRKAN War er heute nicht bei der Arbeit?
YUNG SU … Er ist immer da.
AYSCHA Moment … ! Da ist er … !

B The students in the German class at the Volkshochschule give their reasons for
learning German. Complete each sentence with the modal verb suggested in the
appropriate form of the present tense.
e.g. Ich … in Deutschland bleiben.   (<u>müssen</u>)   →   Ich <u>muß</u> in Deutschland bleiben.

Flüchtling, Aussiedler, Gastarbeiter

YUNG SU Ich bin Flüchtling. Ich mußte aus Vietnam fliehen. Ich … jetzt in
      Deutschland bleiben.   (<u>dürfen</u>)
      Ich … Deutsch lernen, um eine bessere Stelle zu bekommen.   (<u>müssen</u>)
AYSCHA Meine Familie kommt aus Kasachstan. Wir sind Aussiedler. Ich … mein
      Deutsch verbessern, damit ich eine gute Lehre finde.   (<u>wollen</u>)
GÜRKAN Ich wohne seit 30 Jahren in Deutschland. Meine Kinder haben mir
      gesagt, daß ich Deutsch richtig lernen …   (<u>sollen</u>)

C Now answer these questions based on the information given above, transposing the
information from the first to the third person.
e.g. Warum muß Yung Su Deutsch lernen?
  →   Yung Su muß Deutsch lernen, um eine bessere Stelle zu bekommen.

Deutsch als Fremdsprache

1 Wo darf Yung Su jetzt bleiben?
2 Warum will Ayscha ihr Deutsch verbessern?
3 Was haben ihm Gürkans Kinder gesagt?

Help Yourself to Essential German Grammar

Revision test 25–27

A Herr Braun tells his wife the information the travel agent has given him about their hotel in Zürich. Fill in each gap with the correct form of **haben** or **sein** in the present indicative or imperfect subjunctive as required.

e.g. Das Büro [is] gegenüber vom Bahnhof.
→ Das Büro ist gegenüber vom Bahnhof.

Im Reisebüro
1 Das Hotel [is] im Stadtzentrum.
2 Der Angestellte im Reisebüro meint, wir [would have] keine Probleme, das Hotel zu finden.
3 Wenn wir mit der Straßenbahn fahren, [would be] wir in etwa zehn Minuten da.
4 Der Verkehrsverein [has] ein Büro gleich gegenüber dem Bahnhof.

B Herr Braun repeats the conversation with the travel agent. Change the direct questions into indirect questions, using **ob** + subjunctive.

e.g. Ich habe ihn gefragt, „Haben Sie die Zugkarten gebucht?"
Ich habe ihn gefragt, ob er die Zugkarten gebucht habe.

Indirekte Fragen
Ich habe ihn gefragt:
Haben Sie die Flugtickets gebucht?
Sind Sie schon mit dieser Firma gereist?

Er hat uns gefragt:
Sind Sie schon in Zürich gewesen?
Haben Sie schon Geld gewechselt?

C The travel agent also asked if there were any dietary requirements. Replace the English words in Herr Braun's answers with German.

e.g. Ich kann [nothing] trinken, [that] Alkohol enthält.
→ Ich kann nichts trinken, was Alkohol enthält.

Diätbedürfnisse
1 Ich kann [everything] essen, [that] auf der Speisekarte steht.
2 Meine Frau kann [nothing] essen, [that] Erdnüsse enthält.
3 Als wir in Rußland waren, haben wir [something] gegessen, [that] uns beide krank gemacht hat.

D A customer tells the travel agent of her holiday experiences. Complete her report (which contains passive and active sentences) in the perfect with the appropriate auxiliary verb, **haben** or **sein**.

e.g. Mein Auto … gestohlen worden.   →   Mein Auto ist gestohlen worden.

Eine unglückliche Erfahrung

1 Meine Handtasche … gestohlen worden.
2 Die Polizei … die Handtasche später gefunden.
3 Mein Reisepaß, meine Brieftasche und meine Autoschlüssel … vom Dieb behalten worden.
4 Glücklicherweise … ich eine Reiseversicherung gehabt.

E Some travellers to Romania describe their experiences. Replace the English with the equivalent German.

e.g. Sie sind mit [a few] Freunden gefahren.
   →   Sie sind mit ein paar Freunden gefahren.

Eine Reise in den Osten

1 Wir wollten ein neues Reiseziel. Nur [a few] Ausländer fahren nach Rumänien.
2 Wir sind mit [some] Freunden dorthin gefahren.
3 Es hat fast [everybody] in der Gruppe Spaß gemacht.
4 Meine Frau und ich wollen [both] wieder in den Osten reisen.
5 Wegen des Mangels an Medikamenten nehmen wir [everything] mit.

F The travel agent discusses with a customer some differences between the USA and the UK. Complete where appropriate the weak masculine nouns.

Amerika/Großbritannien

1 Amerika hat einen Präsident … Großbritannien hat eine Königin.
2 Die Tochter des Präsident … hat keinen Titel.
3 Die Söhne der Königin sind Prinz …

G At a holiday resort in Austria a survey is carried out amongst the holidaymakers. Complete their statements with the present tense of the modal verb given.

e.g. Ich … früher aufstehen. (sollen)   →   Ich soll früher aufstehen.

Wie gefällt es Ihnen hier?

1 Hier … man schwimmen, surfen und so weiter.   (können)
2 Wir … uns ausruhen. Das ist uns am wichtigsten.   (können)
3 Wir werden Wien besichtigen. Wien … sehr schön sein.   (sollen)
4 Gäste … keine Shorts im Restaurant tragen.   (dürfen)
5 Hier im Hotel … man nicht rauchen.   (dürfen)
6 Ich … lieber nächstes Jahr nach Skandinavien fahren.   (wollen)
7 Ich … etwas Englisch lernen. Hier sind immer viele Engländer.   (sollen)
8 Wir … einen Ausflug nach Salzburg machen.   (wollen)

Help Yourself to Essential German Grammar

Appendices

1 Verb Tables

a Weak (regular) verbs

INFINITIVE	PRESENT	IMPERFECT	PERFECT	IMPERATIVE
wählen	ich wähle	ich wählte	ich habe gewählt	wähl(e)
	du wählst	du wähltest	du hast gewählt	wählt
(to choose)	er wählt	er wählte	er hat gewählt	wählen Sie
	wir wählen	wir wählten	wir haben gewählt	
	ihr wählt	ihr wähltet	ihr habt gewählt	
	sie wählen	sie wählten	sie haben gewählt	

PLUPERFECT	CONDITIONAL	FUTURE	PRESENT SUBJ
ich hatte gewählt	ich würde wählen	ich werde wählen	ich wähle
du hattest gewählt	du würdest wählen	du wirst wählen	du wählest
er hatte gewählt	er würde wählen	er wird wählen	er wähle
wir hatten gewählt	wir würden wählen	wir werden wählen	wir wählen
ihr hattet gewählt	ihr würdet wählen	ihr werdet wählen	ihr wählet
sie hatten gewählt	sie würden wählen	sie werden wählen	sie wählen

PASSIVE PRESENT	PASSIVE IMPERFECT	PASSIVE PERFECT
ich werde gewählt	ich wurde gewählt	ich bin gewählt worden
du wirst gewählt	du wurdest gewählt	du bist gewählt worden
er wird gewählt	er wurde gewählt	er ist gewählt worden
wir werden gewählt	wir wurden gewählt	wir sind gewählt worden
ihr werdet gewählt	ihr wurdet gewählt	ihr seid gewählt worden
sie werden gewählt	sie wurden gewählt	sie sind gewählt worden

b Common irregular and auxiliary verbs: *haben, sein, werden*

INFINITIVE	PRESENT	IMPERFECT	PERFECT	IMPERATIVE
haben	ich habe	ich hatte	ich habe gehabt	hab(e)
	du hast	du hattest	du hast gehabt	habt
(to have;	er hat	er hatte	er hat gehabt	haben Sie
forms past tenses)	wir haben	wir hatten	wir haben gehabt	
	ihr habt	ihr hattet	ihr habt gehabt	
	sie haben	sie hatten	sie haben gehabt	

PLUPERFECT	CONDITIONAL*	FUTURE	PRESENT SUBJ
ich hatte gehabt	ich hätte	ich werde haben	ich habe
du hattest gehabt	du hättest	du wirst haben	du habest
er hatte gehabt	er hätte	er wird haben	er habe
wir hatten gehabt	wir hätten	wir werden haben	wir haben
ihr hattet gehabt	ihr hättet	ihr werdet haben	ihr habet
sie hatten gehabt	sie hätten	sie werden haben	sie haben

*Also imperfect subjunctive.

Help Yourself to Essential German Grammar

INFINITIVE	PRESENT	IMPERFECT	PERFECT	IMPERATIVE
sein	ich bin	ich war	ich bin gewesen	sei
	du bist	du warst	du bist gewesen	seid
(to be;	er ist	er war	er ist gewesen	seien Sie
forms past	wir sind	wir waren	wir sind gewesen	
tenses)	ihr seid	ihr wart	ihr seid gewesen	
	sie sind	sie waren	sie sind gewesen	

PLUPERFECT	CONDITIONAL*	FUTURE	PRESENT SUBJ
ich war gewesen	ich wäre	ich werde sein	ich sei
du warst gewesen	du wärst	du wirst sein	du sei(e)st
er war gewesen	er wäre	er wird sein	er sei
wir waren gewesen	wir wären	wir werden sein	wir seien
ihr wart gewesen	ihr wäret	ihr werdet sein	ihr sei(e)t
sie waren gewesen	sie wären	sie werden sein	sie seien

INFINITIVE	PRESENT	IMPERFECT	PERFECT	IMPERATIVE
werden	ich werde	ich wurde	ich bin geworden	werd(e)
	du wirst	du wurdest	du bist geworden	werdet
(to become;	er wird	er wurde	er ist geworden	werden Sie
forms future	wir werden	wir wurden	wir sind geworden	
and passive)	ihr werdet	ihr wurdet	ihr seid geworden	
	sie werden	sie wurden	sie sind geworden	

PLUPERFECT	CONDITIONAL*	FUTURE	PRESENT SUBJ
ich war geworden	ich würde	ich werde werden	ich werde
du warst geworden	du würdest	du wirst werden	du werdest
er war geworden	er würde	er wird werden	er werde
wir waren geworden	wir würden	wir werden werden	wir werden
ihr wart geworden	ihr würdet	ihr werdet werden	ihr werdet
sie waren geworden	sie würden	sie werden werden	sie werden

c Mixed verbs

INFINITIVE	PRESENT	IMPERFECT	PERFECT	IMPERATIVE
bringen	ich bringe	ich brachte	ich habe gebracht	bring(e)
	du bringst	du brachtest	du hast gebracht	bringt
(to bring)	er bringt	er brachte	er hat gebracht	bringen Sie
	wir bringen	wir brachten	wir haben gebracht	
	ihr bringt	ihr brachtet	ihr habt gebracht	
	sie bringen	sie brachten	sie haben gebracht	
denken	ich denke	ich dachte	ich habe gedacht	denk(e)
	du denkst	du dachtest	du hast gedacht	denkt
(to think)	er denkt	er dachte	er hat gedacht	denken Sie
	wir denken	wir dachten	wir haben gedacht	
	ihr denkt	ihr dachtet	ihr habt gedacht	
	sie denken	sie dachten	sie haben gedacht	

*Also imperfect subjunctive.

Help Yourself to Essential German Grammar

kennen	ich kenne	ich kannte	ich habe gekannt	kenn(e)
	du kennst	du kanntest	du hast gekannt	kennt
(to know)	er kennt	er kannte	er hat gekannt	kennen Sie
	wir kennen	wir kannten	wir haben gekannt	
	ihr kennt	ihr kanntet	ihr habt gekannt	
	sie kennen	sie kannten	sie haben gekannt	

Like bringen: verbringen *(to spend – time)*, verbringt, verbrachte, verbracht
Like kennen: erkennen *(to recognise)*, erkennt, erkannte, erkannt
           brennen *(to burn)*, brennt, brannte, gebrannt
           nennen *(to name)*, nennt, nannte, genannt
           rennen *(to run)*, rennt, rannte, gerannt

d Strong verbs

i e - i - a - e pattern – **e**ssen, **i**ßt, **a**ß, geg**e**ssen

INFINITIVE	PRESENT	IMPERFECT	PERFECT	IMPERATIVE
essen	ich esse	ich aß	ich habe gegessen	iß
	du ißt	du aßt	du hast gegessen	eßt
(to eat)	er ißt	er aß	er hat gegessen	essen Sie
	wir essen	wir aßen	wir haben gegessen	
	ihr eßt	ihr aßt	ihr habt gegessen	
	sie essen	sie aßen	sie haben gegessen	
geben	ich gebe	ich gab	ich habe gegeben	gib
	du gibst	du gabst	du hast gegeben	gebt
(to give)	er gibt	er gab	er hat gegeben	geben Sie
	wir geben	wir gaben	wir haben gegeben	
	ihr gebt	ihr gabt	ihr habt gegeben	
	sie geben	sie gaben	sie haben gegeben	

Like essen: messen *(to measure)*, mißt, maß, gemessen
           vergessen *(to forget)*, vergißt, vergaß, vergessen

ii long e - ie - long a - long e pattern – **l**esen, **lie**st, **la**s, gel**e**sen

INFINITIVE	PRESENT	IMPERFECT	PERFECT	IMPERATIVE
lesen	ich lese	ich las	ich habe gelesen	lies
	du liest	du lasest	du hast gelesen	lest
(to read)	er liest	er las	er hat gelesen	lesen Sie
	wir lesen	wir lasen	wir haben gelesen	
	ihr lest	ihr last	ihr habt gelesen	
	sie lesen	sie lasen	sie haben gelesen	
sehen	ich sehe	ich sah	ich habe gesehen	sieh
	du siehst	du sahst	du hast gesehen	seht
(to see)	er sieht	er sah	er hat gesehen	sehen Sie
	wir sehen	wir sahen	wir haben gesehen	
	ihr seht	ihr saht	ihr habt gesehen	
	sie sehen	sie sahen	sie haben gesehen	
geschehen	es geschieht	es geschah	es ist geschehen	
(to happen)	sie geschehen	sie geschahen	sie sind geschehen	

Like lesen: liegen *(to lie)*, liegt, lag, gelegen
bitten *(to ask)*, bittet, bat, gebeten
treten *(to step)*, tritt, trat, getreten

iii i - a - o pattern – beg**i**nnt, beg**a**nn, beg**o**nnen

INFINITIVE	PRESENT	IMPERFECT	PERFECT	IMPERATIVE
beginnen	ich beginne	ich begann	ich habe begonnen	beginn(e)
	du beginnst	du begannst	du hast begonnen	beginnt
(to begin)	er beginnt	er begann	er hat begonnen	beginnen Sie
	wir beginnen	wir begannen	wir haben begonnen	
	ihr beginnt	ihr begannt	ihr habt begonnen	
	sie beginnen	sie begannen	sie haben begonnen	

Like beginnen: gewinnen *(to win)*, gewinnt, gewann, gewonnen
schwimmen *(to swim)*, schwimmt, schwamm, geschwommen

iv e - i - a - o pattern – helfen, h**i**lft, h**a**lf, geh**o**lfen
long e - ie - long a - long o – stehlen, st**ie**hlt, st**a**hl, gest**o**hlen

INFINITIVE	PRESENT	IMPERFECT	PERFECT	IMPERATIVE
helfen	ich helfe	ich half	ich habe geholfen	hilf
	du hilfst	du halfst	du hast geholfen	helft
(to help)	er hilft	er half	er hat geholfen	helfen Sie
	wir helfen	wir halfen	wir haben geholfen	
	ihr helft	ihr halft	ihr habt geholfen	
	sie helfen	sie halfen	sie haben geholfen	
nehmen	ich nehme	ich nahm	ich habe genommen	nimm
	du nimmst	du nahmst	du hast genommen	nehmt
(to take)	er nimmt	er nahm	er hat genommen	nehmen Sie
	wir nehmen	wir nahmen	wir haben genommen	
	ihr nehmt	ihr nahmt	ihr habt genommen	
	sie nehmen	sie nahmen	sie haben genommen	
stehlen	ich stehle	ich stahl	ich habe gestohlen	stiehl
	du stiehlst	du stahlst	du hast gestohlen	stehlt
(to steal)	er stiehlt	er stahl	er hat gestohlen	stehlen Sie
	wir stehlen	wir stahlen	wir haben gestohlen	
	ihr stehlt	ihr stahlt	ihr habt gestohlen	
	sie stehlen	sie stahlen	sie haben gestohlen	
sprechen	ich spreche	ich sprach	ich habe gesprochen	sprich
	du sprichst	du sprachst	du hast gesprochen	sprecht
(to speak)	er spricht	er sprach	er hat gesprochen	sprechen Sie
	wir sprechen	wir sprachen	wir haben gesprochen	
	ihr sprecht	ihr spracht	ihr habt gesprochen	
	sie sprechen	sie sprachen	sie haben gesprochen	
treffen	ich treffe	ich traf	ich habe getroffen	triff
	du triffst	du trafst	du hast getroffen	trefft
(to meet)	er trifft	er traf	er hat getroffen	treffen Sie
	wir treffen	wir trafen	wir haben getroffen	
	ihr trefft	ihr traft	ihr habt getroffen	
	sie treffen	sie trafen	sie haben getroffen	

werfen	ich werfe	ich warf	ich habe geworfen	wirf
	du wirfst	du warfst	du hast geworfen	werft
(to throw)	er wirft	er warf	er hat geworfen	werfen Sie
	wir werfen	wir warfen	wir haben geworfen	
	ihr werft	ihr warft	ihr habt geworfen	
	sie werfen	sie warfen	sie haben geworfen	

Like stehlen: befehlen *(to order)*, befiehlt, befahl, befohlen
empfehlen *(to recommend)*, empfiehlt, empfahl, empfohlen
Like sprechen: brechen *(to break)*, bricht, brach, gebrochen
versprechen *(to promise)*, verspricht, versprach, versprochen
Like werfen: sterben *(to die)*, stirbt, starb, gestorben

v i - a - u pattern – f**i**ndet, f**a**nd, gef**u**nden

INFINITIVE	PRESENT	IMPERFECT	PERFECT	IMPERATIVE
finden	ich finde	er fand	ich habe gefunden	find(e)
	du findest	du fandst	du hast gefunden	findet
(to find)	er findet	er fand	er hat gefunden	finden Sie
	wir finden	wir fanden	wir haben gefunden	
	ihr findet	ihr fandet	ihr habt gefunden	
	sie finden	sie fanden	sie haben gefunden	
singen	ich singe	ich sang	ich habe gesungen	sing(e)
	du singst	du sangst	du hast gesungen	singt
(to sing)	er singt	er sang	er hat gesungen	singen Sie
	wir singen	wir sangen	wir haben gesungen	
	ihr singt	ihr sangt	ihr habt gesungen	
	sie singen	sie sangen	sie haben gesungen	
trinken	ich trinke	ich trank	ich habe getrunken	trink(e)
	du trinkst	du trankst	du hast getrunken	trinkt
(to drink)	er trinkt	er trank	er hat getrunken	trinken Sie
	wir trinken	wir tranken	wir haben getrunken	
	ihr trinkt	ihr trankt	ihr habt getrunken	
	sie trinken	sie tranken	sie haben getrunken	

Like finden: binden *(to tie)*, bindet, band, gebunden
verschwinden *(to disappear)*, verschwindet, verschwand, verschwunden
Like singen: klingen *(to sound)*, klingt, klang, geklungen
schwingen *(to swing)*, schwingt, schwang, geschwungen
springen *(to jump)*, springt, sprang, gesprungen
zwingen *(to force)*, zwingt, zwang, gezwungen
gelingen *(to succeed)*, gelingt, gelang, gelungen
mißlingen *(to fail)*, mißlingt, mißlang, mißlungen
Like trinken: sinken *(to sink)*, sinkt, sank, gesunken
stinken *(to stink)*, stinkt, stank, gestunken

Help Yourself to Essential German Grammar

vi ei - ie - ie pattern – bl**ei**bt, bl**ie**b, gebl**ie**ben

INFINITIVE	PRESENT	IMPERFECT	PERFECT	IMPERATIVE
bleiben	ich bleibe	ich blieb	ich bin geblieben	bleib(e)
	du bleibst	du bliebst	du bist geblieben	bleibt
(to stay)	er bleibt	er blieb	er ist geblieben	bleiben Sie
	wir bleiben	wir blieben	wir sind geblieben	
	ihr bleibt	ihr bliebt	ihr seid geblieben	
	sie bleiben	sie blieben	sie sind geblieben	
scheinen	ich scheine	ich schien	ich habe geschienen	schein(e)
	du scheinst	du schienst	du hast geschienen	scheint
(to seem, shine)	er scheint	er schien	er hat geschienen	scheinen Sie
	wir scheinen	wir schienen	wir haben geschienen	
	ihr scheint	ihr schient	ihr habt geschienen	
	sie scheinen	sie schienen	sie haben geschienen	
steigen	ich steige	ich stieg	ich bin gestiegen	steig(e)
	du steigst	du stiegst	du bist gestiegen	steigt
(to climb)	er steigt	er stieg	er ist gestiegen	steigen Sie
	wir steigen	wir stiegen	wir sind gestiegen	
	ihr steigt	ihr stiegt	ihr seid gestiegen	
	sie steigen	sie stiegen	sie sind gestiegen	

Like bleiben: leihen *(to lend)*, leiht, lieh, geliehen
reiben *(to rub)*, reibt, rieb, gerieben
schreiben *(to write)*, schreibt, schrieb, geschrieben
schreien *(to shout)*, schreit, schrie, geschrie(e)n
treiben *(to drive)*, treibt, trieb, getrieben
Like scheinen: erscheinen *(to appear)*, erscheint, erschien, erschienen

vii ei - i - i pattern – b**ei**ßen, b**i**ß, geb**i**ssen

INFINITIVE	PRESENT	IMPERFECT	PERFECT	IMPERATIVE
beißen	ich beiße	ich biß	ich habe gebissen	beiß(e)
	du beißt	du bissest	du hast gebissen	beißt
(to bite)	er beißt	er biß	er hat gebissen	beißen Sie
	wir beißen	wir bissen	wir haben gebissen	
	ihr beißt	ihr bißt	ihr habt gebissen	
	sie beißen	sie bissen	sie haben gebissen	
greifen	ich greife	ich griff	ich habe gegriffen	greif(e)
	du greifst	du griffest	du hast gegriffen	greift
(to grasp)	er greift	er griff	er hat gegriffen	greifen Sie
	wir greifen	wir griffen	wir haben gegriffen	
	ihr greift	ihr grifft	ihr habt gegriffen	
	sie greifen	sie griffen	sie haben gegriffen	
reiten	ich reite	ich ritt	ich habe geritten	reit(e)
	du reitest	du rittest	du hast geritten	reitet
(to ride)	er reitet	er ritt	er hat geritten	reiten Sie
	wir reiten	wir ritten	wir haben geritten	
	ihr reitet	ihr rittet	ihr habt geritten	
	sie reiten	sie ritten	sie haben geritten	

Like beißen: reißen *(to tear)*, reißt, riß, gerissen
Like reiten: gleiten *(to glide)*, gleitet, glitt, geglitten
           leiden *(to suffer)*, leidet, litt, gelitten
           schneiden *(to cut)*, schneidet, schnitt, geschnitten

viii ie - o - o pattern – b**ie**gen, b**o**g, geb**o**gen

INFINITIVE	PRESENT	IMPERFECT	PERFECT	IMPERATIVE
biegen	ich biege	ich bog	ich habe gebogen	bieg(e)
	du biegst	du bogst	du hast gebogen	biegt
(to bend)	er biegt	er bog	er hat gebogen	biegen Sie
	wir biegen	wir bogen	wir haben gebogen	
	ihr biegt	ihr bogt	ihr habt gebogen	
	sie biegen	sie bogen	sie haben gebogen	
gießen	ich gieße	ich goß	ich habe gegossen	gieß(e)
	du gießt	du gossest	du hast gegossen	gießt
(to pour)	er gießt	er goß	er hat gegossen	gießen Sie
	wir gießen	wir gossen	wir haben gegossen	
	ihr gießt	ihr goßt	ihr habt gegossen	
	sie gießen	sie gossen	sie haben gegossen	
frieren	ich friere	ich fror	ich habe gefroren	frier(e)
	du frierst	du frorst	du hast gefroren	friert
(to freeze)	er friert	er fror	er hat gefroren	frieren Sie
	wir frieren	wir froren	wir haben gefroren	
	ihr friert	ihr frort	ihr habt gefroren	
	sie frieren	sie froren	sie haben gefroren	

Like biegen: fliegen *(to fly)*, fliegt, flog, geflogen
           ziehen *(to pull)*, zieht, zog, gezogen
           fliehen *(to escape)*, flieht, floh, geflohen
           bieten *(to offer)*, bietet, bot, geboten
           kriechen *(to crawl)*, kriecht, kroch, gekrochen
           riechen *(to smell)*, riecht, roch, gerochen
           schieben *(to push)*, schiebt, schob, geschoben
Like gießen: fließen *(to flow)*, fließt, floß, geflossen
           genießen *(to enjoy)*, genießt, genoß, genossen
           schießen *(to shoot)*, schießt, schoß, geschossen
           schließen *(to shut)*, schließt, schloß, geschlossen
Like frieren: verlieren *(to lose)*, verliert, verlor, verloren

ix a - ä - ie - a pattern – f**a**llen, f**ä**llt, f**ie**l, gef**a**llen

INFINITIVE	PRESENT	IMPERFECT	PERFECT	IMPERATIVE
fallen	ich falle	ich fiel	ich bin gefallen	fall(e)
	du fällst	du fielst	du bist gefallen	fallt
(to fall)	er fällt	er fiel	er ist gefallen	fallen Sie
	wir fallen	wir fielen	wir sind gefallen	
	ihr fallt	ihr fielt	ihr seid gefallen	
	sie fallen	sie fielen	sie sind gefallen	

lassen	ich lasse	ich ließ	ich habe gelassen	lasse, laß
	du läßt	du ließt	du hast gelassen	laßt
(to leave, let)	er läßt	er ließ	er hat gelassen	lassen Sie
	wir lassen	wir ließen	wir haben gelassen	
	ihr laßt	ihr ließt	ihr habt gelassen	
	sie lassen	sie ließen	sie haben gelassen	
laufen	ich laufe	ich lief	ich bin gelaufen	lauf(e)
	du läufst	du liefst	du bist gelaufen	lauft
(to run)	er läuft	er lief	er ist gelaufen	laufen Sie
	wir laufen	wir liefen	wir sind gelaufen	
	ihr lauft	ihr lieft	ihr seid gelaufen	
	sie laufen	sie liefen	sie sind gelaufen	
schlafen	ich schlafe	ich schlief	ich habe geschlafen	schlaf(e)
	du schläfst	du schliefst	du hast geschlafen	schlaft
(to sleep)	er schläft	er schlief	er hat geschlafen	schlafen Sie
	wir schlafen	wir schliefen	wir haben geschlafen	
	ihr schlaft	ihr schlieft	ihr habt geschlafen	
	sie schlafen	sie schliefen	sie haben geschlafen	

Like fallen: halten *(to hold)*, hält, hielt, gehalten
　　　　　　 fangen *(to catch)*, fängt, fing, gefangen
Like schlafen: blasen *(to blow)*, bläst, blies, geblasen

x a - ä - u - a pattern – f**a**hren, f**ä**hrt, f**u**hr, gef**a**hren

INFINITIVE	PRESENT	IMPERFECT	PERFECT	IMPERATIVE
fahren	ich fahre	ich fuhr	ich bin gefahren	fahr(e)
	du fährst	du fuhrst	du bist gefahren	fahrt
(to drive/	er fährt	er fuhr	er ist gefahren	fahren Sie
travel)	wir fahren	wir fuhren	wir sind gefahren	
	ihr fahrt	ihr fuhrt	ihr seid gefahren	
	sie fahren	sie fuhren	sie sind gefahren	
tragen	ich trage	ich trug	ich habe getragen	trag(e)
	du trägst	du trugst	du hast getragen	tragt
(to carry)	er trägt	er trug	er hat getragen	tragen Sie
	wir tragen	wir trugen	wir haben getragen	
	ihr tragt	ihr trugt	ihr habt getragen	
	sie tragen	sie trugen	sie haben getragen	
waschen	ich wasche	ich wusch	ich habe gewaschen	wasch(e)
	du wäschst	du wuschst	du hast gewaschen	wascht
(to wash)	er wäscht	er wusch	er hat gewaschen	waschen Sie
	wir waschen	wir wuschen	wir haben gewaschen	
	ihr wascht	ihr wuscht	ihr habt gewaschen	
	sie waschen	sie wuschen	sie haben gewaschen	

Like tragen: schlagen *(to beat)*, schlägt, schlug, geschlagen
Like waschen: wachsen *(to grow)*, wächst, wuchs, gewachsen

Irregular

INFINITIVE	PRESENT	IMPERFECT	PERFECT	IMPERATIVE
gehen *(to go)*	ich gehe du gehst er geht wir gehen ihr geht sie gehen	ich ging du gingst er ging wir gingen ihr gingt sie gingen	ich bin gegangen du bist gegangen er ist gegangen wir sind gegangen ihr seid gegangen sie sind gegangen	geh(e) geht gehen Sie
kommen *(to come)*	ich komme du kommst er kommt wir kommen ihr kommt sie kommen	er kam du kamst er kam wir kamen ihr kamt sie kamen	ich bin gekommen du bist gekommen er ist gekommen wir sind gekommen ihr seid gekommen sie sind gekommen	komm(e) kommt kommen Sie
rufen *(to call)*	ich rufe du rufst er ruft wir rufen ihr ruft sie rufen	ich rief du riefst er rief wir riefen ihr rieft sie riefen	ich habe gerufen du hast gerufen er hat gerufen wir haben gerufen ihr habt gerufen sie haben gerufen	ruf(e) ruft rufen Sie
sitzen *(to sit)*	ich sitze du sitz(es)t er sitzt wir sitzen ihr sitzt sie sitzen	ich saß du saßest er saß wir saßen ihr saßt sie saßen	ich habe gesessen du hast gesessen er hat gesessen wir haben gesessen ihr habt gesessen sie haben gesessen	sitz(e) sitzt sitzen Sie
stehen *(to stand)*	ich stehe du stehst er steht wir stehen ihr steht sie stehen	ich stand du standst er stand wir standen ihr standet sie standen	ich habe gestanden du hast gestanden er hat gestanden wir haben gestanden ihr habt gestanden sie haben gestanden	steh(e) steht stehen Sie
tun *(to do)*	ich tue du tust er tut wir tun ihr tut sie tun	ich tat du tat(e)st er tat wir taten ihr tatet sie taten	ich habe getan du hast getan er hat getan wir haben getan ihr habt getan sie haben getan	tu(e) tut tun Sie
wissen *(to know)*	ich weiß du weißt er weiß wir wissen ihr wißt sie wissen	ich wußte du wußtest er wußte wir wußten ihr wußtet sie wußten	ich habe gewußt du hast gewußt er hat gewußt wir haben gewußt ihr habt gewußt sie haben gewußt	wisse wißt wissen Sie

Modal verbs

INFINITIVE	PRESENT	IMPERFECT	PERFECT
dürfen *(to be allowed to, may)*	ich darf du darfst er darf wir dürfen ihr dürft sie dürfen	ich durfte du durftest er durfte wir durften ihr durftet sie durften	ich habe gedurft* du hast gedurft er hat gedurft wir haben gedurft ihr habt gedurft sie haben gedurft
können *(to be able to, can)*	ich kann du kannst er kann wir können ihr könnt sie können	ich konnte du konntest er konnte wir konnten ihr konntet sie konnten	ich habe gekonnt* du hast gekonnt er hat gekonnt wir haben gekonnt ihr habt gekonnt sie haben gekonnt
müssen *(to have to, must)*	ich muß du mußt er muß wir müssen ihr müßt sie müssen	ich mußte du mußtest er mußte wir mußten ihr mußtet sie mußten	ich habe gemußt* du hast gemußt er hat gemußt wir haben gemußt ihr habt gemußt sie haben gemußt
sollen *(to be supposed to, should)*	ich soll du sollst er soll wir sollen ihr sollt sie sollen	ich sollte du solltest er sollte wir sollten ihr solltet sie sollten	ich habe gesollt* du hast gesollt er hat gesollt wir haben gesollt ihr habt gesollt sie haben gesollt
wollen *(to want to)*	ich will du willst er will wir wollen ihr wollt sie wollen	ich wollte du wolltest er wollte wir wollten ihr wolltet sie wollten	ich habe gewollt* du hast gewollt er hat gewollt wir haben gewollt ihr habt gewollt sie haben gewollt
mögen *(to like/want to, may)*	ich mag du magst er mag wir mögen ihr mögt sie mögen	ich mochte du mochtest er mochte wir mochten ihr mochtet sie mochten	ich habe gemocht* du hast gemocht er hat gemocht wir haben gemocht ihr habt gemocht sie haben gemocht

Reflexive verbs

INFINITIVE	PRESENT	IMPERFECT	PERFECT
sich freuen *(to be glad)*	ich freue mich du freust dich er freut sich wir freuen uns ihr freut euch sie freuen sich	ich freute mich du freutest dich er freute sich wir freuten uns ihr freutet euch sie freuten sich	ich habe mich gefreut du hast dich gefreut er hat sich gefreut wir haben uns gefreut ihr habt euch gefreut sie haben sich gefreut

*These past participles are not used with an infinitive (see section 27.7).

The imperative forms are **freue dich**, **freut euch**, and **freuen Sie sich**.

See also section 3.3 and Appendix page 148 below on Personal pronouns

Some common reflexive verbs:

sich ändern	*to change*	sich anziehen	*to dress*
sich ärgern	*to be annoyed*	sich ausruhen	*to rest*
sich ausziehen	*to undress*	sich baden	*to have a bath*
sich bedanken	*to thank*	sich beeilen	*to hurry*
sich beklagen	*to complain*	sich benehmen	*to behave*
sich befinden	*to be (situated)*	sich entscheiden	*to decide*
sich entschuldigen	*to apologise*	sich erholen	*to get better, recover*
sich erinnern an	*to remember*	sich erkälten	*to catch a cold*
sich freuen	*to be glad*	sich fühlen	*to feel*
sich fürchten	*to be afraid*	sich gewöhnen an	*to get used to*
sich hinlegen	*to lie down*	sich interessieren für	*to be interested in*
sich melden	*to report*	sich nähern	*to approach*
sich rasieren	*to shave*	sich setzen	*to sit down*
sich trennen	*to part company*	sich umziehen	*to change (one's*
sich unterhalten	*to talk; to converse*		*clothes)*
sich verlassen auf	*to rely on*	sich verabschieden	*to take one's leave*
sich verletzen	*to hurt oneself*	sich verlaufen	*to get lost*
sich waschen	*to wash (oneself)*	sich verlieben in	*to fall in love with*
sich wundern	*to be surprised*	sich wenden	*to turn round*
		sich zurückhalten	*to restrain oneself*

2 Verbs with **sein** in the perfect and pluperfect

a Verbs of motion

Some of the most common are:

kommen	*to come*	gehen	*to go*	fahren	*to travel*
laufen	*to run*	rennen	*to run*	eilen	*to hurry*
steigen	*to climb*	folgen	*to follow*	erscheinen	*to appear*

In addition, all the many examples of these verbs with a prefix, such as:

hereinkommen	*to come in*	**hinaus**gehen	*to go out*	
abfahren	*to leave*	**weg**laufen	*to run away*	etc.

b Verbs describing a change of state

aufwachen	*to wake up*	einschlafen	*to go to sleep*
sterben	*to die*	schmelzen	*to melt*
wachsen	*to grow*	werden	*to become*

Help Yourself to Essential German Grammar

c Two verbs describing lack of motion

sein *to be*   bleiben *to stay*

d Impersonal verbs expressing success, failure or happening

gelingen *to succeed*   mißlingen *to fail*   geschehen *to happen*

3 Verbs with the dative

A number of verbs are followed by a dative object. The most common are:

antworten	*to answer (somebody)*	gratulieren	*to congratulate*
danken	*to thank*	helfen	*to help*
drohen	*to threaten*	raten	*to advise*
folgen	*to follow*	schmeicheln	*to flatter*
gehorchen	*to obey*	vertrauen	*to trust*
gehören	*to belong to*	gefallen	*to please*

4 Impersonal expressions *(see also sections 15.1–3)*

a General

es gibt + accusative   *there is/there are*
es ist/es sind + nominative *there is/there are*

b Feelings (with dative for the person)

es geht mir… /es ist mir…   *I feel…*
Wie geht's dir?/Wie geht es Ihnen? *How are you?*
es tut mir leid   *I'm sorry*
es tut mir weh   *it hurts (me)*

c Feelings (with accusative for the person)

es freut mich *I'm glad*   es ärgert mich *I'm annoyed*

d Liking (with dative for the person)

es gefällt mir   *I like it*
es schmeckt mir   *I like the taste*   es schmeckt gut *it tastes good*

e Suiting (with dative for the person)

es paßt dir *it suits/fits you*   es steht dir *it suits you*

f Success or failure (with dative for the person)

es gelingt mir	*I succeed*	es mißlingt mir	*I fail*

g Weather

es regnet	*it's raining*	es schneit	*it's snowing*
es donnert	*it's thundering*	es blitzt	*there's lightning*
es friert	*it's freezing*		

h Noises

es kracht	*there's a crash*	es raschelt	*there's a rustle*

5 Verbs followed by infinitive

a Verbs followed by *zu* + infinitive (see also section 16.5)

In the great majority of cases where English uses the infinitive with *to* after a verb, German uses the infinitive with **zu** (the exceptions are given in section 5b opposite). The following are a few of the many verbs followed by **zu** + infinitive:

anfangen	*to begin*	beginnen	*to begin*
beschließen	*to decide*	sich entschließen	*to decide*
aufhören	*to stop*	bitten	*to ask*
brauchen	*to need*	drohen	*to threaten*
fürchten	*to fear*	helfen	*to help*
hoffen	*to hope*	scheinen	*to seem*
versprechen	*to promise*	versuchen	*to try*
wagen	*to dare*	wünschen	*to wish*

There is no comma before the **zu** + infinitive if it stands alone:

Es fing an zu regnen	*It began to rain*
Er beschloß zu warten	*He decided to wait*

There is a comma before the **zu** + infinitive as soon as there is something else with it (an object or adverb, for instance):

Es fing an, stark zu regnen	*It began to rain hard*
Er beschloß, auf den nächsten Zug zu warten	*He decided to wait for the next train*

There is no comma even in this case with **brauchen** and **scheinen**:

Sie brauchen nicht heute zu kommen	*You don't need to come today*
Er scheint das Rauchen aufgegeben zu haben	*He seems to have given up smoking*

Remember that where purpose is expressed, **um zu** + infinitive must be used (see sections 9.1–3).

b Verbs followed by infinitive without *zu*

The infinitive needs no **zu** after:

i MODAL VERBS: **dürfen, können, müssen, sollen, wollen, mögen** (see sections 8.5–7 and 27.3–7).

ii **werden** when it is used to form the future and conditional tenses.

iii VERBS OF MOTION particularly **gehen**:

Wir gehen morgen schwimmen	*We are going swimming tomorrow*
Sie gehen früh schlafen	*They go to bed early*

iv Certain other verbs, including **hören, sehen, lehren, lernen**:

Sie hörte/sah ihn hereinkommen	*She heard/saw him come in*
Er lehrt die Kinder lesen	*He is teaching the children to read*
Ich lerne Gitarre spielen	*I am learning to play the guitar*

6 Verbs followed by prepositions *(see also sections 14.3–5)*

A large number of verbs in German are followed by a particular preposition:

an	denken an (+ accusative)	*to think of*
	erinnern an (+ accusative)	*to remind of*
sich	erinnern an (+ accusative)	*to remember*
	erkennen an (+ dative)	*to recognise by*
sich	gewöhnen an (+ accusative)	*to get used to*
	glauben an (+ accusative)	*to believe in*
	leiden an (+ dative)	*to suffer from*
	schicken an (+ accusative)	*to send to*
	schreiben an (+ accusative)	*to write to*
	sterben an (+ dative)	*to die of*
	teilnehmen an (+ dative)	*to take part in*
auf	achten auf (+ accusative)	*to pay attention to*
	aufpassen auf (+ accusative)	*to look after, keep an eye on*
	bestehen auf (+ dative)	*to insist on*
sich	freuen auf (+ accusative)	*to look forward to*
	hoffen auf (+ accusative)	*to hope for*
	reagieren auf (+ accusative)	*to react to*
sich	verlassen auf (+ accusative)	*to rely on*
	warten auf (+ accusative)	*to wait for*
aus	bestehen aus (+ dative)	*to consist of*
	machen aus (+ dative)	*to make from*
	werden aus (+ dative)	*to become of*
für	halten für (+ accusative)	*to regard as, consider*
sich	interessieren für (+ accusative)	*to be interested in*
	sorgen für (+ accusative)	*to look after, see to*
mit	sprechen mit (+ dative)	*to speak to*
	telefonieren mit (+ dative)	*to telephone (somebody)*
nach	fragen nach (+ dative)	*to ask about*
	riechen nach (+ dative)	*to smell of*

	schmecken nach (+ dative)	*to taste of*
sich	sehnen nach (+ dative)	*to long for*
	urteilen nach (+ dative)	*to judge by*
um	bitten um (+ accusative)	*to ask for*
	kämpfen um (+ accusative)	*to fight for*
sich	kümmern um (+ accusative)	*to take care of, look after*
	spielen um (+ accusative)	*to play for (money, etc.)*
von	abhängen von (+ dative)	*to depend on*
	sprechen von (+ dative)	*to talk about*
	träumen von (+ dative)	*to dream of*
vor	Angst haben vor (+ dative)	*to be afraid of*
sich	fürchten vor (+ dative)	*to be afraid of*
	retten vor (+ dative)	*to rescue from*
	schützen vor (+ dative)	*to protect from*
	warnen vor (+ dative)	*to warn of*
	zittern vor (+ dative)	*to tremble with*
zu	gratulieren zu (+ dative)	*to congratulate on*

7 Prepositions *(see also sections 5.3–4 and 6.1–5)*

a Prepositions with the accusative

bis* (expressing time) *until*; (expressing place) *as far as*

durch (expressing place) *through*; (expressing time) *throughout*; (expressing means) *through, by means of, by*

für (with person or time) *for*

gegen (expressing opposition or place) *against*

ohne *without*

um (expressing place) *around, round*; (with time) *at; around*

b Prepositions with the dative

aus (expressing place, motive) *from, out of*; (expressing material) *made of*

außer *apart from, except*

bei (expressing place) *near; at the house of*; (with occasion) *at*

gegenüber *opposite*

mit *with*; (with means of transport) *by*

nach (expressing place) *to*; (expressing time) *after*

seit *since*; (with period) *for*

von (with time, place) *from*; (instead of genitive) *of*; (with cause, creator) *by*

zu (with place, person) *to*; (with time) *at*; (expressing purpose) *for*

---

*Note that **bis** by itself is never followed by the definite article; **bis zu** is used where this is necessary: Bis zum nächsten Mal! *Until (the) next time!*

c Prepositions with the accusative or the dative

These prepositions can all express either POSITION (when they are followed by the DATIVE) or MOVEMENT (when they are followed by the ACCUSATIVE):

an + dative (with place) *at, on*; (with day) *on*; + accusative *to, on*

auf + dative *on*; + accusative *on, onto*

entlang* + dative (rare) or accusative *along*

hinter + dative or accusative *behind*

in + dative *in*; + accusative *in, into*; *to*

neben + dative or accusative *next to, beside*

über + dative *over, above*; + accusative *over, across*; (writing, talking) *about*

unter + dative or accusative *under, below*; *among*

vor + dative (with place) *in front of*; (with time) *before*; + accusative *in front of*

zwischen + dative or accusative *between*

d Prepositions with the genitive

anstatt, statt	*instead of*	**außerhalb**	*outside*
innerhalb	*inside*	**oberhalb**	*above*
trotz	*instead of*	**unterhalb**	*below*
während	*during*	**wegen**	*because of*

8 Conjunctions and other linking words

a Co-ordinating conjunctions

The most common are:

und	*and*	**oder**	*or*
aber	*but*	**sondern**	*but (after a negative)*
denn	*as, for*		

See also sections 14.1–2

b Subordinating conjunctions

Most conjunctions in German are subordinating conjunctions and send their verb to the end of the clause:

als	*when; than*	**als ob**	*as though*
bevor	*before*	**bis**	*until*
da	*as, since*	**damit**	*so that*
daß	*that*	**ehe**	*before*
falls	*if, in case*	**indem**	*while, as*

---

*Note that **entlang** is usually after the noun with the accusative, and before the noun with the dative.

nachdem	after	ob	whether, if
obgleich, obwohl	although	seit, seitdem	since
sobald	as soon as	so daß	so that
solange	as long as	während	while
weil	because	wenn	when, if

*See also sections 15.4–6 and 16.1–4, and 17.3–4 for **when***

c Question words

After **fragen** *(to ask)*, **wissen** *(to know)*, etc., many question words behave in the same way as conjunctions in the middle of a sentence and send the verb to the end. They include:

wann	*when*	warum	*why*	was	*what*
wer	*who*	wie	*how*	wo	*where*

A question word or conjunction can also be formed by placing **wo(r)-** in front of the preposition (see section 16.4).

9 Cases

A 'case' in German is the form which shows how certain words (nouns or pronouns) function within a sentence. It is usually indicated by the ending of an article or adjective coming before it. There are four cases:

a NOMINATIVE

The basic form, used for the subject of a sentence. The subject is the person or thing responsible for the action or happening or situation described by the verb. To find it look for the verb and ask 'Who or what before the verb?'

b ACCUSATIVE

The form used for the direct object in a sentence, and after certain prepositions. The direct object is the person or thing that receives the action of the verb. To find the direct object ask 'Whom or what after the verb?'

c GENITIVE

The form used to show possession, and after certain prepositions. It shows that one noun or pronoun belongs to or is part of another.

d DATIVE

The form used to show the indirect object in a sentence, and after certain prepositions. To find the indirect object ask 'For or to whom or what after the verb?'

10 Articles

a Definite article (= *the*)

	MASCULINE	FEMININE	NEUTER	PLURAL
NOMINATIVE	der	die	das	die
ACCUSATIVE	den	die	das	die
GENITIVE	des	der	des	der
DATIVE	dem	der	dem	den

b Indefinite article (= *a*)

	MASCULINE	FEMININE	NEUTER
NOMINATIVE	ein	eine	ein
ACCUSATIVE	einen	eine	ein
GENITIVE	eines	einer	eines
DATIVE	einem	einer	einem

c *Kein* (*no, not a*) and the possessive adjectives *mein, dein, sein, ihr, unser* have the same endings as *ein* and also of course a plural

	MASCULINE	FEMININE	NEUTER	PLURAL
NOMINATIVE	kein/ihr	keine/ihre	kein/ihr	keine/ihre
ACCUSATIVE	keinen/ihren	keine/ihre	kein/ihr	keine/ihre
GENITIVE	keines/ihres	keiner/ihrer	keines/ihres	keiner/ihrer
DATIVE	keinem/ihrem	keiner/ihrer	keinem/ihrem	keinen/ihren

d *Dieser** (*this*) has similar endings to *der*

	MASCULINE	FEMININE	NEUTER	PLURAL
NOMINATIVE	dieser	diese	dieses	diese
ACCUSATIVE	diesen	diese	dieses	diese
GENITIVE	dieses	dieser	dieses	dieser
DATIVE	diesem	dieser	diesem	diesen

---

*Note that **jeder** (*every*) and **welcher** (*which*) have exactly the same endings as **dieser**.

Help Yourself to Essential German Grammar

11 Adjective endings

The endings on the adjective before a noun depend on case and gender, and of course whether the noun is singular or plural. But the gender makes no difference in the plural – the adjective endings are the same for all genders.

a First here are the NOMINATIVE and ACCUSATIVE

i after the definite article, also **dieser**, **jeder** and **welcher**:

	NOMINATIVE	ACCUSATIVE
MASCULINE	der schwarze Kaffee	den schwarzen Kaffee
FEMININE	die klassische Musik	die klassische Musik
NEUTER	das milde Wetter	das milde Wetter
PLURAL	die langen Haare	die langen Haare

ii after the indefinite article, and **kein** and the possessive adjectives:

	NOMINATIVE	ACCUSATIVE
MASCULINE	ein schwarzer Kaffee	einen schwarzen Kaffee
FEMININE	eine klassische Musik	eine klassische Musik
NEUTER	ein mildes Wetter	ein mildes Wetter
PLURAL	keine langen Haare	keine langen Haare

iii if there is no article:

	NOMINATIVE	ACCUSATIVE
MASCULINE	schwarzer Kaffee	schwarzen Kaffee
FEMININE	klassische Musik	klassische Musik
NEUTER	mildes Wetter	mildes Wetter
PLURAL	lange Haare	lange Haare

Note that the accusative is only different from the nominative in the masculine singular, with its characteristic **-en** ending.

b Here are the GENITIVE and DATIVE endings

i after the definite article, **dieser**, **welcher** and **jeder**:

	GENITIVE	DATIVE
MASCULINE	des schwarzen Kaffees	dem schwarzen Kaffee
FEMININE	der klassischen Musik	der klassischen Musik
NEUTER	des milden Wetters	dem milden Wetter
PLURAL	der langen Haare	den langen Haaren

ii after the indefinite article and **kein** and the possessive adjectives:

	GENITIVE	DATIVE
MASCULINE	eines schwarz**en** Kaffee**s**	einem schwarz**en** Kaffee
FEMININE	einer klassisch**en** Musik	einer klassisch**en** Musik
NEUTER	eines mild**en** Wetter**s**	einem mild**en** Wetter
PLURAL	meiner lang**en** Haare	meinen lang**en** Haar**en**

iii if there is no article:

	GENITIVE	DATIVE
MASCULINE	schwarz**en** Kaffee**s**	schwarz**em** Kaffee
FEMININE	klassisch**er** Musik	klassisch**er** Musik
NEUTER	mild**en** Wetter**s**	mild**em** Wetter
PLURAL	lang**er** Haare	lang**en** Haar**en**

See also sections 7.1–5 and 9.6

12 Noun changes

German nouns sometimes have endings in the singular, while the plural forms vary depending on gender and type. It is always best to learn the plural of a noun along with its gender, although there are certain rules:

a SINGULAR

Masculine and neuter nouns add **-s** in the genitive, and sometimes **-es** if the noun is short (one syllable):

> der Vater   → des Vater**s**
> der Hund   → des Hund**(e)s**
> das Paket   → des Paket**s**

Otherwise the only changes in the singular are to masculine weak nouns (e.g. **Student**, **Präsident**, **Graf**) which add **-en** in all cases apart from the nominative singular, or just **-n** in some cases (e.g. **Herr**) (see section 27.2). But note:

> der Name   → des Namen**s**

b PLURAL

The typical German noun plurals add **-e** if the noun ends in a consonant, but there are many exceptions so this should not be taken as a rule:

> der Hund   → die Hund**e**   das Schiff   → die Schiff**e**

Feminine nouns with one syllable add an umlaut as well, and so do some masculine ones:

> die Hand   → die H**ä**nd**e**   der Sohn   → die S**ö**hn**e**

Some common neuter nouns with one syllable add an Umlaut and **-er**:

das Haus	→ die Häus**er**	das Dorf	→ die Dörf**er**

However, it is safe enough to say that nouns ending in **-e** always add **-n**:

die Blume	→ die Blume**n**	der Name	→ die Name**n**

and that words ending in **-en** do not change:

das Mädchen	→ die Mädchen	der Wagen	→ die Wagen

Masculine nouns ending in **-er** do not usually change, but there are important exceptions (with relations):

der Berliner	→ die Berliner	der Lehrer	→ die Lehrer

BUT

der Vater	→ die Väter	der Bruder	→ die Brüder

13 Personal pronouns

These also have different forms for the different cases:

	NOMINATIVE	ACCUSATIVE	DATIVE
SINGULAR	ich *(I)*	mich *(me)*	mir *(to me)*
	du *(you)*	dich *(you)*	dir *(to you)*
	er *(he)*	ihn *(him)*	ihm *(to him)*
	sie *(she)*	sie *(her)*	ihr *(to her)*
	es *(it)*	es *(it)*	ihm *(to it)*
	man *(one)*	einen *(one)*	einem *(to one)*
PLURAL	wir *(we)*	uns *(us)*	uns *(to us)*
	ihr *(you pl.)*	euch *(you)*	euch *(to you)*
	sie *(they)*	sie *(them)*	ihnen *(to them)*
	Sie *(you formal)*	Sie *(you)*	Ihnen *(to you)*

The genitive forms of the personal pronouns are rare and not shown. The accusative forms listed are also used with reflexive verbs, with the exception of all those for the third person (**ihn**, **sie**, **es**, **einen**, **sie**) where **sich** is used in all cases. This also applies to cases where the action is done to the subject, which may be several people doing something to one another:

Sie hat sich geschnitten	*She cut herself*
Sie haben sich in der Schule kennengelernt	*They got to know one another at school*

See also section 3.3

14 Numbers

a Numbers 0–900

0	null	40	vierzig	80	achtzig
1	ein(s)*	41	einundvierzig	81	einundachtzig
2	zwei	42	zweiundvierzig	82	zweiundachtzig
3	drei	43	dreiundvierzig	83	dreiundachtzig
4	vier	44	vierundvierzig	84	vierundachtzig
5	fünf	45	fünfundvierzig	85	fünfundachtzig
6	sechs	46	sechsundvierzig	86	sechsundachtzig
7	sieben	47	siebenundvierzig	87	siebenundachtzig
8	acht	48	achtundvierzig	88	achtundachtzig
9	neun	49	neunundvierzig	89	neunundachtzig
10	zehn	50	fünfzig	90	neunzig
11	elf	51	einundfünfzig	91	einundneunzig
12	zwölf	52	zweiundfünfzig	92	zweiundneunzig
13	dreizehn	53	dreiundfünfzig	93	dreiundneunzig
14	vierzehn	54	vierundfünfzig	94	vierundneunzig
15	fünfzehn	55	fünfundfünfzig	95	fünfundneunzig
16	sechzehn	56	sechsundfünfzig	96	sechsundneunzig
17	siebzehn	57	siebenundfünfzig	97	siebenundneunzig
18	achtzehn	58	achtundfünfzig	98	achtundneunzig
19	neunzehn	59	neunundfünfzig	99	neunundneunzig
20	zwanzig	60	sechzig	100	(ein)hundert
21	einundzwanzig	61	einundsechzig		
22	zweiundzwanzig	62	zweiundsechzig	101	(ein)hundert(und)eins*
23	dreiundzwanzig	63	dreiundsechzig	110	(ein)hundertzehn
24	vierundzwanzig	64	vierundsechzig	200	zweihundert
25	fünfundzwanzig	65	fünfundsechzig	201	zweihundert(und)eins*
26	sechsundzwanzig	66	sechsundsechzig	251	zweihunderteinundfünfzig
27	siebenundzwanzig	67	siebenundsechzig	300	dreihundert
28	achtundzwanzig	68	achtundsechzig	333	dreihundertdreiunddreißig
29	neunundzwanzig	69	neunundsechzig		
30	dreißig	70	siebzig	400	vierhundert
31	einunddreißig	71	einundsiebzig	500	fünfhundert
32	zweiunddreißig	72	zweiundsiebzig	600	sechshundert
33	dreiunddreißig	73	dreiundsiebzig	700	siebenhundert
34	vierunddreißig	74	vierundsiebzig	800	achthundert
35	fünfunddreißig	75	fünfundsiebzig	900	neunhundert
36	sechsunddreißig	76	sechsundsiebzig		
37	siebenunddreißig	77	siebenundsiebzig		
38	achtunddreißig	78	achtundsiebzig		
39	neununddreißig	79	neunundsiebzig		

*You usually only say **eins** when you are counting, calculating, giving the time or the score, or quoting decimals. However, with larger numbers the form with **eins** is also used before a noun. The bracketed **ein** is for emphasis, and the bracketed **und** is often used in numbers from 101 to 109, 201 to 209, etc.

Help Yourself to Essential German Grammar

b Numbers 1,000–1,000,000,000

1 000	(ein)tausend	10 000	zehntausend
1 001	(ein)tausend(und)eins	20 000	zwanzigtausend
1 050	(ein)tausend(und)fünfzig	30 000	dreißigtausend
1 200	(ein)tausendzweihundert	40 000	vierzigtausend
1 250	(ein)tausendzweihundert(und)fünfzig	50 000	fünfzigtausend
1 500	(ein)tausendfünfhundert *or*	60 000	sechzigtausend
	fünfzehnhundert	70 000	siebzigtausend
1 980	(ein)tausendneunhundert(und)achtzig	80 000	achtzigtausend
2 000	zweitausend	90 000	neunzigtausend
2 001	zweitausend(und)eins	100 000	(ein)hunderttausend
2 010	zweitausendzehn	500 000	fünfhunderttausend
9 000	neuntausend	1 000 000	eine Million
		2 000 000	zwei Millionen
		2 500 000	zwei Millionen fünfhunderttausend
		1 000 000 000	eine Milliarde

c Written numbers

All German numbers, when written out, are in one word until you get to **eine Million**, which is a noun and therefore separate. It also has to be used in the plural for 2 000 000 upwards.

d Numbers over a thousand

Numbers over a thousand in figures do not have commas, but spaces in continental usage:

2,560 → 2 560   256,845 → 256 845   3,560,000 → 3 560 000

However, a comma is used to indicate the decimal point:

19·75 → 19,75   250·965 → 250,965

e Years (up to 2000)

When written out or spoken always include the **hundert**:

1901	neunzehnhundert(und)eins
1985	neunzehnhundertfünfundachtzig
2000	zweitausend
2001	zweitausend(und)eins
2005	zweitausend(und)fünf
2010	zweitausendzehn

To give the year when something happened, either add **im Jahre** or nothing at all:

Sie wurde **im Jahre 1980** geboren *or* Sie wurde **1980** geboren
She was born in 1980

15 Telling the time

a Telling the time

Wie spät ist es? Wie viel Uhr ist es?	*What time is it?*
Es ist fünf Uhr	*It's five o'clock*
Es ist kurz nach zehn	*It's just after ten*
Es ist sechs Uhr vorbei	*It's gone six*

To express minutes *past* and *to* the hour use **nach** and **vor.** You can include **Minuten,** or in colloquial speech leave it out:

Es ist fünf (Minuten) nach drei	*It's five (minutes) past three*
Es ist zwanzig (Minuten) vor eins	*It's twenty (minutes) to one*

To express *a quarter past* and *a quarter to* use **Viertel nach** and **Viertel vor.** But note that **halb,** the equivalent of *half past,* is thought of as being halfway to the next hour instead of after the one before:

Es ist Viertel nach sechs	*It's a quarter past six*
Es ist Viertel vor sieben	*It's a quarter to seven*
Es ist halb **acht**	*It's half past **seven***

To say what time of day you mean, add **morgens, nachmittags, abends** or **nachts**:

Es ist sieben Uhr **morgens**	*It is seven o'clock in the morning*
Ich arbeite bis sechs Uhr **abends**	*I work until six in the evening*

To express *at* use **um,** which cannot be omitted in a reply:

Er kommt um acht Uhr	*He is coming at eight o'clock*
Ich fahre um halb sechs	*I'm going at half past five*
Wann fährt dein Zug? Um neun	*When does your train leave? At nine*

b The 24-hour clock

Unlike English, German uses the 24-hour clock very widely, and it is always used for quoting times in print or on notices, as well as on radio and television. In using it, the word **Uhr,** which is followed by the number of minutes, is never omitted. **Nach** and **vor** cannot be used, nor can **Viertel** or **halb.**

Even up to midday there is a difference. If one says for instance:

zehn Uhr dreißig (*written* 10.30 Uhr)	*instead of*	halb elf
zehn Uhr fünfundvierzig (*written* 10.45 Uhr)	*instead of*	Viertel vor elf

this is the more formal style of the 24-hour clock, and the morning is meant.

Here are the hours of the day according to the 24-hour clock and their equivalents in terms of the 12-hour clock:

1.00 Uhr	ein Uhr	ein Uhr (morgens)	*1 a.m.*
2.00 Uhr	zwei Uhr	zwei Uhr (morgens)	*2 a.m.*
3.00 Uhr	drei Uhr	drei Uhr (morgens)	*3 a.m.*
4.00 Uhr	vier Uhr	vier Uhr (morgens)	*4 a.m.*
5.00 Uhr	fünf Uhr	fünf Uhr (morgens)	*5 a.m.*
6.00 Uhr	sechs Uhr	sechs Uhr (morgens)	*6 a.m.*
7.00 Uhr	sieben Uhr	sieben Uhr (morgens)	*7 a.m.*
8.00 Uhr	acht Uhr	acht Uhr (morgens)	*8 a.m.*
9.00 Uhr	neun Uhr	neun Uhr (morgens)	*9 a.m.*
10.00 Uhr	zehn Uhr	zehn Uhr (vormittags)	*10 a.m.*
11.00 Uhr	elf Uhr	elf Uhr (vormittags)	*11 a.m.*
12.00 Uhr	zwölf Uhr	zwölf Uhr (mittags), Mittag	*12 p.m*
13.00 Uhr	dreizehn Uhr	ein Uhr (nachmittags)	*1 p.m.*
14.00 Uhr	vierzehn Uhr	zwei Uhr (nachmittags)	*2 p.m.*
15.00 Uhr	fünfzehn Uhr	drei Uhr (nachmittags)	*3 p.m.*
16.00 Uhr	sechzehn Uhr	vier Uhr (nachmittags)	*4 p.m.*
17.00 Uhr	siebzehn Uhr	fünf Uhr (nachmittags)	*5 p.m.*
18.00 Uhr	achtzehn Uhr	sechs Uhr (abends)	*6 p.m.*
19.00 Uhr	neunzehn Uhr	sieben Uhr (abends)	*7 p.m.*
20.00 Uhr	zwanzig Uhr	acht Uhr (abends)	*8 p.m.*
21.00 Uhr	einundzwanzig Uhr	neun Uhr (abends)	*9 p.m.*
22.00 Uhr	zweiundzwanzig Uhr	zehn Uhr (abends)	*10 p.m.*
23.00 Uhr	dreiundzwanzig Uhr	elf Uhr (abends)	*11 p.m.*
24.00 Uhr	vierundzwanzig Uhr	zwölf Uhr (nachts)	*12 a.m.*
00.00 Uhr*	null Uhr*	Mitternacht	

Other examples:

8.15 Uhr	acht Uhr fünfzehn	Viertel nach acht (morgens)	*8.15 a.m.*
13.30 Uhr	dreizehn Uhr dreißig	halb zwei (nachmittags)	*1.30 p.m.*
20.45 Uhr	zwanzig Uhr fünfundvierzig	Viertel vor neun (abends)	*8.45 p.m.*

---

*24.00 Uhr indicates the end of the day, 00.00 Uhr the beginning. So times between midnight and 1 a.m. are for instance:

00.22 Uhr	null Uhr zweiundzwanzig	zweiundzwanzig (Minuten) nach zwölf	*12.22 a.m.*

16 Letter writing

a At the top of the letter, you just put the name of the place and the date

Birmingham, den 20. Mai 1998

Your address should go on the back of the envelope with **Abs.** in front of it (which is short for **Absender**).

b To someone you are on first name terms with, you start

Liebe Maria,	*Dear Maria,*	Lieber Peter,	*Dear Peter,*
(or more breezily)			
Hallo Maria!	*Hi Maria!*	Hallo Peter!	*Hi Peter!*

To someone you are not on first name terms with, in a personal letter, you start:

Liebe Frau Maier,	*Dear Frau Maier,*
Lieber Herr Braun,	*Dear Herr Braun,*

If it is a formal business letter, you start either:

Sehr geehrter Herr Roth!	*Dear Herr Roth,*
Sehr geehrte Frau Seitz!	*Dear Frau Seitz,*

or if it is to an organisation, not to a particular person:

Sehr geehrte Damen und Herren!	*Dear Sirs,*

c The usual endings for a letter to a friend are

Herzliche Grüße/Mit herzlichen Grüßen   *Yours/With best wishes*

or more affectionately:

Alles Liebe   *All my/our love*

The standard ending for all more formal letters is:

Mit freundlichen Grüßen   *Yours sincerely*

German–English glossary

A

ab (1 adv) off, away

ab (2 prep + dat) from

Abend (m -s, -e) evening

Abendessen (n -s, -) dinner, supper

abends (adv) in the evening

aber (conj) but, however

abfahren (sep, irreg *) to leave, depart

abfliegen (sep, irreg *) to take off, fly off

Abitur (n -s) A levels = school leaving exam

abschließen (sep, irreg) to lock, conclude

Abschluß (m -sses, -schlüsse) final examination

absolvieren (insep) to graduate, complete

Agent (m en, -en) agent

Ägypten (n -s) Egypt

ähnlich, etwas Ähnliches (adj) similar, something similar

Ahnung (f, -en) idea

Alarm (m -(e)s, -e) alarm

Alkohol (m -s, -e) alcohol

alle(r,s) (indef pron) all, everything, everyone

allein(e) (adj) alone

allerlei (adj does not decline) all sorts of

Alltag (m -(e)s, -e) weekday

Alptraum (m -(e)s, -träume) nightmare

als (conj) as, when

als (in comparison) than

also (conj) so, therefore

alt (adj) old

älter (adj comp of alt) older

älteste(r,s) (adj superl of alt) oldest, eldest

Altersheim (n -(e)s, -e) old people's home

altmodisch (adj) oldfashioned

Amerika (n -s) America

Ampel (f, -n) traffic lights

amusieren to amuse

an (prep + acc/dat) at, on, against, to

andere(r,s) (indef pron) different, other

Anfang (m -(e)s, Anfänge) beginning, start

anfangen (sep, irreg) to begin, start

angehen (sep, irreg *) to tackle

Angestellte(r) (mf decl as adj) salaried employee

Angst haben to be afraid, scared

ankommen (sep, irreg *) to arrive

Anlage (f, -n) system, equipment

Anruf (m -(e)s, -e) call

anrufen (sep, irreg) to phone, call

anschalten (sep) to switch on

Ansichtskarte (f, -n) postcard

anstatt (prep + gen) instead of

anstatt (conj) instead of

Antwort (f, -en) answer, reply

anwerben (sep, irreg) to recruit

anziehen (sep, irreg, refl) to put on, dress

Anzug (m -(e)s, Anzüge) suit

Apfel (m -s, Äpfel) apple

Apotheke (f, -n) dispensing chemist

April (m -s, -) April

Arbeit (f, -en) work

arbeiten to work

Arbeiter (m -s, -) worker

Arbeiterin (f, Arbeiterinnen) female worker

Arbeitsbedingungen (pl) working conditions

Arbeitsplatz (m -es, -plätze) place of work

Arbeitsstunde (f, -n) work hour

Argentinien (n -s) Argentina

Art (f, -en) kind, sort, type

Arzt (m -es, Ärzte) medical doctor

Ärztin (f, -nen) female medical doctor

Athlet (m -en, -) athlete
Athletin (f, -nen) female
  athlete
Atmosphäre (f, -n) atmosphere
Attentat (n -(e)s, -e)
  assassination, assassination
  attempt
auch (adv) also, too, as well
auf (prep + acc/dat) on, upon,
  onto
aufdrücken (sep) to push open
Aufenthalt (m -(e)s, -e) stay
aufhängen (sep) to hang up
aufhören (sep) to stop
aufheben (sep, irreg) to lift up,
  pick up
aufmachen (sep) to open
aufpassen (sep) to look, watch
  out
aufregend (adj) exciting
Aufsatz (m -es, -sätze) essay
aufstehen (sep, irreg *) to get
  up, stand up
aufwachen (sep) to wake up
Aufzug (m -(e)s, -züge) lift
Auge (n -s, -n) eye
August (m -(e)s, -e) August
aus (prep + dat) out of, from
Ausblick (m -(e)s, -e) view,
  outlook
Ausflug (m -(e)s, -flüge)
  excursion, trip, outing
ausgebucht (adj) booked up,
  fully booked
Ausland (n -(e)s, -) abroad,
  foreign countries
ausruhen (sep, irreg) to relax
ausschalten (sep) to switch off,
  turn off
aussehen (sep, irreg *) to look,
  appear
außerhalb (prep + gen) outside
Aussicht (f, -en) view,
  prospect
Aussiedler (m) emigrant
aussteigen (sep, irreg *) to get
  out, get off
Ausstellung (f, -en) exhibition
ausziehen (sep, irreg, refl) to
  undress, take off
Auto (n -s, -s) car
Autobahn (f, -en) motorway
Automat (m -en, -en) machine

automatisch (adj) automatic
Autoreisezug (m -(e)s, -züge)
  Motorail
Autowerkstatt (f, -stätten)
  garage, car repair shop

B

Baby (n -s, -s) baby
Bäcker (m -s, -) baker
Bäckerin (f, -nen) female baker
Bäckerei (f, -en) bakery,
  baker's shop
Bad (n -(e)s, Bäder) bath
Badewanne (f, -n) bath(tub)
Badezimmer (n -s, -) bathroom
Bahnhof (m -(e)s, -höfe)
  railway station
Bahnübergang (m -(e)s, -gänge)
  railway crossing
bald (adv) soon
Balkon (m -s, -s or -e) balcony
Ball (m -(e)s, Bälle) ball
Banane (f, -n) banana
Bank (f, -en) bank
bankrott (adj) bankrupt
Basketball (m -s, -) basketball
basteln to make things with
  one's hands
Bauch (m -(e)s, Bäuche)
  stomach, belly
Bauernhof (m -(e)s, -höfe) farm
Baum (m -(e)s, Bäume) tree
beängstigend (adj) frightening,
  alarming
bedeuten to mean
Bedürfnis (n -ses, -se) need
beginnen to begin, start
behaupten to claim
bei (prep + dat) near, at, with,
  in
beide (pron) both
Bekannte(r) (mf decl as adj)
  friend, acquaintance
bekommen (irreg) to receive,
  get
Belgien (n -s) Belgium
benutzen to use
beobachten to notice, see
bequem (adj) comfortable
beraten (irreg) to advise, give
  advice

Berg (m -(e)s, -e) mountain
Bericht (m -(e)s, -e) report, account
Beruf (m -(e)s, -e) occupation, profession
berühmt (adj) famous
beschließen (irreg) to decide
beschreiben (irreg) to describe
besichtigen to visit, tour, have a look at
Besitz (m -es, -) possession, property
besondere(r,s) (adj) special, particular
besprechen (irreg) to discuss, talk about
besser (adj, adv comp of gut) better
beste(r,s) (adj superl of gut) best
Besteck (n -(e)s, -e) cutlery
bestehen (irreg) to pass, consist of
bestellen to order (in restaurant, etc.)
bestimmt (adj) certain
Besuch (m -(e)s, -e) visit
besuchen to visit
Betätigung (f, -en) activity
Bevölkerung (f, -en) population
bevor (conj) before
bezaubernd (adj) charming, enchanting
Bibliothek (f, -en) library
Bier (n -(e)s, -e) beer
Bild (n -(e)s, -er) picture
billig (adj) cheap
bis (prep + acc, adv) until, till
bitte (interj) please
bitten (um + acc) to ask sb for sth
blöd (adj informal) silly, stupid
blau (adj) blue
bleiben (*) to stay
Bleistift (m -(e)s, -e) pencil
blitzen, es blitzt (impersonal) there is lightening
blond (adj) fair-haired
Blume (f, -n) flower
Bohne (f, -n) bean
Boot (n -(e)s, -e) boat
brauchen to need
braun (adj) brown

Brief (m -(e)s, -e) letter
Brieffreund (m -(e)s, -e) penfriend
Brieffreundin (f, -nen)
Briefkasten (m -s, -kästen) letter box
Briefmarke (f, -n) stamp
Brieftasche (f, -n) wallet
bringen to bring
Brot (n -(e)s, -e) bread
Brötchen (n -s, -) roll
Bruder (m -s, Brüder) brother
Buch (n -(e)s, Bücher) book
buchen to book, reserve
Bücherei (f, -en) library
Bücherregal (n -s, -e) bookshelf
Bundeskanzler (m) German chancellor
Bundesrepublik (f) federal republic
Bundestag (m) German parliament (lower house)
Büro (n -s, -) office
Bus (m -ses, -se) bus
Busch (m -(e)s, Büsche) bush, shrub
Butterbrot (n -(e)s, -e) sandwich

C

Café (n -s, -s) café
Campingplatz (m -(e)s, -plätze) campsite
Chef (m -s, -s) boss, head
Cola (f, -s) coca cola
Computer (m -s, -) computer

D

da (adv) there, here
dafür (adv) for that/it
damals (adv) then, at that time
Dame (f, -n) woman, lady
damit (adv) with that/it
danach (adv) after that/it
Dank (m -(e)s, -) thanks
danken (+ dat) to thank
dann (adv) then
darin (adv) in there, in it/them
daß (conj) that

dasselbe (dem pron see derselbe)
the same
dauern to last
davon (adv) from there/it
DDR (f abbr Deutsche
Demokratische Republik)
East Germany
dein (poss adj) your
denken to think
denn (conj) because
denn (adv) then
derselbe (dem pron) the same
deshalb (adv, conj) therefore
Detektiv (m -s, -e) detective
deutlich (adj) clear
deutsch (adj) German
Deutschland (n -s, -) Germany
Dezember (m -s, -) December
Diät (f, -en) diet
dich (per pron acc of du) you
dicht (adj) thick, dense
dick (adj) fat, thick (colloq ein
dickes Auto = a big car)
Dieb (m -(e)s, -e) thief
Dienstag (m -(e)s, -e) Tuesday
Dienstmädchen (n -s, -) maid
dieselbe (dem pron see derselbe)
the same
Dieselöl (n -(e)s, -e) diesel oil
dieser, diese, dies(es) (dem pron
pl diese) this, that, these
direkt (adj, adv) direct, directly
Direktor (m -s, -en) principal,
headteacher
Disko/Disco (f, -s) disco
Diskussion (f, -en) discussion
diskutieren to discuss
DM (f abbr Deutsche Mark)
German Mark (currency)
doch (conj) anyway, really;
after neg. yes I do, etc.
Dom (m -(e)s, -e) cathedral
donnern, es donnert (impersonal)
there is thunder
Donnerstag (m -(e)s, -e)
Thursday
dort (adv) there
dorthin (adv) there, to there
Dose (f, -n) can, tin
drüben, da drüben (adv) over
there
drücken to push, press
draußen (adv) outside

drogensüchtig (adj) addicted to
drugs
du (per pron nom) you
durch (prep + acc) through, by
means of
dürfen (modal) to be allowed,
permitted
Dusche (f, -n) shower

E

echt (adj, adv) real, really
Ecke (f, -n) corner
Effekt (m -(e)s, -e) effect
ehemalig (adj) former
eigen (adj) own
eigenartig (adj) peculiar, strange
ein, eine, ein (indef article)
one, a
einfach (adj, adv) simple,
simply
Eingang (m -(e)s, -gänge)
entrance
einige(r,s) (indef pron) some
einkaufen to shop
Einkaufszentrum (n -s, -zentren)
shopping centre
einladen (sep, irreg) to invite
Einladung (f, -en) invitation
einmalig (adj) unique
einpacken (sep) to pack, pack
up
einschalten (sep) to switch on
einstecken (sep) to put in
einsteigen (sep, irreg *) to get
on, in
eintippen (sep) to type in
einwickeln (sep) to wrap up, in
Einzelzimmer (n -s, -) single
room
einzig (adj) only, sole
Eishalle (f, -n) ice rink
eislaufen (sep, irreg *) to ice
skate
Elektroware (f, -n) electrical
good(s)
Eltern (pl) parents
Empfangsdame (f, -n)
receptionist
empfehlen to recommend
Ende (n -s, -n) end
endlich (adv) finally, at last

eng (adj)　narrow
englisch (adj)　English
Enkelkind (n -(e)s, -er)
　grandchild
enorm (adj)　enormous
entfernt (adj)　distant, (away)
　from
entlang (prep + acc)　along
entlassen (irreg)　to dismiss,
　make redundant
entscheiden (refl)　to decide
enttäuschen　to disappoint
Enttäuschung (f, -en)
　disappointment
entweder... oder (conj)
　either... or
er (pers pron)　he
Erbse (f, -en)　pea
Erdkunde (f, -)　geography
Erdnuß (f, Erdnüsse)　peanut
Erfahrung (f, -en)　experience
erhöhen　to raise, increase
erinnern sich an (+ dat)　to
　remember
Erinnerung an (+ acc) (f, -en)
　memory (of)
erkennen (irreg)　to recognise
ermordern　to murder
erschaffen　to create
erschießen (irreg)　to shoot
　dead
erschrecken　to frighten, scare
erschrocken (ptp, adj)
　frightened, scared
erst (adv)　first, only, until
Erwachsene(r) (mf decl as adj)
　adult
erwarten　to expect
erzählen　to tell, relate
es (pers pron)　it
Eßecke (f, -n)　dining corner
essen　to eat
Eßtisch (m -(e)s, -e)　dining
　table
Etikett (n -(e)s, -e, od -e)　label
etwa (adv)　about,
　approximately
etwas (indef pron)　something
euch (pers pron dat & acc of ihr)
　you
euer (poss adj)　your
Exkursion (f, -en)　study trip or
　tour

F

Fach (n -(e)s, Fächer)　subject
Fähre (f, -en)　ferry
Fahrer (m -s, -)　driver
Fahrkarte (f, -n)　ticket
Fahrrad (n -(e)s, Fahrräder)
　bicycle
Fahrt (f, -en)　journey
Fall, auf jeden Fall (m -(e)s,
　Fälle)　case, in any case
fallen (*)　to fall
falsch (adj)　wrong
Familie (f, -n)　family
Familienkreis (m -es, -e)
　family circle
fantastisch (adj)　fantastic
Farbe (f, -n)　colour
faul (adj)　lazy
Februar (m -(s), -e)　February
Federball (m -(e)s, Federbälle)
　badminton
Fehler (m -s, -)　mistake, error
feiern　to celebrate
Feiertag (m -(e)s, -e)　holiday
Fenster (n -s, -)　window
Ferien (pl)　holidays
fernsehen (sep, irreg)　to watch
　TV
Fernseher (m -s, -)　television
Fernsprecher (m -s, -)
　telephone, TV announcer
Festessen (n -s, -)　Christmas
　dinner, banquet
Film (m -(e)s, -e)　film
finanziell (adj)　financial
finden　to find
Finger (m -s, -)　finger
Firma (f, Firmen)　company,
　firm
Flasche (f, -n)　bottle
fleißig (adj)　hardworking
fliegen (*)　to fly
fliehen (*)　to flee
Fließband (n -(e)s, Fließbänder)
　conveyor-belt
Florenz (n)　Florence
Flüchtling (m -s, -e)　refugee
Flug (m -(e)s, Flüge)　flight
Flughafen (m -s, Flughäfen)
　airport
Flugschein (m -s, -e)　air ticket
Flugticket (n -s, -s)　air ticket

Flur (m -(e)s, -e)   corridor
folgen (* + dat)   to follow
Foto (n -s, -s)   photograph
Fotoapparat (m -(e)s, -e)   camera
Frage (f, -n)   question
fragen   to ask
Frankreich (n -s)   France
französisch (adj)   French
Frau (f, -en)   woman, wife
frei (adj)   free
Freibad (n -(e)s, Freibäder)
   (open air) swimming pool
Freitag (m -(e)s, -e)   Friday
Freizeit (f)   freetime, leisure
Fremdenverkehrsamt (n -(e)s,
   -ämter)   tourist information
   office
Fremdsprache (f, -n)   foreign
   language
freuen, sich freuen auf (+ acc)
   to look forward to
Freund (m -(e)s, -e)   (male)
   friend
Freundin (f, -nen)   (female)
   friend
freundlich (adj)   friendly
friedlich, sei friedlich (adj)
   peaceful, calm down
Friseursalon (m -s, -s)
   hairdresser (shop)
froh (adj)   happy
früh (adj/adv)   early
früher (comp of früh)   earlier
Frühstück, zum Frühstück (n -s,
   -e)   breakfast, for breakfast
frühstücken (insep)   to have
   breakfast
fühlen (refl)   to feel
Fundbüro (n -s, -s)   lost
   property office
funktionieren   to work, function
für (prep + acc)   for
furchtbar (adj)   terrible, awful
Fuß, zu Fuß (m -es, Füße)   foot,
   on foot

G

Gabel (f, -n)   fork
ganz (adj)   whole, entire
ganz (adv)   quite completely
gar (adv)   at all

Garten (m -s, Gärten)   garden
Gastarbeiter (m -s, -)   foreign
   worker
Gästebett (n -(e)s, -en)   guest
   bed, spare bed
geben, es gibt   to give, there
   is/are
Geburtstag (m -(e)s, -e)
   birthday
gefährlich (adj)   dangerous
gefallen (+ dat)   to please
Gegend (f, -en)   area
gegenüber (prep + dat)
   opposite
Gehalt (n -(e)s, Gehälter)
   salary
Geheimdienst (m -(e)s, -e)
   secret service
Geheimzahl (f, -en)   PIN
   number (bank)
gehen (*)   to go, walk
gehören (+ dat)   to belong to
gelb (adj)   yellow
Geld (n -(e)s, -er)   money
Geldautomat (m -en, -en)   cash
   dispenser
genau, genauso gut wie (adj/adv)
   exact, just as good as
genug (adj)   enough
Gepäck (n -(e)s, pl)   luggage
gerade (adj)   straight
gerade (adv)   just
Gerät (n -(e)s, -e)   appliance
Gericht (n -(e)s, -e)   dish, course
gern(e) (adv)   with pleasure,
   willingly
Gesamtschule (f, -n)
   comprehensive school
Geschäft (n -(e)s, -e)   shop,
   business
geschäftig (adj)   busy
geschehen (*)   to happen, occur
Geschenk (n -(e)s, -e)   present,
   gift
Geschichte (f, -n)   story, history
Geschirr (n -(e)s, -e)   crockery
Geschwister (pl)   brothers and
   sisters
Gesicht (n -(e)s, -er)   face
gesperrt (ptp, adj)   closed
gestern (adv)   yesterday
gestohlen (ptp, adj)   stolen
gestorben (ptp)   died

getan (ptp) did
gewaltsam (adj) violent
gewesen (ptp) been
gewinnen to win
Gewinner (m -s, -) winner
gewöhnlich (adj) usual
geworfen (ptp) thrown
gezogen (ptp) pulled
gib (imperative sing of geben)
  give
Gießkanne (f, -n) watering can
Glas (n -es, Gläser) glass
glauben to believe
gleich (adj) same, similar
Gleis (n -es, -e) platform, line,
  track
glücklich (adj) happy, lucky
glücklicherweise (adv) luckily,
  fortunately
Glühbirne (f, -n) light bulb
Goldmedaille (f, -n) gold medal
Grammatik (f, -) grammar
Griechenland (n) Greece
groß (adj) big
Großbritannien (n) Britain
Größe (f, -n) size
Großeltern (pl) grandparents
größer (adj comp of groß)
  bigger
größte(r,s) (adj superl of groß)
  biggest
Großvater (m -s, -väter)
  grandfather
grün (adj) green
Grundschule (f pl -n) primary
  school
Gruß (m -es, Grüße) greeting
grüßen to greet
gut (adj) good
Gymnasium (n -s, Gymnasien)
  grammar school

H

Haar (n -(e)s, -e) hair
haben to have, have got
Halle (f, -n) hall
Hallenbad (n -(e)s, -bäder)
  (indoor) swimming pool
Haltestelle (f, -n) stop (i.e.
  bus), stopping place
Hamburger (m -s, -)
  hamburger, burger

Hand (f, Hände) hand
Handschuh (m -(e)s, -e) glove
häßlich (adj) ugly
hätte (imperf subj of haben)
  had, would have
Haupt- main, principal
Hauptbahnhof (m -(e)s, -höfe)
  main station
Hauptstraße (f, -n) main road
Haus, zu Hause, nach Hause
  (n -es, Häuser) house, at
  home, (to) home
Hausaufgabe (f, -n) homework
Hausfrau (f, -en) housewife
Hausmeister (m -s, -) caretaker,
  janitor
Heimfahrt, gute Heimfahrt!
  (f, -en) journey home; have
  a good journey!
heiraten to marry
heißen to call, be called
helfen (+ dat) to help
hell (adj) light
Hemd (n -(e)s, -en) shirt
herein (adv) in
Herr (m -(e)n, -en) Mr, sir
herstellen (sep) to produce
herum (adv) round, around
herzlich (adj) warm, sincere
Herzog (m -s, Herzöge) duke
Heuhaufen (m -s, -) hayrick,
  haystack
heute (adv) today
heute abend (adv) this evening
heutzutage (adv) nowadays
Hexe (f, -n) witch
hier (adv) here
hierher (adv) here
Hilfe (f, -n) help
hinein (adv) in
hinlegen (sep) to put down
hinter (prep + acc/dat) behind
historisch (adj) historic
Hobby (n -s, -s) hobby
hoch (adj) high, tall
höchste(r,s) (superl of hoch)
  highest
Hochzeitstag (m -(e)s, -e)
  wedding anniversary
Hof (m -(e)s, -höfe) yard,
  courtyard
höher (comp of hoch) higher
holen to fetch

hören to hear
Hörer (m -s, -) telephone receiver
Hose (f, -n) trousers
Hotel (n -s, -s) hotel
Hürdenlauf (m -(e)s, -läufe) hurdles

I

ich (pers pron) I
identifizieren to identify
ihm (pers pron dat see er)
ihn (pers pron acc see er)
Ihnen, ihnen (pers pron dat see Sie, sie pl)
ihr (2nd pers pl pers pron; dat sing see sie; poss adj)
Ihr (poss adj sing & pl) your
im (contr of in dem)
immer, immer mehr (adv) always, more and more
in (prep + acc/dat) into, in
Information (f, -en) information
informieren to inform
innerhalb (prep + gen) within, inside
ins (contr of in das)
Insel (f, -n) island
Instruktion (f, -en) instruction
intelligent (adj) intelligent
interessant (adj) interesting
Interesse (n -s, -n) interest
interessieren sich für (+ acc) to be interested in
Interview (n -s, -s) interview
irgendwie (adv) somehow
Irland (n -s) Ireland, Eire
Italien (n) Italy

J

ja (adv) yes
Jacke (f, -n) jacket
Jahr (n -(e)s, -e) year
Januar (m -s, -e) January
japanisch (adj) Japanese
Jeanshose (f, -n) jeans
jede(r,s) (indef pron) each, every

jemand (indef pron) somebody, someone
jetzt (adv) now
Job (m -s, -s) job
Jugend (f, -) youth
Jugendherberge (f, -n) youth hostel
Juli (m -(s), -s) July
jung (adj) young
jünger (comp of jung) younger
Juni (m -(s), -s) June

K

Kabel (n -s, -) wire, flex
Kaffee (m -s, -s) coffee
Kaiser (m -s, -) emperor
kalt (adj) cold
kämmen to comb
Kämpfer (m -s, -) fighter, warrior
Kanal (m -s, Kanäle) canal, channel
Kantine (f, -n) canteen
Kanzler (m -s, -) Chancellor (Germany)
kaputt (adj) broken
Karriere (f, -n) career
Karte (f, -n) ticket, card
Kasse (f, -n) cash desk, till
Kassette (f, -n) cassette
Kasten (m -s, Kästen) box
Katze (f, -n) cat
kaufen to buy
Kaufhaus (n -(e)s, -häuser) department store
Kaufmann (m -(e)s, Kaufleute) businessman
kaum (adv) hardly, scarcely
kein(e) (indef pron) no, not a
Keks (m -es, -e) biscuit
Kellner (m -s, -) waiter
kicken to kick
Kilo (n -s, -(s)) kilo
Kind (n -(e)s, -er) child
Kindergarten (m -s, -gärten) nursery school
Kinderwagen (m -s, -) pushchair, pram
Kino (n -s, -s) cinema
Klasse (f, -n) class
Klassenfahrt (f, -en) school trip

Klassenlehrer (m -s, -) class teacher

Klassenlehrerin (f, -nen) (female) class teacher

klassisch (adj) classical

Kleiderschrank (m -(e)s, -schränke) wardrobe

Kleidung (f, -) clothes, clothing

klein (adj) little, small

klopfen to knock

Klub (m -s, -s) club

Kneipe (f, -n) pub

Kochen (n -s, -) cooking

Koffer (m -s, -) suitcase, bag

Kollege (m -n, -n) colleague

Kommode (f, -n) chest of drawers

Konferenz (f, -en) conference

König (m -s, -e) king

Königin (f, -nen) queen

können (modal) to be able to

Konsum- (m -s,) consumption

Konsument (m -en) consumer

konzentrieren (auf + acc) to concentrate (on)

Kopf (m -(e)s, Köpfe) head

Kopfhörer (m -s, -) headphone

Kopfschmerz (m usually plural Kopfschmerzen) headache

kosten to cost

krank (adj) sick, unwell

Krankenhaus (n -es, -häuser) hospital

Krankheit (f, -en) illness, sickness

kriegen to get

Krimi (m -s, -s) thriller, detective (novel), crime (film)

Kriminalität (f, -en) crime

Kroatien (n -s) Croatia

Küche (f, -n) kitchen

Kugel (f, -n) ball, bullet

Kugelschreiber (m -s, -) biro, ballpoint pen

Kunde (m -n, -n) customer

Kundin (f, -nen) (female) customer

kündigen to dismiss; (+ dat) give someone notice

Kündigung (f, -en) dismissal, notice to quit

L

lachen (über + acc) to laugh (about)

Laden (m -s, Läden) shop

Land; auf dem Lande (n -(e)s, Länder) land; in the country

Landkarte (f, -n) map

lang (adj) long

langsam (adj/adv) slow(ly)

langweilig (adj) boring

Lärm (m -(e)s, -) noise

lassen to leave

laufen (*) to run, go, (film) be playing

laut (adj) loud

Leben (n -s, -) life

Lebenslauf (m -(e)s, -läufe) curriculum vitae, CV

Lebensmittel (pl) food

Leder (n -s, -) leather

legen to put, place, lay down

Lehre (f, -n) training, apprenticeship

Lehrer (m -s, -) teacher

Lehrerin (f, -nen) (female) teacher

Lehrling (m -s, -e) trainee, apprentice

Lehrstelle (f, -n) position (as an apprentice)

Lehrzeit (f, -en) apprenticeship

Leiche (f, -n) corpse, body

leid; es tut mir leid (adj) sorry; I'm sorry

leider (adv) unfortunately

leihen to lend

Leinwand (f, -wände) screen (cinema)

leise (adj) quiet

Leistung (f, -en) performance, power

lernen to learn

lesen to read

letzte(r,s) (adj) last

Licht (n -(e)s, -er) light

lieber (adv comp of gern) rather, sooner

Lieblings- favourite

liebste(r,s) (adv superl of gern) most of all, best of all

liegen to lie, be situated

Liegestuhl (m -(e)s, -stühle)
  deckchair
Lineal (n -s, -e)   ruler
Linie (f, -n)   line, route
linke(r,s) (adj)   left
links (adv)   on the left
Liste (f, -n)   list
Liter (m or n -s, -)   litre
Löffel (m -s, -)   spoon
los: was ist los?   what's up,
  what's wrong?
lösen   to solve
Lotto (n -s, -s)   lottery
Löwe (m -n, -n)   lion
Luft (f, Lüfte (rare))   air
Lust, Lust haben (f, Lüste)
  pleasure, joy; to feel like
  something
lustig (adj)   funny, amusing
Luxemburg (n -s)   Luxembourg

M

machen   to make
Mädchen (n -s, -)   girl
Mai (m -(e)s, -)   May
mal (adv)   times
Mal (n -(e)s, -e)   time
man (indef pron)   you, one
Mangel an (+ dat) (m -s, Mängel)
  lack of, shortness of
Mann (m -(e)s, Männer)   man,
  husband
Mannschaft (f, -en)   team
Mantel (m -s, Mäntel)   coat
Markt (m -(e)s, Märkte)   market
März (m -(es), -)   March
Maschine (f, -n)   machine
Mathe, Mathematik (f, -)
  maths, mathematics
Mechaniker (m -s, -)   mechanic
Medikament (n -s, -e)   medicine
mehr (indef pron comp of viel,
  sehr)   more
mein (poss adj)   my
meinen   to think, mean
Meinung (f, -en)   opinion
meiste(r,s) (indef pron superl of
  viel)   most
Meisterschaft (f, -en)
  championship
Menge (f, -n)   quantity, amount,
  lots of

Menü (n -s, -s)   menu
Messer (n -s, -)   knife
Metall (n -s, -e)   metal
Meter (m or n -s, -)   metre
mich (pers pron acc of ich)   me
mieten   to rent, hire
Milch (f, -)   milk
Millionär (m -s, -e)   millionaire
mindestens (adv)   at least
Minister (m -s, -)   minister
Minute (f, -n)   minute
mir (pers pron dat of ich)   me,
  to me
mit (prep + dat)   with
Mitglied (n -(e)s, -er)   member
mitnehmen (sep, irreg)   to take
  (with one)
Mitte (f, -n)   middle, centre
mittelgroß (adj)   medium-sized
mitten (adv)   in the middle of
  something
Mitternacht (f no article)
  midnight
Mittwoch (m -s, -e)   Wednesday
möchte (imperf subj of mögen)
  would like
Modell (n -s, -e)   model
mögen (modal)   to like
Monat (m -(e)s, -e)   month
Montag (m -(e)s, -e)   Monday
morgen (adv)   tomorrow
Morgen (m -s, -)   morning
morgens (adv)   in the morning
müde (adj)   tired
Müll (m -(e)s, -)   rubbish
Müllmann (m -(e)s, -männer or
  Mülleute)   dustman
Münze (f, -n)   coin
Museum (n -s, Museen)
  museum
Musik (f, -en)   music
müssen (modal)   to have to,
  must
Mutter (f, Mütter)   mother
Mutti (f, -s)   mummy, mum

N

nach (prep + dat)   to, after
  (time phrases), according to
Nachbar (m -n or -s)   neighbour
Nachbarin (f, -nen)   (female
  neighbour)

nachdem (conj) after, since
nachmittag (adv) afternoon
Nachricht (f, -en) news
Nacht (f, Nächte) night
nachts (adv) at night
nächste(r,s) (adj superl of nah)
    nearest, next
Nähe (f, -) vicinity,
    neighbourhood
Name (m -ns, -n) name
Nashorn (n -(e)s, -hörner)
    rhinoceros
naß (adj) wet
natürlich (adj/adv) natural(ly)
neben (prep + acc/dat) beside,
    next to
Neffe (m -n, -n) nephew
nehmen to take
nein (adv) no
Nervensäge (f, -n) pest, pain in
    the neck (informal)
nett (adj) nice
neu; was gibt's Neues? (adj)
    new; what's new then?
neueste(r,s) (superl of neu)
    newest, most recent
Neujahr (n -(e)s, -e) New Year
nicht (adv) not
nichts (indef pron invariable)
    nothing
nie (adv) never
niedrig (adj) low
niedrigste(r,s) (superl of niedrig)
    lowest
niemand (indef pron) nobody,
    no one
nirgends (adv) nowhere
noch (adv) still, yet
Norden (m -s, -) north
normalerweise (adv) normally,
    usually
Note (f, -n) mark, grade
November (m -s, -) November
Nummer (f, -n) number
nur (adv) only, just
nützen to use
Nylon (n -(s), -) nylon

O

ob (conj) if, whether
obgleich (conj) although

obwohl (conj) although
oder (conj) or
offen (adj) open
oft (adv) often, frequently
öfter(s) (adv) on occasion
ohne (prep + acc) without
Ohr (n -(e)s, -en) ear
Oktober (m -s, -) October
Olympiade (f, -n) Olympic
    games
olympisch (adj) olympic
Oma (f, -s) granny, nanny
Onkel (m -s, -) uncle
Opa (m -s, -s) grandad,
    grandpa
organisieren to organise
original (adj) original
Ort (m -(e)s, -e) place
Osten (m -s, -) east
Österreich (n -s) Austria

P

Paar (n -s, -e) pair
Packung (f, -en) packet, pack
Papier (n -s, -e) paper
Park (m -s, -s) park
Parlament (n -s, -e) parliament
Party (f, -s or Parties) party
Passant (m -en, -en) passerby
passieren (*) to happen
Peking Beijing
perfekt (adj) perfect
Person (f, -en) person
Personal (n -s, -) staff,
    personnel
Pferd (n -(e)s, -e) horse
Pflanze (f, -n) plant
pflanzen to plant
Plätzchen (n -s, -) biscuit
plötzlich (adj/adv) sudden(ly)
planen to plan
Plastik (n -s, -s) plastic
Platz (m -es, Plätze) place,
    seat, square
plaudern to chat, talk
Plaudertasche (f, -n) chatterbox
Politik (f, -) politics, policy
Politiker (m -s, -) politician
Polizei (f, en) police
Polizist (m -en, -en) policeman
Polizistin (f, -nen) policewoman

Pommes (pl)   chips, french fries
Portugal (n -s)   Portugal
Postamt (n -(e)s, -ämter)   post office
Poster (n -s, -(s))   poster
Postkarte (f, -n)   postcard
praktisch (adj)   practical
Präsident (m -en, -en)   president
Preis (m -es, -e)   price, prize
preisgünstig (adj)   inexpensive
preiswert (adj)   good value
Prinz (m -en, -en)   prince
Prinzessin (f, -nen)   princess
pro (prep (no article))   per
Problem (n -s, -e)   problem
Prospekt (m -(e)s, -e)   brochure, leaflet
Pulli (m -s, -s)   pullover
Pullover (m -s, -)   pullover
pünktlich (adj/adv)   punctual, on time

Q

Quittung (f, -en)   receipt

R

Rad (n -(e)s, Räder)   wheel
radfahren (sep, irreg *)   to cycle
Rasenmäher (m -s, -) lawn mower
rasieren (refl)   to shave
Raststätte (f, -n)   services, service area
Rathaus (n -es, -häuser)   town hall
Ratschlag (m -(e)s, -schläge)   advice, piece of advice
Rätsel (n -s, -)   puzzle, riddle
Räuber (m -s, -)   robber
Raubtier (n -(e)s, -e)   predator, beast of prey
rauchen   to smoke
Raum (m -(e)s, Räume)   room, space
realistisch (adj)   realistic
Realschule (f, -n)   secondary school
recht, recht haben (adj)   right, to be right
rechts (adv)   right
reduzieren   to reduce

Regal (n -s, -e)   shelf, shelves
regelmäßig (adj)   regular
Regen (m -s, -)   rain
Regierung (f, -en)   government
regional (adj)   regional
regnen (impersonal)   to rain
reich (adj)   rich
reichen   to reach, stretch, extend
Reichstag (m)   German parliament 1871–1945
Reise; gute Reise! (f, -n)   journey; have a good journey!
Reisebüro (n -s, -s)   travel agency
Reisebus (m -ses, -se)   coach
Reiseführer (m -s, -)   guidebook
reisen (*)   to travel
Reisepaß (m -passes, -pässe)   passport
Reisepläne (pl)   plans for a journey
Reisescheck (m -s, -s)   traveller's check
Reisetasche (f, -n)   travel bag
Reiseziel (n -(e)s, -e)   travel destination
Rekord (m -s, -e)   record
Rente (f, -n)   pension
Rentner (m -s, -)   pensioner
Reparatur (f, -en)   repair
reparieren   to repair
Reportage (f, -n)   report
Reporter (m -s, -)   reporter
Restaurant (n -s, -s)   restaurant
Resultat (n -(e)s, -e)   result
Revolver (m -s, -)   revolver
richtig (adj/adv)   correct(ly)
Rolltreppe (f, -n)   escalator
Roman (m -s, -e)   novel
romantisch (adj)   romantic
rot (adj)   red
Routine (f, -n)   routine
Rowdytum (n, -)   hooliganism
Rückblick (m -(e)s, -e)   look back
Rucksack (m -(e)s, -säcke)   rucksack
Ruhe (f, -)   quiet, silence
ruhig; du kannst ruhig gehen (adj/adv)   quiet; feel free to go
Rußland (n)   Russia

S

S-Bahn (f abbr Stadtbahn, Schnellbahn) suburban train, express
S-Bahnhof (m -(e)s, -höfe) suburban line station
Sänger (m -s, -) singer
süß (adj) sweet
Süßigkeit (f, -en) sweets (pl), sweetness
Südafrika (n) South Africa
Süden (m -s, -) south
Safe (m or n -s, -s) safe (money)
sammeln to collect
Samstag (m -(e)s, -e) Saturday
Sardine (f, -n) sardine
sauber (adj) clean
Sauberkeit (f, -en) cleanliness
Schaden (m -s, Schäden) damage
Schal (m -s, -s or -e) scarf
Schallplatte (f, -n) record
schalten to switch
Schatten (m -s, -) shadow
schauen to look
Schaufenster (n -s, -) shop window
Scheibe (f, -n) window pane
scheinen to shine, seem
schenken to give something as a present
scheußlich (adj) dreadful
schick (adj) elegant, stylish
schicken to send
Schiff (n -(e)s, -e) ship, boat
Schlacht (f, -en) battle
Schlafanzug (m -(e)s, -züge) pyjamas
schlafen to sleep
Schlafenszeit (f, -en) bedtime
Schlafzimmer (n -s, -) bedroom
Schlange (f, -n) snake, queue
schlecht (adj/adv) bad(ly)
schließen to close
Schließfach (n -(e)s, -fächer) locker
schlimm (adj) bad
Schlitz (m -es, -e) slit, opening
Schloß (n schlosses, Schlösser) castle, palace, stately home

Schlüssel (m -s, -) key
Schlüsselbund (m or n -(e)s, -bunde) bunch of keys
Schlußverkauf (m -(e)s, -verkäufe) sale (end of season)
schmal (adj) narrow, slim
schmutzig (adj) dirty
schneiden to cut
schnell (adj) quick
schon (adv) already
schön (adj) beautiful, lovely
Schönheit (f, -en) beauty
schönste(r,s) (superl of schön) most beautiful
Schottland (n -s) Scotland
Schraubenzieher (m -s, -) screwdriver
schrecklich (adj) terrible
schreiben to write
schreien to shout, scream
Schriftsteller (m -s, -) author, writer
Schuh (m -(e)s, -e) shoe
Schulbildung (f, -en) education (school)
Schule (f, -n) school
Schüler (m -s, -) schoolboy
Schülerin (f, -nen) schoolgirl
Schulhof (m -(e)s, -höfe) playground (school)
Schulmappe (f, -n) schoolbag
schwach (adj) weak
schwarz (adj) black
schwatzen to chatter
Schweiz (f) Switzerland
schwer (adj/adv) difficult; really, deeply
Schwester (f, -n) sister
Schwiegertochter (f, -töchter) daughter-in-law
schwierig (adj) difficult
Schwierigkeit (f, -en) difficulty
Schwimmbad (n -(e)s, -bäder) swimming pool
schwimmen (* also haben) to swim
schwindelig (adj) dizzy
See (f, -en) sea
See (m -s, -n) lake
seekrank (adj) seasick
sehr (adv) very
sei (imperative sing of sein) be!

seien (imperative pl of sein) be!

Seifenpulver (n -s,-) soap powder

sein (*) to be

sein (poss adj) his, it's

seit (prep + dat) since

seitdem (adv) since then

Seite (f, -n) side

Sekt (m -(e)s, -e) sparkling wine

Sendung (f, -en) programme (radio, TV)

September (m -(s), -) September

setzen, sich setzen to put, place, to sit down

sich (3rd pers sing refl pron) him, her, it; himself, herself, itself

Sicherheit (f, -en) safety, security, certainty

sie (pers pron 3rd pers sing/plural) she, they

Sie (pers pron 2nd pers sing/plural (formal)) you

sitzen to sit

skandalös (adj) scandalous

Skandinavien (n) Scandinavia

Ski (m -s, - or -e) ski

Skilaufen (* sep) to ski

skrupellos (adj) unscrupulous

so (adv) so

Sofa (n -s, -s) sofa, settee

sofort (adv) immediately

Sohn (m -(e)s, Söhne) son

sollen (modal) to ought, should, be supposed to

Sommer (m -s, -) summer

Sonderangebot (n -es, -e) special offer

sondern (conj) but

Sonnabend (m -s, -e) Saturday

Sonne (f, -n) sun

Sonnenschirm (m -(e)s, -e) sunshade, parasol

Sonntag (m -(e)s, -e) Sunday

sonst (adv) else, otherwise

Sorge (f, -n) worry, trouble

Sorte (f, -n) sort, type

Sozialarbeiter (m -s, -) social worker

spät (adj/adv) late

Spaß (m -es, Späße) fun

Spanien (n) Spain

sparen to save

Spaziergang (m -(e)s, -gänge) walk

Speisekarte (f, -n) menu

Spiegel (m -s, -) mirror

Spiel (n -(e)s, -e) game, match

spielen to play

Spieler (m -s, -) player

Spielplatz (m -es, -plätze) playground

Sport (m -(e)s, -e) sport

Sportart (f, -en) sport (type of)

Sportler (m -s, -) sportsman, athlete

sportlich (adj) sporting

Sprache (f, -n) language

sprechen to speak

Staat (m -(e)s, -en) state

Stadt (f, Städte) town

Stadtteil (m -(e)s, -e) district, part of town

Station (f, -en) station

Stau (m -(e)s, -e) traffic jam

staunen to be astonished, amazed

stechen to bite, sting

Stechkahn (m -(e)s, -kähne) punt

Steckdose (f, -n) socket (electrical)

Stecker (m -s, -) plug (electrical)

stehen to stand

stehlen to steal

steigend (adj) increasing

Stelle (f, -n) place, spot

Stellenangebot (n -es, -e) job offer

sterben (*) to die

Stereoanlage (f, -n) stereo system

Stimme (f, -n) voice

stimmen to be right

Straßenbahn (f, -en) tram

Strecke (f, -en) route, road

streiten to argue, quarrel

streng (adj) strict

Strickjacke (f, -n) cardigan

Strumpf (m -(e)s, Strümpfe) sock, stocking

Student (m -en, -en) student

studieren to study

Studio (n -s, -s) studio

Stuhl (m -(e)s, Stühle)   chair
Stunde (f, -n)   hour
stürmisch (adj)   stormy, rough
suchen   to look for
Supermarkt (m -(e)s, -märkte)
   supermarket
surfen   to surf
sympathisch (adj)   pleasant, nice
System (n -s, -e)   system

T

T-Shirt (n -s,-s)   T-shirt
Tablette (f, -n)   pill, tablet
Tag (m -(e)s, -e)   day
Tagebuch (n -(e)s, -bücher)
   diary
täglich (adj/adv)   daily, every
   day
tagsüber (adv)   during the day
tanken   to tank up, fill up
Tankstelle (f, -n)   petrol station
Tante (f, -n)   aunt
tanzen   to dance
Tasche (f, -n)   bag
Taschenbuch (n -(e)s, -bücher)
   paperback book
Tasse (f, -n)   cup
Tat (f, -en)   deed, act, crime
taub (adj)   deaf
Teilzeitarbeit (f -n)   part time
   work
Telefax (n -, -e)   fax
Telefon (n -s, -e)   telephone
telefonieren   to telephone
Teller (m -s, -)   plate
Tennis (n -, -)   tennis
Tennischläger (m -s, -)   tennis
   racquet
Teppich (m -s, -e)   carpet
Terrasse (f, -n)   patio, terrace
Terrorismus (m -)   terrorism
teuer (adj)   expensive
Theater (n -s, -)   theatre
Thema (n -s, Themen)   topic,
   theme
tippen   to type
Tisch (m -(e)s, -e)   table
Tischler (m -s, -)   carpenter,
   joiner
Titel (m -s, -)   title
Tochter (f, Töchter)   daughter
Toilette (f, -n)   toilet, WC

toll (adj)   great, fantastic
Tomate (f, -n)   tomato
Topf (m -(e)s, Töpfe)   pot,
   (sauce) pan
Tor (n -(e)s, -e)   goal
Tormann (m -(e)s, -männer)
   goalkeeper
töten   to kill
Tourismus (m -, -)   tourism
Tourist (m -en, -en)   tourist
tragen   to carry, wear
trainieren   to train, coach
Traum (m -(e)s, Träume)   dream
träumen   to dream
traurig (adj)   sad
Traurigkeit (f, -en)   sadness
treffen (refl)   to meet
trinken   to drink
Tritt (m -(e)s, -e)   step
trocknen   to dry
trotzdem (adv)   nevertheless
Truthahn (m -(e)s, -hähne)
   turkey
Tube (f, -n)   tube
tun   to do
Tunnel (m -s, - or -s)   tunnel
Tür (f, -en)   door
Türkei (f)   Turkey
Turm (m -(e)s, Türme)   tower
Tüte (f, -n)   bag
typisch (adj)   typical

U

U-Bahn (f, -en)   underground
   (train)
üben   to practise
über (prep + acc/dat)   above,
   over, across, about
überall (adv)   everywhere
Überfall (m -(e)s, -fälle)   attack,
   assault
Übersetzung (f, -en)   translation
Uhr (f, -en)   clock, watch,
   o'clock
um (prep + acc)   around, round
um... zu (conj)   in order to
Umfrage (f, -n)   survey
umgeben (insep, irreg)   to (be)
   surrounded by
Umleitung (f, -en)   detour,
   diversion

Umschlag (m -(e)s, -schläge) envelope

umweltfreundlich (adj) environmentally friendly

umwerfen (sep, irreg) to knock down

umziehen (sep, irreg) to move (house)

unbedingt (adj) really, absolutely

und (conj) and

und so weiter, usw and so on, etc.

unerfahren (adj) inexperienced

Unfall (m -s, Unfälle) accident

ungebraucht (adj) unused

ungefähr (adv) approximately

unglaublich (adj) incredible, unbelievable

unglücklich (adj) sad, unhappy

Uni (f, -s) university

Uniform (f, -en) uniform

Universität (f, -en) university

uns (pers pron acc of wir; refl pron acc/dat) us, ourselves

unser (poss adj) our

unter (prep + acc/dat) under, beneath

Unterkunft (f, -künfte) accommodation

Unterricht (m -(e)s, -) lessons

Untertasse (f, -n) saucer

unvergleichbar (adj) incomparable

Urlaub (m -(e)s, -e) holiday(s)

USA (pl) USA

V

Vater (m -s, Väter) father

Vati (m -s, -s) daddy, dad

verabredet (ptp, adj) engaged, prior engagement

verabschieden (refl) to say goodbye

verantwortlich (adj) responsible

verbessern to improve

Verbindung (f, -en) connection, telephone line

verboten (adj) forbidden

verbringen to spend (time)

verdienen to earn

Vereinigten Staaten, die (pl) the United States

Vergangenheit (f, -en) past

vergessen to forget

Vergleich, im Vergleich mit/zu (m -(e)s, -e) comparison, comparison with/to

Vergnügen (n -s, -) pleasure

verherrlichen to glorify

Verkäufer (m -s, -) shop assistant

Verkäuferin (f, -nen) shop assistant

Verkehr (m -(e)s, -) traffic

verlassen (irreg) to leave

verletzen, sich verletzen to injure, to hurt oneself

verletzt (ptp, adj) injured

verpassen to miss

verschieden (adj) different, various

Verschiedenheit (f, -en) difference, variety

verschmutzen to pollute, make dirty

Versicherung (f, -en) insurance

verstecken to hide, conceal

verstehen (irreg) to understand

Verteidiger (m -s, -) defender

Verwandte(r) (mf decl as adj) relative, relation

viel(e) (adj) a lot of, much, many

vielleicht (adv) perhaps

Viertel (n -s, -) quarter, district

Villa (f, Villen) villa

Volkshochschule (f, -n) adult education centre

voll (adj/adv) full, fully

von (prep + dat) from, of, about

vor (prep + acc/dat) before, in front of

vorbeifahren (sep, irreg *) to drive past

vorhaben (sep, irreg) to intend, to plan, have planned

Vorhang (m -s, -hänge) curtain

vorn(e) (adv) forwards, in front, at the front

Vorschrift (f, -en) regulation, rules

Vorsicht! (f, -) Watch out!

W

wählen   to choose, dial

während (prep + dat/gen; conj)
during; while

wahr (adj)   true

Wahrheit (f, -en)   truth

Wald (m -(e)s, Wälder)   wood(s)

Wand (f, Wände)   wall (indoor)

wandern (*)   to hike, wander

wann? (interrog adv)   when?

war (imperf of sein)   was

Ware (f, -n)   product, goods

wäre (imperf subj of sein)
were, would be

Wärme (f, (rare) -n)   warmth

warten auf (+ acc)   to wait
(for)

Wartezeit (f, -en)   waiting time

warum? (interrog adv)   why?

was (interrog pron; relative pron)
what; which

waschen (also refl)   to wash

Waschmaschine (f, -n)   washing
machine

Wasser (n -s, -)   water

Wasserhahn (m -(e)s, -hähne)
tap

WC (n -s, -s)   toilet, WC

wechseln   to change, exchange

weder... noch (conj)   neither...
nor

Weg (m -(e)s, -e)   path, track,
road

wegen (prep + gen)   because of,
due to

wegnehmen (sep, irreg)   to take
away, remove

weh tun   to hurt

weiß (adj)   white

weiß (1st/3rd pers sing of
wissen)   know

Weihnachten (n -, -)   Christmas

Wein (m -(e)s, -e)   wine

weinen   to cry, weep

weit (adj; adv)   wide; far

weiter (comp of weit)   further

welche(r,s) (interrog pron)
which

Welt (f, -en)   world

wem (dat of wer)   who, whom

wenig(e) (adj/adv)   little, few

wenn (conj)   if, whenever

wer (interrog pron; rel pron;
indef pron)   who, somebody

Werbung (f, -en)   advertising

werden (*)   to become

werfen   to throw

Werkstatt (f, -stätten)   garage,
workshop

Wertsache (f, -n)   object of
value , (pl) valuables

Westen (m -s, -)   west

Wetter (n -s, -)   weather

Wettervorhersage (f, -n)
weather forecast

wichtig (adj)   important

wichtigste(r,s) (superl of
wichtig)   most important

Widerspruch (m -(e)s, -sprüche)
contradiction

wie (interrog adv; conj)   how,
what; as

wiederverwendbar (adj)
reusable

Wien (n -s)   Vienna

wieso (interrog adv)   why

wie viel? (interrog adv)   how
much?, how many?

will, willst (1st, 2nd pers sing of
wollen)   want

willkommen (adj)   welcome

windsurfen (insep)   to windsurf

Winter (m -s, -)   winter

winzig (adj)   tiny

wir (1st pers plural pron)   we

wirklich (adj/adv)   real(ly)

wissen   to know

wo? (interrog)   where?

Woche (f, -n)   week

Wochenende (n -s, -n)
weekend

wohl (adv)   well, happy

wohltätig (adj)   charitable

wohnen   to live, stay

Wohnhaus (n -(e)s, -häuser)
residential building

Wohnung (f, -en)   flat

Wohnzimmer (n -s, -)   living
room

Wolldecke (f, -n)   blanket

wollen (modal)   to want (to)

worüber (relat interrog)   about
what, which

Wortstellung (f, -en)   word
order

wunderschön (adj)   beautiful, lovely
wünschen   to wish, ask for something
würde (imperf subj of werden) would

Z

Zahnpasta (f, -pasten) toothpaste
zeigen   to show, point
Zeit (f, -en)   time
Zeitschrift (f, -en)   magazine
Zeitung (f, -en)   newspaper
Zentrum (n -s, Zentren)   centre
zersplittern   to shatter
Zettel (m -s, -)   note
Zeugnis (n -ses, -se)   report (school), certificate
ziehen   to pull

ziemlich (adv)   rather, quite
Zimmer (n -s, -)   room
Zoo (m -s, -s)   zoo
zu (prep + dat)   to, at, in
zuerst (adv)   first
Zug (m -(e)s, Züge)   train
zugig (adj)   draughty
Zukunft (f, -)   future
zuletzt (adv)   last, in the end
zum (contr of zu dem)   to the
zumachen (sep)   to close
zur (contr of zu der)   to the
zurück (adv)   back
Zuschauer (m -s, -)   spectator, viewer
zuschließen (sep, irreg)   to lock
zweifellos (adv)   undoubtedly, unquestionably
zweimal (adv)   twice
zweitens (adv)   secondly
Zwilling (m -s, -e)   twin

English–German glossary

*	*auxiliary verb sein*
abbr	*abbreviation*
acc	*accusative case*
adj	*adjective*
adv	*adverb*
comp	*comparative*
conj	*conjunction*
contr	*contraction*
dat	*dative case*
f	*feminine*
gen	*genitive case*
imperf	*imperfect*
indef	*indefinite*
insep	*inseparable*
interj	*interjection*
interrog	*interrogative*
irreg	*irregular*
m	*masculine*
n	*neuter*
per	*personal*
pl	*plural*
poss	*possessive*
prep	*preposition*
pron	*pronoun*
ptp	*past participle*
refl	*reflexive*
sep	*separable*
sing	*singular*
subj	*subjunctive*
superl	*superlative*
zB	*eg*

After a masculine, neuter noun the genitive and plural endings are shown.
After a feminine noun the plural ending is shown.

A

to be able to   können (modal)
about   von + dat, um + acc,
    über + acc (prep)
according to   nach (prep + dat)
after   nachdem (conj)
after   nach (prep + dat)
all   alle(r,s) (indef pron)
to be allowed, permitted   dürfen
    (modal)

although   obwohl/obgleich
    (conj)
America   Amerika (n -s)
and   und (conj)
to arrive   ankommen (sep, irreg *)
as   wie/da (conj)
as, when   als (conj)
to ask sb for sth   bitten um (+ acc)

B

bad(ly)   schlecht (adj/adv)
bathroom   Badezimmer (n -s, -)
to be   sein (*)
most beautiful   schönste(r,s) (superl
    of schön)
beautiful, lovely   schön (adj)
because   denn/weil (conj)
because of   wegen (prep + gen)
to become   werden (*)
before   bevor (conj)
before, in front of   vor (prep +
    acc/dat)
to begin   beginnen
Belgium   Belgien (n -s)
beside   neben (prep + acc/dat)
best   beste(r,s) (adj superl of
    gut)
best of all, most of all
    liebste(r,s) (adv superl of
    gern)
better   besser (adj, adv comp of
    gut)
big   groß (adj)
bigger   größer (comp of groß)
biggest   größte(r,s) (superl of
    groß)
book   Buch (n -(e)s, Bücher)
bookcase   Bücherregal (n -s, -e)
bookshelf   Bücherregal (n -s, -e)
boring   langweilig (adj)
both   beide (pron)
to bring   bringen
busy   geschäftig (adj)
but (after a negative)   sondern
    (conj)
but, however   aber (conj)

C

to change   wechseln
cheap   billig (adj)
to choose   wählen
clever   gescheit, klug (adj)
to comb   kämmen
to cry (weep)   weinen
curtain   Vorhang (m -s, -hänge)

D

dangerous   gefährlich (adj)
to decide   entscheiden
to dial   wählen
difficult   schwierig (adj)
to draw (through)   ziehen
to dress   anziehen (sep, irreg)
to drink   trinken
to dry   trocknen
due to   wegen (prep + gen)
during   während (prep + dat or
    gen; conj)

E

each   jede(r,s) (indef pron)
to eat   essen
enough   genug (adj)
every   jede(r,s) (indef pron)
everything   alle(r,s) (indef pron)
to exchange   wechseln
expensive   teuer (adj)

F

fascinating   bezaubernd (adj)
few   wenig(e) (adj/adv)
to find   finden
to follow   folgen (* + dat)
France   Frankreich (n -s)
from   von, aus (country) (prep
    + dat)
in front of, before   vor (prep +
    acc/dat)
full, fully   voll (adj/adv)
funny, amusing   lustig (adj)

G

to get on/in   einsteigen (sep, irreg *)

to get out/off   aussteigen (sep,
    irreg *)
to get up   aufstehen (sep, irreg *)
to get, receive   bekommen (irreg)
to give, there is/are   geben, es
    gibt
gladly   gern(e) (adv)
to go   gehen (*)
good   gut (adj)

H

to happen   geschehen (*)
hardworking   fleißig (adj)
to have to, must   müssen
    (modal)
to have, have got   haben
to hear   hören
to help   helfen (+ dat)
her   ihr (dat sing of sie)
high   hoch (adj)
higher   höher (comp of hoch)
highest   höchste(r,s) (superl of
    hoch)
his   sein (poss adj)
historic   historisch (adj)
house, at home, (to) home
    Haus, zu Hause, nach Hause
    (n -es, Häuser)
how?   wie? (interrog adv)
how many?   wieviel? (interrog
    adv)
how much?   wieviel? (interrog
    adv)

i

if   ob (conj)
if (whenever)   wenn (conj)
in, into   in (prep + acc/dat)
to insist (on)   bestehen (auf + dat)
    (irreg)
interesting   interessant (adv)
Ireland, Eire   Irland (n -s)
there is/are   es gibt (impersonal)
its   sein, ihr (poss adj)

K

kitchen   Küche (f, -n)

L

to leave   lassen
there is lightening   blitzen, es blitzt
     (impersonal)
would like   möchte (imperf subj of
     mögen)
to like   mögen
to listen   hören
little, few   wenig(e) (adj)
to live   wohnen
to look forward to   freuen, sich
     freuen auf (+ acc)
loud   laut (adj)
Luxembourg   Luxemburg (n, -s)

M

more   mehr (indef pron comp of
     viel, sehr)
most   meiste(r,s) (indef pron
     superl of viel)
my   mein (poss adj)

N

next to   neben (prep + acc/dat)
nice   sympathisch, nett (adj)
no, not a   kein(e) (indef pron)
to notice   beobachten

O

of   von (prep + dat)
opposite   gegenüber (prep + dat)
or   oder (conj)
to ought   sollen (modal)
our   unser (poss adj)
outside   außerhalb (prep + gen)

P

to pass (an exam)   bestehen (irreg)
patio   Terrasse (f, -n)
to play   spielen
pleasant   sympathischnett (adj)
with pleasure   gern(e) (adv)
polluted   Verschmutzt (adj)
Portugal   Portugal (n -s)
prefer   lieber (adv comp of gern)
to pull   ziehen

to push, press   drücken
to put   stecken
to put on (dress)   anziehen (sep,
     irreg)

Q

quick   schnell (adj)
quiet   ruhig (adj/adv)

R

to rain   regnen, es regnet
     (impersonal)
to read   lesen
to receive   empfangen
regular   regelmäßig (adj)

S

to say goodbye   verabschieden
     (reflex)
to see   sehen
shelf, shelves   Regal (n -s, -e)
to shoot dead   erschießen (irreg)
should   sollen (modal)
simple, simply   einfach
     (adj/adv)
since (because)   denn (conj)
since then (time since)   seitdem
     (adv)
to sit   sitzen
to sleep   schlafen
slow(ly)   langsam (adj/adv)
some   einige(r,s) (indef pron)
something   etwas (indef pron)
to speak (about)   sprechen (von +
     dat)
to spend (time)   verbringen
in spite of, despite   trotz (prep +
     gen)
to stand up   aufstehen (sep,
     irreg *)
to start   beginnen
to stay   wohnen, bleiben (*)
to be supposed to   sollen (modal)
Switzerland   die Schweiz (f)

T

tall   hoch (adj)

terrace   Terrasse (f, -n)
to thank   danken (+ dat)
to thunder   donnern, es donnert
   (impersonal)
to   zu, nach (prep + dat), in
   (+ acc/dat)
to type   tippen
to type in   eintippen (sep)

U

until, till   bis (prep + acc/adv)
USA   USA (pl die)

V

to visit   besuchen

W

to wake up   aufwachen (sep)
to want (to)   wollen (modal)
to wash   waschen (also refl)
to watch TV   fernsehen (sep,
   irreg)

what?   was? (interrog pron)
when?   wann? (interrog adv)
whenever   wenn (conj)
where?   wo? (interrog)
whether, if   ob (conj)
which   was (relative pron)
while   während (prep + dat or
   gen)
why?   warum? (interrog adv)
window   Fenster (n -s, -)
with   mit (prep + dat)
within   innerhalb (prep + gen)
to work   arbeiten
worrying   beängstigend (adj)
to write   schreiben

Y

you (plural informal)   ihr (2nd
   pers pl pers pron)
your (formal)   Ihr (poss adj 2nd
   pers sing & pl)
your (informal sing)   dein (poss
   adj 2nd pers sing)
your (informal plural)   euer
   (poss adj)

Grammar index

For definitions of terms see:

Help Yourself to Essential German Grammar

Key to exercises
Detachable answer section for class use

Chapter 1 – What do you know? (page 1)

A *Meine Wohnung*

den 18. September

Lieber/Liebe X,

du fragst, wie unsere Wohnung aussieht. **Die** Küche ist rechts von der Eingangstür.
Neben der Küche ist **das** Badezimmer. Links ist **das** Wohnzimmer.
Die Wohnung hat drei Schlafzimmer.
Der Balkon hat eine sehr schöne Aussicht auf den Garten.
Der Garten liegt vor und hinter dem Haus.
Hier ist ein Foto von dem Wohnhaus.
Kannst Du mir ein Foto von Deinem Haus schicken?
Schreib bald!
Maria

B *Meine Brüder*
1 Mein Bruder Peter ist sehr sportlich. Er **spielt** gern Tennis und Federball.
2 Mein jüngerer Bruder Moritz ist dreizehn Jahre alt. Er **bastelt** sehr gerne.
Meine Eltern
3 Meine Mutter **lernt** abends Englisch in der Volkshochschule.
4 Mein Vater **sammelt** Briefmarken von der ehemaligen DDR.
Meine Großeltern
5 Mein Großvater **hört** gern Musik, obwohl er jetzt ziemlich taub ist.
6 Meine Oma **wandert** gern auf dem Lande.

Chapter 1 – What have you learnt? (page 4)

A *Was gibt es in der Gegend zu tun?*
1 Berlin ist eine sehr interessante Stadt. In unserem Stadtteil gibt es eine Disko, ein
Kino, ein Museum und ein Sportzentrum. In der Disko **tanzt** man und man
hört Musik. Das Kino **zeigt** die neuesten Filme.
2 Ich **besuche** jede Woche das Sportzentrum. Da **spiele** ich Squash und danach
kaufe ich mir eine Cola.
3 Meine Freunde und ich **besichtigen** ungefähr zweimal pro Jahr das Museum. In
dem Museum sind Ausstellungen über die regionale Geschichte. Ich **wohne** gerne
hier in Berlin. Es gibt immer viel zu tun.
4 An der Ecke ist eine Bibliothek. Dort **mache** ich meine Hausaufgaben. Meine
Freunde und ich **arbeiten** auf den Computers. Die Bibliothek ist prima!
5 Berlin hat mehrere Seen und Wälder. Im Sommer **segeln** wir auf dem Wannsee.
Im Herbst **macht** meine Schulklasse eine Wanderung im Grünewald.

B *Mein Haus*

Hier ist ein Foto von meinem Haus.
Die Küche ist zu eng und **das Badezimmer** zu groß.
Die Vorhänge im Wohnzimmer sind scheußlich. **Der Bücherschrank** nimmt zu viel
Platz ein. **Die Terrasse** ist für kleine Kinder sehr gefährlich. **Das Haus** liegt direkt an
einer Hauptstraße. **Die Fenster** sind undicht. Ja, mir gefällt das Haus gar nicht!

Chapter 2 – What do you know? (page 5)

A *Mein Zimmer*

FREUND   Hast du dein eigenes Zimmer?

MARIA   Ja. Mein Zimmer ist ziemlich groß. Neben der Tür ist **ein** Kleiderschrank
und **eine** Kommode.

FREUND   Hat das Zimmer **ein** Fenster?

MARIA   Das Fenster ist auf der rechten Seite des Kleiderschrankes. Unter dem
Fenster ist **ein** Gästebett. In der Mitte ist **ein** kleiner Teppich.

FREUND   Hast du Bilder oder Posters an der Wand?

MARIA   An der Wand über meinem Bett sind – Posters von meinen
Lieblingssportlern. Wie sieht dein Zimmer aus?

B *Was macht die Familie?*

MUTTI   Peter! Wo bist du?

PETER   Ich bin im Wohnzimmer. Ich **sehe** fern.

MUTTI   Wo ist dein Bruder?

PETER   Moritz ist noch nicht zu Hause. Er **trifft** um drei Uhr seinen Freund am
Kinderspielplatz.

MUTTI   Ist Maria zu Hause?

MARIA   Ich bin hier in meinem Schlafzimmer. Ich bin müde. Ich **lese**.

MUTTI   Was macht dein Vater?

VATI   Ich **schreibe** einen Brief an Tante Irmi. Opa Maier **sitzt** mit mir im
Wohnzimmer und **schläft**.

OMA   Und ich bin hier in der Küche und **schneide** Brot für das Abendessen.

Chapter 2 – What have you learnt? (page 8)

A *Im Sonderangebot*

1

MARIA   **Ein** Kassettenrekorder kostet nur DM 89,- und **eine** Stereoanlage kostet DM
249,-. Und schau mal Mutti, **ein** Kopfhörer kostet DM 18,-. **Ein** Mini-CD-
Spieler kostet DM 149,- und hier gibt es noch was: **eine** Packung von fünf
Kassetten DM 9,89. **Ein** Hi-Fi System kostet nur DM 429,-!

2

MARIA   Na ja, aber Gabis CD-Spieler allein hat DM 400 gekostet.

MUTTER   Aber Maria, Gabi arbeitet jetzt. Sie ist – Empfangsdame in einem Hotel, nicht wahr?

MARIA   Wir haben aber keinen CD-Spieler.

MUTTER   Maria, ich kriege langsam – Kopfschmerzen. Wir brauchen keinen CD-Spieler. Vati und ich haben auf jeden Fall nur Schallplatten.

3

MARIA   Ich muß irgendwie – Geld verdienen.

MUTTER   Dann kannst du ruhig die Stellenangebote auch durchlesen!

B *Zu Hause*
1 Ich **schreibe** auch im Wohnzimmer Briefe und **sehe** fern.
2 Wir **essen** und **trinken** in der Küche.
3 Ich **höre** in meinem Zimmer Musik und **schlafe**.
4 Wir **sitzen** im Sommer im Garten.
5 Meine Eltern **arbeiten** gern im Garten.

Chapter 3 – What do you know? (page 9)

A *Mein Körper*
Ich habe zwei Auge**n**, zwei Ohr**en**, und fünf Finger – an einer Hand.

B *Meine Alltagsroutine*
1 Der Bus **kommt** pünktlich um viertel nach sieben **an**.
2 Ich **steige** in den Bus **ein**.
3 Ich **steige** an der Bushaltestelle direkt vor meinem Kindergarten **aus**.

C *Meine tägliche Routine*
1 Zuerst gehe ich ins Badezimmer. Ich **wasche mich** schnell.
2 Ich **rasiere mich**.
3 Ich **kämme mich** im Schlafzimmer vor dem Spiegel.

D *Was spielen wir?*
1 KIND   Ich **bin** Batman, und du **bist** Robin.
2 KIND   Nein, er **ist** Superman. Wir **sind** Batman und Robin.
3 KIND   Superman **ist** besser als Batman.

Chapter 3 – What have you learnt? (page 12)

A *In meinem Zimmer*
1 In meinem Zimmer habe ich **einen Vorhang/zwei Vorhänge** und **einen Kleiderschrank/zwei Kleiderschränke**.
2 Neben meinem Bett habe ich **einen Nachttisch/zwei Nachttische**.
3 An der Wand habe ich **ein Foto/zwei Fotos** und **ein Bild/zwei Bilder**.
4 Das Zimmer hat **ein Fenster/zwei Fenster**.
5 Ich habe **ein Bücherregal/zwei Bücherregale, einen Kassettenrekorder/zwei Kassettenrekorder** und **einen Fernseher/zwei Fernseher**.

B *Ich stehe langsam auf*
  1 Ich wache um sieben Uhr **auf**.
    Zuerst höre ich etwas Musik.
  2 Ich stehe nur langsam **auf**.
    Dann gehe ich ins Badezimmer.
  3 Ich wasche **mich**.
    Danach gehe ich ins Schlafzimmer zurück.
  4 Ich kämme **mich**.
    Ich frühstücke schnell.
    Ich verlasse das Haus um 8.25 Uhr.
  5 Der Bus kommt um 8.30 Uhr **an**.
    Ich steige in den Bus **ein**.
    Die Fahrt zur Schule dauert 15 Minuten.
  6 Ich steige vor der Schule **aus**.
    Die Schule beginnt um neun Uhr.

Chapters 1–3 – Revision (pages 13–14)

A *Im Kaufhaus*

1 Besteck (das)	2 Messer (das)	3 Gabel (die)	4 Löffel (der)
5 Geschirr (das)	6 Teller (der)	7 Untertasse (die)	8 Tasse (die)
9 Glas (das)	10 Bier (das)	11 Wein (der)	12 Sekt (der)

B *Meine Familie (1)*

MARIA Hast du Geschwister?

DU Ich **habe** zwei Brüder und eine Schwester.

MARIA Wie heißen sie?

DU Meine Brüder **heißen** John und Stephen. Sie **sind** Zwillinge. Meine Schwester **heißt** Jayne. Jayne **ist** 21.

C *Meine Familie (2)*

MARIA Was sind deine Hobbys?

DU Ich **spiele** gern Tennis und ich **lese** sehr gern und **gehe** gern ins Kino.

MARIA Was macht dein Vater gern in seiner Freizeit?

DU Er **hört** sehr gern Musik und **arbeitet** jedes Wochenende im Garten.

MARIA Arbeitet deine Mutter?

DU Meine Mutter **hilft** jeden Mittwoch in einem Wohltätigkeitsladen. Sie **bekommt** kein Geld dafür. Sie **bringt** mir oft alte Taschenbücher nach Hause.

D *Zum Einpacken*
1   **eine** Hose
2   **eine** Jacke
3   **ein** Pullover
4   **ein** T-Shirt
5   **ein** Sporthemd
6   **ein** Paar Schuhe
7   **ein** Regenmantel
8   **ein** Schlafanzug

E *Grüße aus Österreich*

Bad Gastein, 18.7.98 Grüße aus Österreich. Wir amüsieren **uns** hier. Wir stehen jeden Tag früh **auf**! Peter wäscht **sich** schnell und zieht **sich** gleich **an**. Danach hat er eine Tennisstunde in die Tennishalle. Danach machen wir normalerweise einen Spaziergang. Wir fühlen **uns** alle sehr wohl. Eure Familie Maier	Familie XYZ 10 High St _____

F *Vergessen Sie nicht!*
1 e   Schalten Sie das Licht **aus**.
2 c   Bringen Sie den Müll **hinaus**.
3 a   Ziehen Sie den Stecker des Fernsehers **heraus**.
4 b   Schalten Sie den Sicherheitsalarm **an/ein**.
5 d   Schließen Sie die Tür **ab/zu**.

Chapter 4 – What do you know? (page 15)

A *In meiner Gegend*
Nicht weit von meiner Wohnung gibt es **ein** Einkaufszentrum, **ein** Schwimmbad und **einen** Park mit Tennisplätzen. Im Einkaufszentrum gibt es **eine** Bank. Jeden Samstag gibt es **einen** Markt auf dem Marktplatz. Es gibt **einen** Bahnhof fünf Minuten von hier entfernt.

B *Liebe Maria,*   *den 11. November*
ich freue mich schon auf meinen Besuch in Berlin. Also ich möchte **das** *Rote Rathaus,* **den** *Fernsehturm und* **den** *Alexanderplatz sehen. Ich möchte auch* **das** *Brandenburgertor,* **den** *Reichstag und* **das** *Schloß Charlottenburg besichtigen. Meine Freundin hat mir auch* **die** *Babelsberger Filmstudios empfohlen.*
                                                    Bis bald,
                                    _____

C *Richtig oder falsch?*
1 falsch
2 richtig
3 falsch
4 falsch

Chapter 4 – What have you learnt? (page 18)

A *Im Verkehrsbüro*
1 Gibt es **einen** Ausflug nach Salzburg?
2 Gibt es denn **kein** Freibad in der Nähe?
3 Ich möchte **eine** Karte für **die** Stadtrundfahrt reservieren.
4 Gibt es **einen** Bus nach Potsdam?
5 Kann man hier Karten für **das** Theater kaufen?
6 Ich möchte **einen** Stadtplan bitte.
7 Ich möchte **das** Schloß besichtigen. Gibt es morgen **eine** Führung?
8 Wo kann ich hier **ein** Fahrrad mieten?

B *Herr Maiers Kalender*
1 falsch;   um zehn Uhr
2 falsch;   um 13 Uhr
3 richtig
4 richtig
5 falsch;   um neun Uhr
6 falsch;   um 13 Uhr
7 falsch;   um 18.15 Uhr
8 richtig

Chapter 5 – What do you know? (page 19)

A *Ich verstehe nicht*
1 Das Auto gehört **der** Frau.
2 Die alte Dame dankt **dem** Mädchen.
3 Sie gibt **dem** Mann ein Buch.
4 Der Arzt hilft **der** Studentin.
5 Der Detektiv folgt **den** Kindern.

B *Hast du Lust, ins Kino zu gehen?*
1 PETER   Hallo Ingrid, hier Peter. Hast du Lust heute abend ins Kino zu gehen?
   INGRID   Tag Peter. Leider kann ich nicht. **Nach** der Schule gehe ich **mit** meinen
   Freunden eislaufen.
2 PETER   Tag Max, hier Peter. Willst du heute abend **mit** mir **zu** dem (**zum**)
   See gehen?
   MAX   Tut mir leid. Ich gehe **mit** Fredi und seinem Freund in die Disko.

3 PETER Hallo Anja. Hast du heute abend schon etwas vor?

ANJA Ja, ich fahre **mit** Ingrid und ihrer Mutter **zu** dem (**zum**) Einkaufszentrum. Wir gehen einkaufen. **Nach** dem Abendessen muß ich unbedingt meine Hausaufgaben machen.

Chapter 5 – What have you learnt (page 22)

A *Weihnachtsgeschenke*
1 Herr Maier gibt **seiner** Tochter ein Buch.
2 Frau Maier gibt **ihrem** Sohn ein Paar Handschuhe.
3 Peter gibt **seinem** Vater eine Krawatte.
4 Maria gibt **ihrer** Mutter eine Vase.

B *Im Einkaufszentrum*
1 falsch. Das Kaufhaus ist gegenüber der Buchhandlung.
2 falsch. Das Schuhgeschäft ist rechts von der Buchhandlung.
3 falsch. Die Bank ist gegenüber dem Kino.
4 richtig

C *Einkaufsliste*
1 b Sie geht zum Reisebüro.
2 d Sie geht zum Fotogeschäft.
3 a Sie geht zur Bibliothek.
4 c Sie geht zur Apotheke.

Chapter 6 – What do you know? (page 23)

A *Wohin gehen wir?*
1 Die Hauptstraße ist um **die** Ecke.
2 Wir gehen **den** Weg entlang.
3 Ich gehe zuerst in **das** Kaufhaus. (accusative: movement)
4 Der Eingang ist an **der** Ecke. (dative: no movement)

B *Was macht ihr in den Ferien?*
1 Ich fahre im Sommer **nach** Spanien. Ich besuche meine Brieffreundin.
2 Wenn ich genug Geld hätte, würde ich **nach** Amerika fliegen.
3 Zu Weihnachten fahren wir **in die** Schweiz. Wir laufen gerne Ski.
4 Meine Familie kommt aus Istanbul. Wir fahren jedes Jahr **in die** Türkei.

C *Befehle*
1 c Come!   2 d Go!
3 e Pull!   4 f Get up!
5 a Push!   6 g Answer!
7 h Begin!   8 b Stop!

Chapter 6 – What have you learnt? (page 26)

A *Die Wahrheit*

Montag besuche ich mit Monika das Kaufhaus **neben der** Bibliothek.
Dienstag? Leider bin ich schon **mit** Peter verabredet. Wir gehen **in die** Disko.
Mittwoch gehe ich **mit** Bernd **ins/zum** Theater.
Donnerstag spielen Michael und ich **im** Park Tennis.
Freitag treffe ich Max **vor dem** Museum.
Samstag treffe ich Sven **gegenüber dem** Kino.

B *Telefon/Fernsprecher*

1 **Werfen Sie** die Münzen in den Schlitz **ein.**
2 **Wählen Sie** die Nummer.
3 Am Ende des Telefonanrufs **legen Sie** den Hörer **auf.**
4 **Warten Sie** auf die ungebrauchten Münzen.

Chapters 4–6 – Revision (pages 27–28)

A *Einmal zum Stadtzentrum bitte*

1 DU   Wie komme ich am besten **zum** Einkaufszentrum?
2 PASSANT Sie müssen entweder 20 Minuten zu Fuß gehen oder fünf Minuten mit **dem** Bus fahren.
3 Sie nehmen **die** Linie 104.
4 PASSANT Die Bushaltestelle liegt direkt vor **der** Bäckerei.
5 PASSANT **Beim** Fahrer.
6 PASSANT **Am** Rathaus.

B *Ich suche...*

DU   Gibt es **eine** Bank in der Nähe?
PASSANT Die Bank ist neben **der** Bäckerei.
DU   Hat die Bank **einen** Geldautomaten?
PASSANT Der Geldautomat ist in **der** Bank.
DU   Wo gibt es hier **ein** Postamt?
PASSANT Das Postamt ist gegenüber **dem** Markt.
DU   Gibt es hier **einen** Briefkasten?
PASSANT Der Briefkasten ist vor **dem** Postamt.

C *Wieviel Uhr ist es in...?*

Es ist 22 Uhr in London.
Es ist 23 Uhr in Berlin.
Es ist 12 Uhr in San Franzisko.
Es ist sieben Uhr in Peking.
Es ist drei Uhr in Delhi.

D *Am Geldautomaten*
1 Um die Tür aufzumachen, **ziehen Sie** die Bankkarte durch den Schlitz.
2 **Drücken Sie** die Tür auf. **Gehen Sie** hinein.
3 Um Geld vom Automaten abzuheben, **folgen Sie** den Anweisungen.
4 **Stecken Sie** die Karte in den Schlitz **ein**. **Wählen Sie** die gewünschte Sprache.
5 Dann **tippen Sie** Ihre Geheimzahl **ein**, und so weiter.

E *Gute Heimfahrt!*
1 Er fährt in die Schweiz.
2 Er fährt nach Italien.
3 Er fährt nach Frankreich.
4 Er fährt nach Luxemburg.

Gute Reise!
1 Er kommt aus Portugal.
2 Er kommt aus Irland.
3 Er kommt aus Belgien.
4 Er kommt aus Amerika/aus den Vereinigten Staaten/aus den USA.

Chapter 7 – what do you know? (page 29)

A *Was soll ich kaufen?*
Eine Videokassette kostet DM 29,-. Das ist nicht **teuer**.
Das T-Shirt kostet nur DM 10,-. Das ist **billig**.
Die Jeanshose kostet DM 59,-. Ich habe nur DM 50,-. Das ist nicht **genug**. Ich kaufe mir die Videokassette.

B *Gehen wir ins Restaurant?*
FRAU MAIER Das neu**e** Restaurant in der Goethestraße soll gut sein.
HERR MAIER Gehen wir lieber zum Restaurant am See. Der schön**e** Ausblick ist unübertroffen und die romantisch**e** Atmosphäre gefällt mir.

Gehen wir lieber ins Theater
FRAU MAIER Ein schön**er** Ausblick nützt uns nicht, wenn wir nichts draußen sehen können.
HERR MAIER Ein voll**es** Restaurant bedeutet ein gutes Restaurant.
FRAU MAIER Ich gehe lieber ins Theater. Was spielt im Schillertheater?

C *Im Laden*
1 die Steckdose
2 die Glühbirne
3 der Wasserhahn
4 der Schraubenzieher

Chapter 7 – What have you learnt? (page 32)

A *Welchen Beruf findest du am besten?*

MARIA Ich möchte Ärztin sein. Aber dann hat man ein langes Studium.

HERR MAIER **Eine** Ärztin ist sehr wichtig. Ohne Ärzte würden wir alle krank sein.

OMA MAIER **Eine** Krankenpflegerin verdient aber sehr wenig.

MORITZ Bankier! Das ist **ein** schöner Beruf! Ich würde **ein** sehr schnelles Auto und **eine** teure Wohnung in Monaco kaufen!

B *Alles für den Garten*
1 Der grüne Rasenmäher
2 Die große Gießkanne
3 Die blauen Blumentöpfe
4 Der bequeme Liegestuhl
5 Die schnönen gelben Sonnenschirme

C *Umweltfreundlich oder nicht?*
1 c Die Straßen sind sehr laut. iii
2 a Die Luft ist verschmutzt. ii
3 d Der Verkehr in der Stadt ist immer stark. iii
4 b Der Stadtrat ist unfahig. iv

Chapter 8 – What do you know? (page 33)

A *Ein Rätsel*
1 Wir müssen am Samstag ein neues Sofa kaufen.
2 Man kann im Supermarkt billig einkaufen.
3 Die Geschäfte sind am Samstag nachmittag offen.

B *Die Plaudertasche*
1 Ja. Das ist unser Bus.
2 Ja. Wir steigen hier aus.
3 Ja. Wir gehen in den Supermarkt.
4 Ja. Wir wollen Bananen.

C *Was wollt ihr heute machen?*
1 Oma Maier will im Supermarkt einkaufen.
2 Ich will im Kino einen Film sehen.
3 Du willst im Park spazierengehen.
4 Peter und Zoran wollen in der Disko tanzen.

D *Den muß ich sehen!*

PETER Was **können** wir machen?

MAX Wann **müßt** ihr zu Hause sein?

PETER Um 11 Uhr. Der neue Film mit Arnold Schwarzenegger läuft im Odeon.

MAX Den **muß** ich unbedingt sehen!

Chapter 8 – What have you learnt (page 36)

A *Was gibt's Neues?*
1 Ja. Wir spielen am Mittwoch Fußball.
2 Nein. Karl und Fredi kommen am Montag zum Abendessen.
3 Ja. Wir gehen am Samstag in die neue Disko im Kurfürstendamm.
4 Nein. Philip kommt am Sonntag ins Kino mit.
5 Ja. Marianne lernt jetzt Auto fahren.
6 Nein. Wir können am Sonntag spät aufstehen.
7 Nein. Wir machen am Dienstag die Klassenfahrt.
8 Ja. Der Film fängt um 21 Uhr an.

B *Der Zettel*
1 Manfred schenkt mir einen Schal.
2 Wann gehst du ins Schwimmbad?
3 Gehst du ins Kino?
4 Morgen kaufe ich einen Computer.

C *Wo bin ich?*
1 Ich **kann** hier Brötchen kaufen.   c in der Bäckerei
2 Wir **müssen** hier tanken.   a an der Tankstelle
3 Vati **will** hier ein Glas Bier trinken.   d in der Kneipe
4 Du **kannst** hier Medikamente kaufen.   b in der Apotheke

Chapter 9 – What do you know? (page 37)

A *Ist Frau Maier zu Hause?*
1 d Sie geht zuerst in den Supermarkt, um Lebensmittel zu kaufen.
2 c Zweitens geht sie ins Blumengeschäft, **um** Blumen **zu** kaufen.
3 a Danach geht sie ins Café, **um** eine Freundin **zu** treffen.
4 b Zuletzt geht sie in die Autowerkstatt, **um** ihr Auto **zu** holen.

B *Im großen Kaufhaus*
VERKÄUFER Guten Tag! Sie wünschen, bitte?
KUNDIN Ich suche einen Pullover, Größe 42.
VERKÄUFER Die gelb**e** Strickjacke ist Größe 42. Gefällt sie Ihnen?
KUNDIN Haben Sie etwas Ähnliches in Hellblau?
VERKÄUFER Der hier ist das letzt**e** Modell in Hellblau.
KUNDIN Der hellblau**e** Pullover sieht sehr schick aus. Welche Größe ist der?
VERKÄUFER Der ist auch Größe 42.
KUNDIN Gut, den nehme ich.

C *Elektrowaren*
VERKÄUFER Ja, Sie haben Recht. Dieses Modell hat einen eigenartig**en** Fehler. Leider können wir hier die japanisch**en** Maschinen nicht reparieren. Ich gebe Ihnen Ihr Geld zurück. Haben Sie die original**e** Quittung dafür? Kommen Sie bitte mit zur Kasse.

Chapter 9 – What have you learnt? (page 40)

A *Wo sind sie denn alle?*
1 Maria geht zur Post, um einen Brief zu schicken.
2 Frau Maier geht zum Arzt, um ein Rezept zu holen.
3 Moritz geht zur Schule, um seine Tasche zu suchen.

B *Der Banküberfall*
Das Auto **der Bankräuber** steht immer noch vor dem Haupteingang **der Bank**. Die Fensterscheiben **des Autos** sind durch die Kugeln **der Polizisten** zersplittert.

C *Im Supermarkt*
Also zwei Kilo von den rot**en** Äpfeln. Eine Tube dieser neu**en** Zahnpasta. Haben sie grün**e** Bohnen? Ach ja, da, neben den groß**en** Packungen Erbsen. Ich möchte eine Dose der best**en** Sardinen. Ich glaube, das war es, oder?

1 **ja**	2 **nein**	3 **ja**
4 **ja**	5 **nein**	6 **ja**

D *Hat es Spaß gemacht?*
1 Wir haben ein Hotel **innerhalb** der Stadt gebucht.
2 Leider war das Hotel weit **außerhalb** des Orts.
3 **Wegen** des Lärms vom Flughafen konnten wir kaum schlafen.
4 **Während** der Nacht haben uns die Insekten gestochen.
5 **Trotz** dieser schlechten Erfahrungen hat es uns Spaß gemacht!

Chapters 7–9 – Revision (pages 41–42)

A *Wie findest du Berlin?*
1 Berlin ist jetzt zu **laut**. Es gibt immer mehr Verkehr.
2 Es gibt zu viele Touristen. Die Straßen im Zentrum sind immer **voll**.
3 Die Kriminalität ist ein großes Problem. Es ist nachts **gefährlich**, allein mit der U-Bahn zu fahren.

a Aber früher war Berlin wie eine Insel umgeben von der DDR. Damals war das Leben in Berlin zu **ruhig**.
b Wir brauchen Tourismus. Berlin und Potsdam sind historisch **wichtig**. Das Schloß Sanssoucis ist **bezaubernd**.
c Das stimmt. Die steigende Kriminalität ist **beängstigend**.

B *Beschreiben Sie bitte den Rucksack*
Er ist ein klein**er** schwarz**er** Rucksack aus Nylon. Er hat zwei Taschen vorne. In diesen klein**en** Taschen sind ein blau**er** Kugelschreiber und drei Postkarten. In der groß**en** Tasche des Rucksacks ist mein grün**er** Regenmantel.

C *Schilder*

1 Kinderspielplatz	Children's playground
2 Wartezeit 20 Minuten	Waiting time 20 minutes
3 Vorsicht Bahnübergang!	Careful railway crossing!
4 Kabelfernsehen	Cable TV
5 Mittwochs Ruhetag	Closed on Wednesday

D *Wortstellung!*
1 Wie komme ich zum Bahnhof?
2 Wir gehen morgen ins Kino, um einen Film zu sehen.
3 Spielen die Kinder auf dem Schulhof?
4 Wann fährt der Zug nach Stuttgart ab?
5 Nächstes Jahr fahren wir in die Schweiz, um meine Oma zu besuchen.

E *Im Schuhgeschäft*

DU	Haben Sie diese Schuhe in einer klein**eren** Größe?
VERKÄUFERIN	Nein, leider nicht.
DU	Vielleicht in einem ähnlich**en** Stil?
VERKÄUFERIN	Wir haben die hier. Welche Farbe möchten Sie?
DU	Ich habe sie lieber im praktisch**en** Schwarz.
VERKÄUFERIN	Ja, Schwarz ist eine praktische Farbe. Wie finden Sie die?
DU	Plastik ist aber unangenehm bei dem warm**en** Wetter. Haben Sie etwas Ähnliches in Leder?

F *Die Familie Maier*
1 c Der Name mein**er** Mutter ist Irmgard.
2 e Die Frau mein**es** Vaters heißt Irmgard.
3 a Die Kinder mein**er** Eltern heißen Moritz und Maria.
4 b Der Name unser**es** Schulleiters ist Gruber.
5 d Der Sohn unser**er** Nachbarn heißt Klaus.

Chapter 10 – What do you know? (page 43)

A *Können wir endlich nach Hause gehen?*
1 Jaja. **Sie** kommen aus Italien.
2 Jaja. **Er** ist für unsere Eßecke zu groß.
3 Jaja. **Sie** ist wirklich preiswert.
4 Jaja. **Es** ist aus Edelstahl.

B *Der Schlußverkauf*
1 Wenn die Schuhe im Schlußverkauf sind, dann kaufe ich **sie**.
2 Wenn ein Pulli im Schlußverkauf ist, dann kaufe ich **ihn**.

C *Weihnachtsgeschenke (1)*
1 Sie schenkt **ihm** eine Videokassette.
2 Sie schenkt **ihnen** Süßigkeiten.
3 Sie schenkt **ihr** einen Mantel.
4 Sie schenkt **ihm** eine Krawatte.

D *Weihnachtsgeschenke (2)*
1 Sie gibt **sie** <u>ihm</u>.
2 Sie gibt **sie** <u>ihnen</u>.
3 Sie gibt **es** <u>ihr</u>.
4 Sie gibt **ihn** <u>ihm</u>.

Chapter 10 – What have you learnt? (page 46)

A *Worüber sprechen sie?*
1 **Das Buch** ist sehr aufregend.
2 **Die Geschichte** ist sehr interessant.
3 **Der Schriftsteller** ist weltberühmt.
4 **Die Fernsehsendungen** sind genau so gut wie die Bücher.

B *Geburtstagsgeschenke*
1 Josef schenkt **sie ihm.**
2 Mutti schenkt **ihn ihm.**
3 Vati schenkt **es ihm.**
4 Maria schenkt **sie ihm.**

C *Geschenke zum Hochzeitstag*
MARIA Mutti möchte Mitglied des Kinoklubs werden.
OMA Dann kaufe ich **ihr** vielleicht eine Mitgliedskarte. Ja, ich kaufe **sie** ihr.
MARIA Vati und Mutti möchten nächstes Jahr nach Ägypten fahren.
OMA Vielleicht sollte ich **ihnen** einen Reiseführer von Ägypten schenken. Vielleicht kaufe ich **ihn** ihnen.
MARIA Vati arbeitet gern im Garten. Er möchte einige Bäume pflanzen.
OMA Ich könnte **ihm** einen Apfelbaum geben. Ja, ich gebe **ihn** ihm.

Chapter 11 – What do you know? (page 47)

A *Die Einladung*
OMA Guten Tag. **Wie** geht es dir? Komm rein.
DU Guten Tag Frau Maier. **Wo** soll ich meinen Mantel aufhängen? Er ist ziemlich naß.
OMA Gib ihn mir. Ich hänge ihn im Badezimmer über die Badewanne. **Wann** triffst du Maria und Peter?
DU Um sieben Uhr.
OPA **Warum** stehst du im Flur? Komm ins Wohnzimmer in die Wärme!

B *Ich habe viel gemacht*
1 Montagmorgen habe ich Tennis mit Maria und Peter **gespielt.**
2 Wir haben danach einen Ausflug nach Potsdam **gemacht.**
3 Am Dienstag hat Peter ein Auto **gekauft.**
4 Peter hat einen Ausflug in das Filmstudio **organisiert.**
5 Wir haben gestern bis Mitternacht in der Disko **getanzt.**
6 Ich habe erst heute Ansichtskarten nach England **geschickt.**

C *Was hast du diese Woche gemacht?*
1 Was **hast** du mit Peter und Maria gemacht?
2 **Hat** Peter einen Ausflug für dich organisiert?
3 Wann **habt** ihr das Filmstudio besucht?
4 **Hast** du Ansichtskarten nach England geschickt?

Chapter 11 – What have you learnt? (page 50)

A *Fragen am Telefon*
1 Der Film beginnt um 20.30 Uhr.
2 Es kostet DM 6 für Erwachsene.
3 Der Film dauert zwei Stunden.
4 Der Film spielt im Odeon.

B *Mein Tagebuch*
Am Dienstag **hat** Peter einen Ausflug **organisiert.**
Am Mittwoch **haben** wir alle bis Mitternacht in der Disko **getanzt.**
Am Donnerstag **habe** ich Oma und Opa Maier **besucht.**
Am Freitag **haben** Herr und Frau Maier bei Aldi **eingekauft.**

C *Grüße aus Berlin!*
Lieber Paul,
ich habe hier viel Spaß gehabt. Wir haben viel gemacht.
Wir haben den Reichstag besichtigt. Ich habe mein Deutsch verbessert.
Was hast Du gemacht?
Bis bald,   ───────────
Dein Freund

Chapter 12 – What do you know? (page 51)

A *Weihnachten*
1 Ich habe die letzten Weihnachtsferien bei meinen Großeltern **verbracht.**
2 Am ersten Weihnachtsfeiertag haben wir unsere Geschenke **bekommen.**
3 Wir haben ein typisches Festessen mit Truthahn **gegessen.**
4 Wir haben eine Flasche Wein **getrunken.**
5 Großvater hat seine neue CD **gespielt.**

B *Was haben Sie gestern gemacht?*
1 Ich bin mit meinen Freunden ins Schwimmbad **gegangen.**
2 Wir sind dort den ganzen Tag **geblieben.**
3 Ich bin schön braun **geworden.**
4 Sonst ist nichts **geschehen.**

C *In meiner Freizeit*
1 **Meine** Lieblingssportart ist Skil aufen.
2 Jedes Jahr verbringen wir **unsere** Weihnachtsferien in Lech.
3 Meine Mutter kommt auch. **Ihre** Familie wohnt in Lech.
4 Wir lachen über meinen Vater, **sein** Ski laufen ist furchtbar!
5 Was ist **dein** Lieblingsurlaub?

Chapter 12 – What have you learnt? (page 54)

A *Die neue Freundin*
   1 Dann **hat** sie mir ihre Telefonnummer **gegeben.**
   2 Ich **habe** ein Einladung zu ihrer Geburtstagsparty **bekommen.**
   3 Meine Schwester **hat** für sie ein tolles Geschenk **empfohlen.**
   4 Wir **haben** stundenlang **gesprochen.**

B *Was ist passiert?*
   1 Der Bus **ist** nie **gekommen.**
   2 Ich **bin** schließlich mit Maria zur U-Bahn-Station **gelaufen.**
   3 Wir **sind** mit der U-Bahn **gefahren**!
   4 Was **ist** denn hier **geschehen**?

C *Lieber Gäste*
   Liebe Gäste, **Sie sind** herzlich willkommen. Wir bitten **Sie**, auf **Ihren** Besitz aufzupassen, und empfehlen **Ihnen**, daß **Sie** die Schließfächer für **Ihre** Wertsachen benutzen.

D *Moment mal!*
   I washed my hair: Ich habe mir **die** Haare gewaschen.
   I'm putting my T-shirt on: Ich ziehe mir **das** T-Shirt an.

Chapters 10–12 – Revision (pages 55–56)

A *Der Sci-fi Film (1)*
   Er ist fantastisch! **Es** hat eine enorme Leinwand. **Sie** sind so realistisch. **Es** sieht toll aus.

   Der Sci-fi Film (2)
   Moritz schenkt mir **das Modell** zum Geburtstag. Ich schenke ihm **den Raumkämpfer.** Mutti, kannst du mir **die Videokassette** kaufen?

B *Was hast du denn hier?*
   Das Buch gehört **ihr.** Das Lineal gehört **ihm.** Die Bleistifte gehören **ihnen.**

C *Meine Geburtstagsparty*
   Ich **möchte** ins Kino gehen. Susanne **möchte** in den Zoo. Mutti und Vati **möchten** hier zu Hause feiern. Moritz und Philipp, ihr **möchtet** eislaufen gehen.

D *Wir gehen eislaufen*
   Wo treffen wir uns? **Wie** fahren wir dorthin? **Was** kostet es?
   Warum kommt Sabine erst um sechs Uhr? **Wann** kommen wir nach Hause?

E *Eine Postkarte aus Spanien*
   Grüße aus Spanien! Ich **habe** einen guten Flug nach Malaga **gehabt.**
   Wir **haben** für die Ferien viel **organisiert.** Jeden Tag **habe** ich Tennis **gespielt.**
   Meine Freundin **hat** windsurfen **gelernt.** Heute morgen **haben** wir ein Boot **gemietet.**
   Kristel **hat** jeden Tag im Supermarkt **eingekauft.**

F *Grüße aus Holland*

verbracht	verbringen	to spend (time)
gewesen	sein	to be
ausgegangen	ausgehen	to go out
mitgenommen	mitnehmen	to take with
gefunden	finden	to find

G *Ein Unfall*

Gestern **bin** ich mit dem Fahrrad in die Stadt gefahren. Ich **habe** das Fahrrad zum Geburtstag bekommen. Plötzlich **bin** ich vom Rad gefallen. Ein Autofahrer **hat** mich ins Krankenhaus gebracht. Mein Kopf **hat** mir weh getan. Der Arzt **ist** sehr freundlich gewesen. Glücklicherweise **habe** ich nur leichte Schäden am Fahrrad gehabt.

H *Am Gepäckfließband*

Ich habe schon **meinen** Koffer. Wo ist **deine** Reisetasche? Ich sehe das Etikett von **unseren** Skiern. Hat Stefan **seinen** Rucksack gefunden? Wo sind Herr und Frau Braun? Ich habe **ihren** Kinderwagen gerade gesehen. Kinder, da kommen endlich **eure** Taschen.

Chapter 13 – What do you know? (page 57)

A *Im Vergleich zu*

1 Die Bundesrepublik ist **größer** als Großbritannien.
2 Der Zugspitze ist **höher** als Snowdon.
3 Schottland ist **schöner** als England.
4 Ben Nevis ist der **höchste** Berg Großbritanniens.
5 Die **schönste** Stadt Deutschlands ist Quedlinburg.
6 Deutschland ist aber das **größte** Land.

B *Ratschläge*

1 b, 2 d, 3 a, 4 c

C *Interessen*

1 Was für Filme siehst du **am liebsten**?
2 Was für Bücher liest du **lieber**?

Chapter 13 – What have you learnt? (page 60)

A *Größer, besser, schneller (1)*

1 Der BMW ist schnell. Mein Auto ist schnell**er**.
2 Der Mercedes ist groß. Mein Auto ist **größer**.
3 Der Audi ist bequem. Mein Auto ist **bequemer**.

B *Größer, besser, schneller (2)*
1 Der BMW hat ein gutes Stereo. Mein Auto hat ein besser**es** Stereo.
2 Der Jaguar hat eine hohe Leistung. Mein Auto hat eine höher**e** Leistung.
3 Der Mercedes hat viel Platz. Mein Auto hat **mehr** Platz.

C *Filme, Musik, Bücher*
1 Maria: Ich höre **gern** klassische Musik.
2 Peter: **Am liebsten** sehe ich Krimis.
3 Maria or Philipp: Ich lese **lieber** Krimis.
4 Philipp: Actionfilme sehe ich **am liebsten**.
5 Peter: Ich lese **lieber** geschichtliche Romane.
6 Maria: Die Musik von Beethoven höre ich **am liebsten**.

Chapter 14 – What do you know? (page 61)

A *Die Hausaufgabe*
1 Ich schreibe meine Hausaufgaben**, denn** ich möchte eine gute Note.
2 Ich wohne in einer Wohnung**, aber** meine Großeltern wohnen in einem Haus.
3 Meine Mutter ist Lehrerin**, und** mein Vater ist Kaufmann.
4 Zum Frühstück esse ich ein Butterbrot **oder** ich trinke ein Glas Milch.

B *Sondern oder aber?*
1 Ich fahre nicht mit dem Bus zur Schule, **sondern** gehe zu Fuß.
2 Peter ist mein Bruder, **aber** er wohnt nicht bei uns.
3 Maria ist meine Schwester, **aber** sie ist eine Nervensäge!
4 Ich bekomme keine schlechte Note, **sondern** eine gute.

C *Worauf wartest du?*
1 Ich warte schon lange **darauf**.
2 Sie lacht oft **darüber**.
3 Er fragt immer wieder **danach**.
4 Du solltest auch **daran** denken.

Chapter 14 – What have you learnt? (page 64)

A *Der unerfahrene Kellner*
KELLNER   Einen Tisch für acht Personen.
HERR MAIER Nein, nicht acht Personen, **sondern** sechs Personen. Für nächsten Samstag.
KELLNER   Es tut mir leid, **aber** wir haben am Samstag nichts frei.

B *Mein Wochenende*
Letzten Samstag bin ich schwimmen gegangen**, denn** das Wetter war schön. Am Abend bin ich zu Hause geblieben**, aber** mein Bruder und meine Schwester sind ausgegangen. Meine Eltern sind ins Kino gegangen**, und** ich habe mir eine Videokassette angesehen.

C *Was ist bis jetzt passiert?*

1 Der Mann hat ein paar Minuten **auf** die blonde Dame gewartet.
2 Sie ist ins Zimmer gekommen. Sie hat **von** ihrer Tochter gesprochen.
3 Sie hat ihn **um** Hilfe gebeten. Ich weiß nicht warum.
4 Sie **auf** einer Antwort bestanden und jetzt streiten sie.
5 Ich freue mich schon **auf** die Werbung!

Chapter 15 – What do you know? (page 65)

A *Wie geht's?*

1 I'm sorry.   Es tut mir leid.
2 I'm not well.   Es geht mir schlecht.
3 I feel dizzy.   Es ist mir schwindelig.
4 I'm well.   Es geht mir gut.

B *Meinungen*

1 Meine Oma findet, daß Fußballspieler zu viel Geld bekommen.
2 Meine Mutter denkt, daß Hausfrauen am wichtigsten sind.
3 Mein Opa findet, daß Rentner mehr Geld brauchen.

C *Ein schrecklicher Tag*

1 Ich habe den Zug verpaßt, weil die Ampel vor dem Büro kaputt ist.
2 Ich habe den Zug verpaßt, weil die Rolltreppe zu den Gleisen wegen Reparatur ausgeschaltet ist.
3 Ich habe den Zug verpaßt, weil es jeden Abend einen Stau auf der Hauptstraße gibt.

Chapter 15 – What have you learnt? (page 68)

A *Macbeth*

Macbeth trifft drei Hexen. **Es regnet. Es donnert. Es blitzt.** Die Frau von Macbeth ermordet den König Malcolm. **Es geht** Macbeths Frau immer schlechter. Ganz am Ende **gibt es** eine große Schlacht und Macbeth stirbt.

B *Warum kommst du so spät nach Hause?*

Ich habe die Schule spät verlassen, weil meine Klassenlehrerin mit mir gesprochen hat, weil sie mit meiner Arbeit nicht zufrieden ist, weil ich zu viele Fehler in meiner Klassenarbeit gemacht habe.

C *Die alten Filme sind besser gewesen*

1 **Ich finde, daß** die neuesten Krimis entsetzlich **sind, weil** sie die Kriminalität verherrlichen.
2 **Ich finde, daß** die alten Liebesgeschichten schöner **sind, weil** sie nicht so viel Sex **bringen.**
3 **Ich finde, daß** die modernen Actionfilme blöd **sind, weil** sie keine normalen Menschen **zeigen.**

Chapters 13–15 – Revision (pages 69–70)

A *Zwei Jungen*

1 Stefan ist jünger als Moritz.
2 Stefan ist größer als Moritz.
3 Moritz ist kleiner als Stefan.

B *Vier Schüler*

1 Stefan ist der großte.
2 Birgit ist die kleinste.
3 Stefan ist der jüngste.
4 Yasmin ist die älteste.

C *Gute Noten*

1 Stefan braucht eine besser**e** Note, wenn er an der Uni studieren will.
2 Moritz schreibt immer einen länger**en** Aufsatz als Stefan.
3 Yasmin hat immer die best**en** Noten in der Klasse.
4 Stefan ist der best**e** Schüler in der Klasse.
5 Moritz bekommt immer das schlechtest**e** Zeugnis.
6 Birgit ist die ruhigst**e** Schülerin.

D

STEFAN	Es gefällt **ihm**, wie er die Klasse behandelt.
YASMIN	Es gefällt **ihr**, wie er spricht.
MORITZ UND BIRGIT	Es gefällt **ihnen**, wie er alles erklärt.

E *Das Schulzeugnis*

Stefan liest sehr gern **und** schreibt gern Aufsätze. Leider schwätzt er zu viel **oder** konzentriert sich nicht gut. Er muß bessere Noten kriegen, **denn** er möchte weiter studieren. Er soll nicht mehr, **sondern** besser arbeiten.

F *Die Sommerferien*

Ich freue mich schon auf **die** Ferien. Wir interessieren uns für **die** Türkei. Erinnert ihr euch an **die** letzten Sommerferien? Meine Freundin erzählt mir viel von **der** Türkei. Wir warten auf **den** Prospekt vom Reisebüro.

G *Mir geht's schlecht*

1 Philip hat Kopfschmerzen. Es geht **ihm** nicht gut.
2 Susanne hat Ohrenschmerzen. Die Ohren tun **ihr** weh.
3 Stefan und Birgit haben Zahnschmerzen. Die Zähne tun **ihnen** weh.
4 Yasmin hat eine Erkältung. Es geht **ihr** schlecht.

H *Ich habe den Film in schon gesehen*

1 Er hat gesagt, daß er den Film in England schon gesehen hat.
2 Er hat gesagt, daß er lieber schwimmen gegangen ist.
3 Er hat gesagt, daß er zu viel Hausaufgaben gehabt hat.
4 Er hat gesagt, daß er lieber mit Yasmin in die Disko gegangen ist.

Chapter 16 – What do you know? (page 71)

A *Du mußt noch...*

Bevor ich Berlin verlasse, möchte ich euch zum Essen im Restaurant einladen. **Obgleich** Samstag mein letzter Tag ist, habe ich mittags Zeit, **da** mein Zug erst um 21 Uhr abfährt.

B *Ich weiß nicht*

1 Ich weiß nicht, wie die Wettervorhersage für Samstag ist.
2 Ich weiß nicht, wann die neue Eishalle auf hat.
3 Ich weiß nicht, wer im Fußballstadion spielt.
4 Ich weiß nicht, was für Musik es in der Disko gibt.
5 Ich weiß nicht, warum Peter nicht mitkommt.

C *Ich muß noch*

1 ja. Ich habe vergessen, Daniela ihr Buch **zu** geben.
2 nein
3 nein
4 nein
5 ja. Ich freue mich darauf, meine Familie wieder**zu**sehen.

Chapter 16 – What have you learnt (page 74)

A *Wir gehen ins Theater*

1 **Obwohl** das Wetter sehr gut **ist, müssen wir** alle Fenster zumachen.
2 Die Katze will bestimmt hereinkommen, **nachdem wir** ausgegangen **sind**.
3 Ich muß meine Schlüssel finden, **bevor wir abfahren**.
4 **Seitdem** ich die Karten gekauft **habe, ist das Theater** ganz ausgebucht.
5 Wir brauchen nicht in der Schlange zu stehen, **da wir** schon Karten **haben**.

B *Die Verbindung ist schlecht*

1 Ich habe keine Ahnung, **wovon du sprichst!**
2 Ich will wissen, **warum dein Telefon nicht funktioniert!**
3 Ich habe nicht gehört, **wann du zurückkommst**.

C *Eine Einladung*

DU   Ich lade euch ein, nächstes Jahr meine Familie und mich **zu besuchen**.
HERR MAIER Nichts **zu danken**. Es war für uns ein Vergnügen, dich **zu begrüßen**.
FRAU MAIER Moritz! Maria! Ihr müßt euch **verabschieden**. Ach nein. Ihr könnt euch nie verabschieden, ohne **zu weinen**!

Chapter 17 – What do you know? (page 75)

A *Wann fährt dein Zug?*

1 Auf der Fähre, **wenn** das Wetter schön ist, kannst du draußen sitzen.
2 Weißt du, **wann** du in London ankommst?
3 **Wenn** du in London ankommst, grüße deine Eltern recht schön von uns.
4 Wir kommen dich besuchen, aber ich bin nicht sicher, **wann**.

B *Wo ist der Schlüssel?*
1 Ich habe das Licht angeschaltet.
  Ich habe den Schlüssel in der Hand gehabt.
2 Peter hat eine Tasse Kaffee gemacht.
  Ich habe das Schlüsselbund auf den Tisch gelegt.
3 Ich bin ins Wohnzimmer gegangen.
  Ich habe den Schlüssel nicht mehr gehabt.

C *Die Millionäre*
1 Meine Eltern **werden** eine Villa in Italien kaufen!
2 Kinder, ihr **werdet** eure Lieblingspopstars treffen!
3 Meine Frau **wird** einen neuen Mercedes fahren!
4 Wir **werden** eine Weltreise machen.

Chapter 17 – What have you learnt? (page 78)

A *Ausflüge*
1 **Wenn** das Wetter schlecht **ist, besuchen wir** das Schloß Charlottenburg.
2 **Wenn** die Sonne **scheint, macht die Familie** einen Spaziergang durch den Wald.
3 **Wenn** es sehr stark **regnet, fahren wir** irgendwohin essen.
4 **Wenn** es sehr warm **ist, können die Jungen** ins Freibad gehen.

B *Der Ausflug war ein Alptraum!*
Ich erinnere mich nicht genau, **wann** das Schiff abgefahren ist. Wahrscheinlich am frühen Nachmittag. **Wenn** wir sonntags einen Ausflug machen, gehen wir gewöhnlich nach dem Mittagessen.
Als das Schiff mitten auf dem See war, hat es einen schrecklichen Sturm gegeben. Wir waren alle seekrank.
Jetzt **wenn** wir ausgehen, passen wir immer auf das Wetter auf!

C *Träume*
1 Frau Maier **wird** jeden Winter in Gstaad **Ski fahren.**
2 Oma und Opa Maier werden ein dickes Auto kaufen.
3 Herr Maier **wird** ein Haus in Spanien **kaufen.**
4 Maria **wird** in alle Konzerte der Berliner Philharmoniker **gehen.**

Chapter 18 – What do you know? (page 79)

A *Das Schulzeugnis*
1 Ich werde **gut** lernen.
2 Ich werde **viel** arbeiten.
3 Ich werde nicht so **viel** plaudern.

B *Am Elternabend (1)*
1 Er lernt **mehr**.
2 Er plaudert **weniger**.
3 Er kann sich **besser** konzentrieren.

C *Am Elternabend (2)*
Moritz lernt **am fleißigsten** und **am meisten**, plaudert **am wenigsten** und konzentriert sich **am besten** von der ganzen Klasse, wenn er allein sitzt.

D *Gehst du denn nicht ins Kino?*
1 b I have saved for four weeks.
2 c I have been working in the baker's for a month.
3 a The film isn't on any more on Saturday!

Chapter 18 – What have you learnt? (page 82)

A *Ein Telefonanruf nach England*
PETER Du sprichst Englisch genauso gut wie ich.
FRAU MAIER Aber du sprichst es **deutlicher** aus. Am Telefon ist das wichtig.
PETER Du hast dein Englisch **mehr** geübt.
FRAU MAIER Ich telefoniere **lieber** heute abend. Ja, ich rufe **später** an.
PETER Es wird heute abend zu spät sein. Gib mir das Telefon!
FRAU MAIER OK. Aber es ist **besser**, wenn ich dir die Fragen aufschreibe.

B *Reisepläne*
1 Wir fahren **am schnellsten** durch den Tunnel.
2 **Am besten** übernachten wir auf einem Campingplatz in der Nähe von Canterbury.
3 Wir kommen **am liebsten** am 20. Juli in Canterbury an.
4 **Am spätesten** fahren wir am 25. Juli ab.
5 Wir kommen **am frühesten** am 31. Juli nach Berlin zurück.

C *Ja, ich spreche Deutsch*
1 richtig
2 falsch. Sie kommen am 20. Juli in Canterbury an.
3 falsch. Die Familie möchte fünf Nächte auf einem Campingplatz bleiben.
4 richtig

Chapters 16–18 – Revision (pages 83–84)

A *Mein Freund und ich*
1 **Bevor** wir heiraten, müssen wir warten.
2 Wir warten, **bis** wir Geld für ein Haus gespart haben.
3 Meine Kinder haben gefragt, **ob** sie uns helfen können.
4 **Obgleich/Obwohl** wir warten müssen, macht es uns keine Sorgen.
5 **Während** wir sparen, wohnen mein Freund und ich hier im Altersheim.
6 **Seitdem** es Satellitenfernsehen hier gibt, schauen wir mehr Sport.

Help Yourself to Essential German Grammar

B *Was hat sie gesagt?*
1 Wann möchten Sie essen?
2 Wo haben Sie die Zeitung gelassen?
3 Warum hat Ihr Sohn ein neues Auto gekauft?
4 Wie sind Sie nach Hause gefahren?

C *Hausvorschriften*
1 ja. Es ist verboten, im Altersheim **zu** rauchen.
2 ja. Wir bitten unsere Gäste, die Bibliothek morgens **zu** benutzen.
3 ja. Wir empfehlen unseren Gästen, ihre Wertsachen im Safe **zu** lassen.
4 ja. Bitte, verlassen Sie das Altersheim nicht, ohne das Personal **zu** informieren.

D *Oma Müller*
Als mein Mann gestorben ist, war ich ganz allein zu Hause. Meine Tochter kommt heute nachmittag, aber ich weiß nicht, **wann** sie ankommt. **Wenn** ich sie wiedersehe, werde ich mich freuen. Ich war sehr froh, **als** ich Herrn Heinrich kennengelernt habe.

E *Das Jahr 2030*
Wir besuchen das Jahr 2030. Der Supermarkt **wird** ganz anders aussehen. Die Kunden **werden** von zu Hause alles durch das Internet bestellen. Es **wird** kein Plastik mehr geben, sondern nur wiederverwendbare Stoffe. Ich **werde** in einem umweltfreundlichen Haus wohnen.

F *Besser*
Yasmin schreibt **besser**. Sie arbeitet **langsamer** aber **genauer**. Sie tanzt **schöner** und läuft **schneller**.

G *Am besten*
1 Du stehst **am langsamsten** auf.
2 Du läufst **am schnellsten** nach der Schule nach Hause.
3 Du singst **am schönsten** in der Badewanne.
4 Du spielst **am besten** auf dem Computer.

H *Wortstellung*
1 jeden Abend   Time phrase
   mit dem Bus   Manner phrase
   nach Hause   Place phrase
2 seit einem Jahr   Time phrase
   in der Jugendherberge Place phrase
3 am Wochenende   Time phrase
   mit meinen Freunden Manner phrase
   im Park   Place phrase

Chapter 19 – What do you know? (page 85)

A *Mein Lebenslauf*

Von 1992 bis 1997 **besuchte** ich eine Gesamtschule in Berlin. Ich **absolvierte** 1997 meine Schulbildung mit dem Realschulabschluß.

B *Die Lehrzeit*

Ab dem Alter von 12 Jahren **ging** ich in ein Gymnasium. Obwohl ich mein Abitur **bestand, beschloß** ich trotzdem eine Lehrzeit als Automechaniker zu machen. Ich **half** meinem Onkel jedes Wochenende in seiner Autowerkstatt.

C *Mein Beruf*

1 Schwierigkeit: schwierig
2 Gesundheit: gesund
3 Müdigkeit: müde
4 Fähigkeit: fähig

Chapter 19 – What have you learnt? (page 88)

A *Das Interview*

SABINE Früher **wohnte** meine Familie in Duisburg. Ich **besuchte** am Anfang ein Gymnasium. Wegen meiner schlechten Noten in Mathe **wechselte** ich meine Schule.

ZORAN Ich **begann** eine Lehrzeit als Tischler, aber die Firma hat bankrott gemacht. Danach **entschied** ich, einen Beruf mit besseren Aussichten zu lernen.

B *Die Diskussion*

1 Ich habe **viel Interessantes** gelernt.
2 Ich habe **allerlei Blödes** gesagt.
3 Wir möchten nächste Woche **etwas Ähnliches** machen.

C *In der Kantine*

1 **Die** einzige Schwierigkeit für mich ist die Fahrt hierher.
2 **Das** Kochen ist ein großes Vergnügen.
3 **Die** Verschiedenheit der Fächer gefällt mir.
4 Ich finde **das** Lernen der vielen Tatsachen sehr schwierig.

Chapter 20 – What do you know? (page 89)

A *Die Familie ist nach Köln umgezogen*

1 Manfred **hatte** keine Wahl, seine Familie ist nach Köln umgezogen.
2 Sein Vater **war** arbeitslos und konnte keine Arbeitsstelle finden.
3 Seine Brüder **hatten** auch in der Schule Schwierigkeiten.
4 Sie **waren** beide unartig.

B *Hast du Peter gesehen?*

1 b Als ich hinkam, saß er in der Ecke. i
2 c Seitdem du hier bist, habe ich ihn nicht gesehen. ii
3 a Er wartete im Flur, als ich ihn sah. iii

C *Ein Widerspruch!*

1 Sabine hat die Hausaufgaben **noch nicht** gemacht.
2 Es geht dem Lehrer **nicht** gut.
3 Stefan versteht **nichts**, was der Lehrer sagt.
4 Der Lehrer hat uns die Arbeit **noch nicht** erklärt.
5 Sie hat ihn **nicht** gut verstanden.

Chapter 20 – What have you learnt? (page 92)

A *Der Ferienjob (1)*

Ich **hatte** eine Stelle in einem Restaurant in Florenz. Die Arbeitsstunden **waren** viel länger als erwartet. Mein Zimmer **war** winzig und **hatte** keinen Fernseher.

B *Der Ferienjob (2)*

1 Als ich mit ihm die Arbeitsbedingungen besprochen habe, **war** der Chef sehr nett zu mir.
2 Während ich in dem Zimmer **wohnte**, hat er mir einen Farbfernseher geliehen.
3 Obwohl ich im Restaurant gern **arbeitete**, war ich froh zuzück nach Deutschland zu kommen.

C *Im Rückblick*

1 Im Rückblick fand ich die ganze Erfahrung interessant.
2 Ich habe eine gute Erinnerung an meine Zeit in Italien.
3 Ich bin alles in allem einer, der gerne im Ausland arbeitet.
4 Ich würde gerne wieder im Ausland arbeiten.

D *Ferienjob mit Unterkunft*

1 Das Wohnzimmer hatte **weder** Vorhänge **noch** Teppich.
2 Die Küche hatte weder Fenster noch Ventilator.
3 Das Büro hatte **weder** Computer **noch** Faxgerät.
4 Die Arbeitskollegen hatten weder Zeit noch Lust, mir zu helfen.

Chapter 21 – What do you know? (page 93)

A *Eine neue Karriere*

1 Ich **hatte** vor einem Jahr eine Lehrstelle als Tischler gefunden.
2 Lange Zeit **hatte** die Firma finanzielle Probleme gehabt.
3 Nachdem die Firma bankrott gemacht **hatte**, mußte ich eine neue Stelle finden.
4 Meine Eltern **waren** sowieso mit der Firma enttäuscht gewesen.

B *Meine Familie stammt aus Kroatien*
1 Seit 1973 wohnt meine Familie in Deutschland, **da** mein Vater damals Arbeit in Berlin gefunden **hatte**.
2 Meine Mutter arbeitete zu der Zeit in seiner Firma, **weil** ihre Eltern nach Berlin umgezogen **waren**.

C *Befehle*
1 c, 2 e, 3 d, 4 b, 5 a

Chapter 21 – What have you learnt? (page 96)

A *Arbeitserfahrungen*
1 Der erste Chef **hatte** früher Probleme mit Lehrlingen gehabt.
2 Die nächste Firma **war** von Stuttgart nach Berlin umgezogen.
3 Die Fahrt zu der dritten Firma **war** zu gefährlich geworden.

B *Kündigung*
1 Die erste Firma hat mich entlassen, **obwohl** sie mehr Arbeitnehmer angeworben hatte.
2 Ich habe der nächsten Firma gekündigt, **weil** die Arbeit zu langweilig geworden war.
3 Die Arbeitsstunden gefielen mir nicht bei der dritten Firma, da ich bei den anderen Firmen mehr Freizeit gehabt hatte.

C *Was machen wir denn?*
PETER   Nein. **Spielen wir** lieber Basketball auf dem Hof!
MICHAEL   **Gib** mir die Zeitung!
SABINE   **Gehen wir** in die Disko.
ZORAN   Peter, **geh** schnell nach Hause und hol dein Auto!

Chapters 19–21 – Revision (pages 97–98)

A *In meiner Jugend*
Als ich Kind **war**, **besuchte** ich eine Grundschule in Neukölln. Die Lehrer **waren** sehr streng. Alle Kinder **trugen** eine Schuluniform. Wir **hatten** viele Hausaufgaben. Nach der Schule **machte** ich eine Lehre als Bäckerin. Ich **arbeitete** nur zwei Jahre lang, dann **traf** ich Opa Maier.

B *In der Bäckerei*
Die Sauberkeit war die Hauptsache. Zu der Zeit gab es eine furchtbare **Krankheit**. Ein Freund ist viel Jahre später daran gestorben. Das war eine **Traurigkeit**. Ich kann mich genau an die **Schönheit** des Schaufensters erinnern. Die **Verschiedenheit** der Brotsorten war erstaunlich.

C *Wie war dein Tag?*
FRAU MAIER Hast du heute etwas **Interessantes** gemacht?
HERR MAIER Nein. Nichts **Neues**. Nur viel **Langweiliges**. Wie war dein Tag?
FRAU MAIER Ich habe allerlei **Verschiedenes** getan.

D *Die Konferenz (1)*

Wir **trafen** uns am Rudower S-Bahnhof. Dann **fuhren** wir zum Busbahnhof. Wir **nahmen** den Reisebus vom Busbahnhof nach Stuttgart. Dort **mußten** wir mit der Straßenbahn ins Zentrum fahren.

E *Die Konferenz (2)*

1 Das war **kein** gutes Hotel.
2 Ich hatte ein Einzelzimmer mit **weder** Dusche **noch** WC.
3 Ich konnte meine Kollegen **nirgends** finden.
4 **Niemand** hat den Direktor getroffen.

F *Als du in Stuttgart warst*

1 Ich **war** um 17 Uhr von der Arbeit **gekommen**.
2 Die Kinder **waren** etwas früher nach Hause **gekommen**.
3 Frau Rust **hatte** an die Tür **geklopft**.
4 Ihre Waschmaschine **hatte** am Morgen nicht richtig **funktioniert**.
5 Sie **war** sofort zum Hausmeister **gegangen**.
6 Leider **hatte** er keine Zeit **gehabt**.

G *In der Kantine (1)*

1 Zoran, **bring** mir bitte eine Flasche Cola.
2 **Holt** mir Messer und Gabel.
3 Michael, **vergiß** nicht Salz und Pfeffer.
4 **Macht** schnell, ihr beiden, ich verhungere!

H *In der Kantine (2)*

1 **Essen wir** Hamburger mit Pommes!
2 **Trinken wir** lieber Milch!
3 **Kaufen wir** einige Süßigkeiten!
4 **Warten wir** einen Moment auf Peter!

Chapter 22 – What do you know? (page 99)

A *Was hat er gesagt?*

1 **Welche** Königin besucht Großbritannien?
2 **Welches** Parlament diskutiert Terrorismus?
3 **Welcher** Minister ist in einen Skandal verwickelt!
4 **Welche** Sportlerin hat einen neuen Rekord erziehlt?

B *Was sagt sie?*

1 c,   2 a,   3 b

C *Ein Staatsbesuch*

1 c,   2 a,   3 b

D *Meine Politik*

1 Moritz **würde** die Preise für Süßigkeiten reduzieren.
2 Meine Eltern **würden** die Renten erhöhen.
3 Ich **würde** mehr Arbeitsplätze schaffen.

Chapter 22 – What have you learnt? (page 102)

A *Sportreportage*

1 **Welcher** Tennisspieler hat die APT Meisterschaften gewonnen?
2 Über **welche** Athletin schreibt man hier?
3 Von **welchem** Pferd spricht der Reporter?

B *Politik*

1 **Wen** hat der Bundeskanzler angekündigt?
2 **Wem** gibt der König einen Preis?
3 Mit **wem** fährt der Präsident nach Italien?

C *Nicht wahr?*

1 Der Tennisspieler sieht dick aus, nicht wahr?
2 Man kann ihn kaum erkennen, nicht wahr?
3 Der Minister hat ein Doppelkinn, nicht wahr?
4 Der Filmstar trägt zu viel Make-up, nicht wahr?

D *Probleme lösen*

1 Dann **würden** meine Kinder mich morgens in Ruhe **lassen**.
2 Mein Mann **würde** auch froh **sein**, seine eigene Zeitung zu lesen.
3 Ich **würde** gerne jeden Morgen die Zeitung **lesen**.

Chapter 23 – What do you know? (page 103)

A *Zeitungsberichte*

1 Der Präsident **ist** bereit, mit den Oppositionsparteien zu verhandeln.
2 Die Gewerkschaften **sind** mit den Arbeitsbedingungen zufrieden.
3 Der Koalitionspartner **hat** finanzielle Schwierigkeiten.
4 Der Vater **ist** des Mords schuldig.

B *Der Vertrag*

1 Ausländische Arbeiter **dürften** ohne Arbeitserlaubnis arbeiten.
2 Studenten **könnten** im Ausland arbeiten.
3 Reisende **müßten** keinen Paß an der Grenze zeigen.

C *Der Lottogewinner*

1 Ich wäre echt faul!
2 Wir wären alle reich.
3 Ich würde jeden Tag spät aufstehen.
4 Ich hätte mindestens vier Autos.
5 Die Familie würde eine Villa in Frankreich kaufen.
6 Das Leben wäre perfekt!

Chapter 23 – What have you learnt? (page 106)

A *Traumferien*

1 Wenn ich viel Geld **hätte**, **würde** ich eine Weltreise machen.
2 Wenn wir reich **wären**, **würden** wir China besuchen.
3 Wenn mein Vater ein Millionär **wäre**, **würde** er uns auf einer Kreuzfahrt mitnehmen.
4 Wenn Peter DM 1000,- **hätte**, **würde** er seine Ferien in Spanien verbringen.
5 Manfred, du **würdest** lieber zu Hause bleiben, auch wenn du reich **wärst**.
6 Ich **würde** an einem Sprachkurs in England teilnehmen.

B *Leserbriefe – Eva Martins antwortet*

1 Sicher **dürften** Sie allein mit dem Auto einkaufen gehen.
2 Ich **würde** einmal versuchen, in Ruhe mit ihr Ihre Probleme zu besprechen.
3 Wenn Sie Ihre Eltern öfter besuchen **könnten**, wäre es schön.
4 Ihr Mann wäre bestimmt glücklicher, wenn er jedes Wochenende nicht arbeiten **müßte**.
5 Ihr Sohn **würde** lieber mit seinen Freunden in Urlaub fahren.
6 Wenn Sie nicht arbeiten **müßten**, hätten sie mehr Zeit für die Kinder.

Chapter 24 – What do you know? (page 107)

A *An der Raststätte*

1 Hier ist die Raststätte. Sie liegt in der Nähe von Köln.
2 Das war das Auto. Es ist schnell vorbeigefahren.
3 Wo sind die Toiletten? Sie sind am nächsten.

B *Der Verkehrsbericht*

1 b Das ist die Autobahn, auf der ich fahren wollte. i
2 d Hier ist der Bericht, auf den ich wartete. ii
3 a Gibt es eine Umleitung, der wir folgen müssen? iii
4 c Hier ist die Raststätte, an der wir tanken können. iv

C *Skandalös*

1 Die Politiker haben Freunde, **deren** Kollegen skrupellos sind. *(Freunde = plural)*
2 Das ist das Kind, **dessen** Eltern im Fernsehen waren. *(Kind = neuter)*
3 Der Parteichef hat eine Kollegin, **deren** Vater berühmter Schauspieler ist. *(Kollegin = feminine)*
4 Die Königin spricht mit dem Soldaten, **dessen** Hand verletzt wurde. *(Soldat = masculine)*

Chapter 24 – What have you learnt? (page 110)

A *Meine Karriere*
1 Ich arbeitete in einem Theater, **das** in der Karl-Marx Straße liegt.
2 Tagsüber arbeitete ich auf einem Markt, **der** nicht mehr da ist.
3 Ich hatte damals eine sehr gute Freundin, **die** jetzt sehr berühmt ist.
4 Alle diese Autos, **die** hier im Foto sind, gehörten meinem dritten Mann.

B *Hollywood*
1 Dürrenmatt war ein guter Freund, **den** ich oft besuchte.
2 Hier ist ein Bild von dem Haus, **das** ich 1937 in Hollywood kaufte.
3 Hier sind die Schuhe, **die** ich in meinem berühmtesten Film trug.
4 Meine tochter, **die** ich 1939 bekam, lebt mit mir in Genf.

C *In der guten alten Zeit*
1 Ich mag die alten Western, **in denen** John Wayne spielt.
2 Das war der Film, **für den/wofür** sie einen Oscar bekommen hat.
3 Richard Tauber war der Sänger, **dessen Stimme** ich immer gern hatte.
4 Ich erinnere mich an die Freundinnen, **mit denen** ich ins Kino ging.

Chapters 22–24 – Revision (pages 111–112)

A *Die Olympiade*
1 **Welcher** Athlet hat den Hürdenlauf gewonnen?
2 **Welche** Mannschaft hat einen neuen Weltrekord?
3 Der Favorit spielt gegen **welchen** Spieler?
4 Die Resultate sind in **welcher** Zeitung?

B *Die Olympischen Spiele*
1 **Wer** gewinnt?
2 Er spielt gegen **wen**?
3 Mit **wem** trainiert er?

C *Der Staatsbesuch*
1 Der Kanzler ist schon nach London abgefahren.
2 Er fliegt mit Lufthansa.
3 Die Königin trägt immer eine Handtasche.
4 Sie hat nichts darin.

D *Südafrika*
1 Der Präsident **will** nächstes Jahr Südafrika besuchen.
2 Er **möchte** Nelson Mandela wieder treffen.
3 Wenn möglich, **würde** er auch Namibia besichtigen.

E *Der Autoreisezug*

1 Während **der** Weihnachtsferien gibt es immer viel Verkehr auf der Autobahn nach Hannover.

2 Wegen **des** Verkehrs fahren wir lieber mit dem Zug.

3 Obwohl unsere Verwandten innerhalb **des** Orts wohnen, nehmen wir lieber das Auto mit.

4 Trotz **der** guten Autobahnen gibt es zu Weihnachten lange Staus.

F *Meinungen*

1 Wenn du intelligent **wärst**, würdest du meinen Standpunkt verstehen.

2 Wenn Peter Lust **hätte**, könnte er gut singen.

3 Wenn ich älter wäre, **hättest** du mehr Respekt.

4 Ich **hätte** Angst, da allein zu sein.

5 Wir **wären** froh, hier zu wohnen.

G *In der Zeitung*

1 Frau Müller zeigt ihm das Büro, in **dem** ich arbeite.

2 Da sind meine Kollegen, von **denen** ich oft spreche.

3 Hinter ihnen ist mein Freund, **dessen** Mutter neben uns wohnt.

4 Auf der linken Seite sind meine Freundinnen Kirsten und Bärbel, mit **denen** ich zur Firma fahre.

5 Sie Können im Foto den Pullover sehen, **den** du mir zum Geburtstag geschenkt hast.

Chapter 25 – What do you know? (page 113)

A *Hier spricht man Deutsch*

liegt : liegen
könnten : können
spricht : sprechen
hätten : haben
gibt : geben

B *Hätten wir genug Geld dafür?*

1 Ich hätte Probleme, genug Geld dafür zu sparen. (*uncertainty*)

2 Es gibt in Südafrika eine Menge zu tun, und zu sehen. (*certainty*)

3 Wenn Michael hier wäre, dann könnten wir ihn fragen. (*uncertainty*)

C *Was hat er gesagt?*

1 Er sagte, daß wir Geld däfür sparen **könnten**.

2 Er sagte, daß er Prospekte vom Reisebüro **hole**.

3 Er sagte, daß Südafrika sehr interessant **sei**.

D *Michael hat recht*

Alles, was er sagt ist richtig. **Nichts**, was er sagt ist falsch. Er hat **etwas** darüber gelesen, was er uns zeigen wird.

Chapter 25 – What have you learnt? (page 116)

A *Im Reisebüro*

Wenn wir letztes Jahr dorthin **gefahren wären**, **hätten** wir die Flugtickets billiger **bekommen**. Er hat mir erzählt, daß du schon öfters in dem Reisebüro gewesen bist. Du **hättest** mir sagen **können**, daß du schon dort warst!

B *Eine Umfrage*

1 20% sagen, daß die Kantine schmutzig ist.
2 Ein Mädchen sagte, daß die internationalen Gerichte interessant waren.
3 Ein Lehrer behauptet, daß das Essen immer kalt ist.
4 Viele Studenten behaupteten, daß die Kantine preisgünstig war.

C *Der internationale Abend*

Der Direktor hat uns eingeladen, **was** wir sehr nett finden. Die Eltern müssen **das** mitbringen, **was** auf der Liste steht. Alles **was** auf dem Menü ist, kommt aus einem anderen Land.

Chapter 26 – What do you know? (page 117)

A *In der Zeitung*

1 past   2 past   3 present   4 past

B *Unglaublich!*

a passive   b active   c active   d passive

C *Wer ist das Kind?*

1 Das Kind konnte von **einem** Arzt identifiziert werden.
2 Die Mutter wird von **einer** Sozialarbeiterin beraten.
3 Das Kind wurde von **einer** Frau ausgesetzt.
4 Das Baby wird von **einer** Familie in Wedding versorgt.

Chapter 26 – What have you learnt? (page 120)

A *Das Attentat*

1 Die Leiche von dem Präsidenten **wurde** im Badezimmer **gefunden**.
2 Er **wurde** fünfmal mit einem Revolver **erschoßen**.
3 Zwei Frauen **wurden** von einem Dienstmädchen **beobachtet**.

B *Der Krimi*

1 Eine Frau **wird** sechsmal mit einem Revolver **erschoßen**.
2 Der Präsident **wird** von Agenten vom Geheimdienst **beobachtet**.
3 Die Leiche der Frau **wird** im Schlafzimmer des Präsidenten **gefunden**.

C *Das Fußballspiel*

1 d,   2 a,   3 c,   4 b

Chapter 27 – What do you know? (page 121)

A *Wir sprechen nur Deutsch*
1 Wieso denn?
2 Doch.
3 Es ist ja blöd.
4 Haben Sie denn keine Fremdsprache in der Schule gelernt?
5 Es gefällt Ihnen sicher in Österreich.

B *Reisepläne*
Wir **sollen** Edinburgh besuchen. Die Burg **soll** sehr schön sein. Dann **sollst** du deine Freundin in Glasgow sehen. Die hast du seit Jahren nicht gesehen. Ich **soll** eine Landkarte kaufen, damit wir unsere Reise besser planen können. Die Polizisten in Großbritannien **sollen** Touristen gegenüber sehr freundlich sein.

C *Wir lernen Englisch*
Unsere Tochter hat uns gesagt, daß wir Englisch lernen **sollen**, damit wir in andere Länder fahren **können**. Wir **müssen** viel lernen. Wir **dürfen** im Unterricht kein Deutsch sprechen!

Chapter 27 – What have you learnt? (page 124)

A *Die Volkshochschüler*
YUNG SU Wo ist Kamal? Was ist **denn** mit ihm los?
AYSCHA Er wird **schon** kommen.
GÜRKAN War er heute nicht an der Arbeit?
YUNG SU **Doch.** Er ist immer da.
AYSCHA Moment **mal**! Da ist er **ja**.

B *Flüchtling, Aussiedler, Gastarbeiter*
YUNG SU Ich bin Flüchtling. Ich mußte aus Vietnam fliehen. Ich **darf** jetzt in Deutschland bleiben.
Ich **muß** Deutsch lernen, um eine bessere Stelle zu bekommen.
AYSCHA Meine Familie kommt aus Kasachstan. Wir sind Aussiedler. Ich **will** mein Deutsch verbessern, damit ich eine gute Lehre finde.
GÜRKAN Ich wohne seit 30 Jahren in Deutschland. Meine Kinder haben mir gesagt, daß ich Deutsch richtig lernen **soll**.

C *Deutsch als Fremdsprache*
1 Yung Su darf jetzt in Deutschland bleiben.
2 Ayscha will ihr Deutsch verbessern, damit sie eine gute Lehre findet.
3 Die Kinder von Gürkan haben ihm gesagt, daß er Deutsch richtig lernen soll.

Chapters 25–27 – Revision (pages 125–126)

A *Im Reisebüro*
1 Das Hotel **ist** im Stadtzentrum.
2 Der Angestellte im Reisebüro meint, wir **hätten** keine Probleme, das Hotel zu finden.
3 Wenn wir mit der Straßenbahn fahren, **wären** wir in etwa zehn Minuten da.
4 Der Verkehrsverein **hat** ein Büro gleich gegenüber dem Bahnhof.

B *Indirekte Fragen*
Ich habe ihn gefragt, ob er die Flugtickets gebucht habe.
Ich habe ihn gefragt, ob er schon mit dieser Firma gereist sei.

Er hat uns gefragt, ob wir schon in Zürich gewesen seien.
Er hat uns gefragt, ob wir schon Geld gewechselt hätten*.

C *Diätbedürfnisse*
1 Ich kann **alles** essen, **was** auf der Speisekarte steht.
2 Meine Frau kann **nichts** essen, **was** Erdnüsse enthält.
3 Als wir in Rußland waren, haben wir **etwas** gegessen, **was** uns beide krank gemacht hat.

D *Eine unglückliche Erfahrung*
1 Meine Handtasche **ist** gestohlen worden.
2 Die Polizei **hat** die Handtasche später gefunden.
3 Mein Reisepaß, meine Brieftasche und meine Autoschlüssel **sind** vom Dieb behalten worden.
4 Glücklicherweise **habe** ich eine Reiseversicherung gehabt.

E *Eine Reise in den Osten*
1 Wir wollten ein neues Reiseziel. Nur **ein paar** Ausländer fahren nach Rumänien.
2 Wir sind mit **einigen** Freunden dorthin gefahren.
3 Es hat fast **jedem** in der Gruppe Spaß gemacht.
4 Meine Frau und ich wollen **beide** wieder in den Osten reisen.
5 Wegen des Mangels an Medikamenten nehmen wir **alles** mit.

F *Amerika/Großbritannien*
1 Amerika hat einen Präsident**en**. Großbritannien hat eine Königin.
2 Die Tochter des Präsident**en** hat keinen Titel.
3 Die Söhne der Königin sind Prinz**en**.

---

*Imperfect subjunctive because the present subjunctive of **haben** looks identical to the present indicative of **haben**.

G *Wie gefällt es Ihnen hier?*
1 Hier **kann** man schwimmen, surfen und so weiter.
2 Wir **können** uns ausruhen. Das ist uns am wichtigsten.
3 Wir werden Wien besichtigen. Wien **soll** sehr schön sein.
4 Gäste **dürfen** keine Shorts im Restaurant tragen.
5 Hier im Hotel **darf** man nicht rauchen.
6 Ich **will** lieber nächstes Jahr nach Skandinavien fahren.
7 Ich **soll** etwas Englisch lernen. Hier sind immer viele Engländer.
8 Wir **wollen** einen Ausflug nach Salzburg machen.